GUNBOAT!

OTHER BOOKS BY BRYAN PERRETT

BRYAN PERRETT

GUNBOAT!

SMALL SHIPS AT WAR

CASSELL&CO

Cassell & Co
Wellington House, 125 Strand
London WC2R OBB

First published 2000

British Library Cataloguing-in-Publication Data
A catalogue record for this book is available from the British Library

ISBN 0-304-35302-7

Distributed in the USA by
Sterling Publishing Co Inc
387 Park Avenue South
New York
NY 10016-8810

Printed and bound in Great Britain by Creative Print and Design (Wales)

CONTENTS

INTRODUCTION

The autocrat of the Victorian breakfast table, empurpled by some outrage committed by foreigners against his humanitarian or commercial interests somewhere in the world, was no more a myth than his strongly worded letter to *The Times*, urging the Admiralty to despatch a gunboat forthwith to restore order and uphold the national honour. Readers of 'The Thunderer' apart, Her Majesty's Government received regular requests for gunboat assistance, sometimes at the rate of two or three a month, from the Foreign and Colonial Offices, colonial governors, consuls in dusty, unheard-of towns, and merchants at home and abroad. Such requests were usually granted and, more often than not, the problem was dealt with quickly and efficiently.

Such a degree of restlessness sits uneasily with the cosy picture we have inherited of a prosperous Great Britain, the workshop of the world, basking in the warmth of the long Victorian summer as, one after another, large tracts of territory were proudly added to her colonial Empire, the security of which rested on the *Pax Britannica* imposed by the mighty Royal Navy. Such, in fact, was the view common at the end of Victoria's long reign, although if we were to examine its origins a little more closely we should see that nothing was really quite what it seemed.

The business of the United Kingdom has, quite simply, always been business. Trade, went the saying, followed the flag, yet in reality the reverse was true. Wherever there was business to be done, the traders arrived first. More often than not, they saw to it that the local ruler benefited from their presence and thus inadvertently created a British sphere of influence.

At the moment when Queen Victoria ascended the throne, annexation and colonisation did not form part of anyone's agenda. True, colonies existed in Canada, Australia and South Africa; likewise, islands in the West Indies, of immense financial worth during the 18th and early 19th centuries because of their sugar crops, also retained colonial status despite their declining importance, as did Malta and other islands captured during the Napoleonic Wars because of their strategic importance. These were a fact of life, but as regards the establishment of further colonies on the land masses of Africa, Asia and the Americas, the government was firmly opposed to the idea of expansion, largely because they were unlikely to repay the cost of their administration and defence. Colonies, too, could be a source of trouble, witness the revolt of thirteen former American colonies, still within the memory of some, and the more recent disintegration of Spain's American empire. In this context it is worth remembering that India, regarded as the very jewel of the Imperial Crown at the end of Victoria's reign, was administered by a commercial organisation, the Honourable East India Company, until the Great Mutiny of 1857.

Yet, human nature being what it is, change was constant. Local rulers within trading spheres might play off British and competing interests against each other for their own personal advantage, or the area might be troubled by dynastic struggles, civil unrest or even invasion by jealous neighbours keen to lay hands on the wealth created by commercially induced profit. There were, too, unexpected causes of friction. The Victorians, living in a stable, prosperous society that practised religion to a much greater degree than is the case today, felt that they had a moral duty to export the benefits of civilisation to less fortunate peoples in Africa and Asia. Unfortunately, attempts by missionaries to preach the Gospel, and the protracted struggle to suppress the evil but lucrative slave trade were just two of several areas which seriously upset local vested interests.

As the Industrial Revolution reached its full potential, British ships carrying British manufactured goods of every kind from railway locomotives to sewing machines delivered their cargoes to every quarter of the globe, returning home with raw materials, foodstuffs and luxury items. The figures involved grew to such proportions that trading companies in Africa and the Far East were able to exert considerable political influence and demand protection for their interests in times of trouble. Sometimes, armed intervention was the only way of restoring stability, and if that did not work the first time around, annexation would follow. Even then, indirect rule through local kings and chiefs was the preferred method of governing these new and not altogether welcome colonies, coupled with an incorruptible civil service and legal system. Most of their inhabitants welcomed the subsequent rule of law, stability and improved communications which enabled them to live out their lives in peace and share in the area's growing prosperity. Thus, large areas of the map became red, almost by accident.

The colonisation process during the latter part of Victoria's reign was somewhat different. Some European nations, feeling that Great Britain's now pre-eminent position in the world detracted from their own interests and prestige, began acquiring colonies of their own. The result was, *inter alia*, the so-called Scramble for Africa, in which, for strategic or commercial reasons, the United Kingdom found it necessary to lay formal claim to hitherto unannexed territories in order to deny them to others.

The process could not have been completed without the *Pax Britannica* imposed by the Royal Navy on the high seas. The term is, perhaps, a little misleading, for in the final analysis it meant the imposition of stable maritime trading conditions by the United Kingdom in its accidental role as world policeman. In reality, there were very few days when, somewhere around the globe, the Royal Navy and the British and Indian Armies were not engaged in active operations.

Likewise, our picture of the Royal Navy itself has been somewhat coloured by the post-Victorian afterglow. Throughout the 19th century the two influences which simultaneously dominated naval life were the Treasury's parsimony and a continuous process of technical innovation. Once Napoleon had been safely packed off to St Helena, the Admiralty was forced to cut the Navy's strength dramatically. By 1817 it had been reduced to just 19,000 men. This figure would rise slowly as commitments expanded, but the cut had gone too deep, and full mobilisation for the Crimean War was delayed because many ships were unable to complete their crews. Thereafter, a naval career was made more attractive by providing the ordinary seaman with a uniform, better pay and conditions of service, and a career structure.

The first technical problem requiring the Navy's attention was steam, and in this its initial reaction mirrored that of many commercial shipowners who declared they would only resort to it when coal was as cheap as wind. Furthermore, said the latter, what was the point of stuffing hulls with costly machinery and coal bunkers at the expense of paying cargo? However, once their competitors began running regular scheduled services regardless of wind and tide, their opinions changed. Likewise, the more conservative admirals were quick to point out that installation of furnaces, engines and boilers meant the removal of guns and crew accommodation, that trained personnel would be needed to service them, and that, worst of all, standards of seamanship would inevitably decline. What they could not deny was that steam provided tactical flexibility, a point which would certainly not be lost on the Navy's enemies. Steam therefore became a reality for both merchant vessels and warships, although difficulties remained. One was that until ships could be built large enough to stow sufficient fuel for an ocean voyage and still perform their intended function, or coaling stations could be established along the major trade routes, engines performed an auxiliary function and the retention of sail was necessary. Sails, in fact, did not disappear from major warship design until the last quarter of the century.

A second difficulty lay in the application of steam propulsion, which could be by paddle or screw. Side paddles enabled a warship to turn within her own axis in calm water, but they exerted a severe drag when the vessel was under sail alone. Because so little was known about their design at the time, screws also exerted a drag, although when not in use they could be raised clear of the water. As to which was the more efficient, the argument was resolved in 1845 by a tug-of-war between two sloops, the paddler *Alecto* and the screw-driven *Rattler*, won easily by the latter. However, as we shall see, circumstances could arise where the paddle was really the only viable alternative.

As technology expanded, the Royal Navy was forced to address many other technical questions. The traditional 'wooden wall' battleship was terribly vulnerable to explosive shells and was clearly obsolete by the 1860s. The ironclad hull provided some protection, and from this the steel hull protected by armour plate was a logical development. Gun and ammunition technology also expanded apace. Bigger guns were unsuited to broadside mounting and instead were positioned on the vessel's centre line with swivelling carriages that enabled them to fire to port or starboard. In due course, this led to protected barbette mountings and ultimately to enclosed armoured turrets. The transition from smooth-bore cannon to rifled gun was less straightforward. Rifling to produce better accuracy and range did not present serious problems, but rifled breech-loading guns introduced in the late 1850s contained a dangerous design flaw and for a while a reversion was made to rifled muzzle-loading. Once more efficient breech-closing mechanisms such as the interrupted screw or sliding block made their appearance, it was possible to adopt breech-loading as standard. Curiously, the machine gun found greater favour with the Navy than it did with the Army. Towards the end of the period other weapons, including the mine (originally known as the torpedo) and the automotive torpedo, and new classes of warship such as the submarine and the torpedo boat, also began to impact seriously on naval thought.

It can thus be seen that, with constant development in hull design, motive power, gunnery and protection, Queen Victoria's Navy lived in a state of constant change. Hardly had a warship been built than she was overtaken by some new improvement in one form or another. The same was naturally true of all navies, and for this reason the Royal Navy was able to maintain its dominant strength, which was set as being equal to that of any two possible antagonists acting in concert.

After the Napoleonic Wars, it fought very few major engagements. In 1816, accompanied by a Dutch frigate squadron, it bombarded Algiers with the object of destroying the power of the Barbary pirates; in 1827, during the Greek War of Independence, it was joined by French and Russian warships and destroyed a Turkish–Egyptian fleet at Navarino; and during the Crimean War it mounted major operations in the Baltic and Black Seas.

For most of the time, however, much of the Royal Navy was underemployed. Its primary responsibility remained the defence of the United Kingdom and the greater portion of its strength was retained in home waters. A sizeable presence was also maintained in the Mediterranean, partly to preserve British interests in the Middle East, and partly to keep an eye on the French fleet in Toulon, the departure of which to reinforce its Atlantic brethren, so producing a dangerous multiplication of French strength in the Channel, remained an Admiralty nightmare for many years. A presence was maintained in North America and the West Indies, China, the East Indies, Australia, the Pacific and South and West Africa, but the global projection of squadrons of capital ships, in the modern sense, was not within the Navy's immediate power, and for that reason most of its business in distant seas remained the responsibility of smaller warships.

That business included exploration and hydrography, the suppression of the slave trade, and the preservation of secure trading conditions, which involved intervention to protect British interests and eliminating piracy. The expanding markets of the East Indies and the China Seas in particular swarmed with pirates who were quite beyond the control of their nominal rulers. To escape the Navy, pirates and slavers alike would vanish up rivers or take refuge in shallow coastal waters where the warships were unable to follow. If a sailing warship entered a river, her progress was governed by wind and current, both of which might be against her. Of necessity, resort was often made to boat action, but as pirates and slavers liked to operate from protected bases, the available armament might be inadequate to deal with these. Experience during the thirty years from the 1820s onwards confirmed that much better results could be obtained using steam-powered gunboats.

In Nelsonian terms a gunboat was simply a boat with a gun propelled by oars or sweeps. What was required now, however, was a shallow-draught, paddle- or screw-driven steamer with remarkably high firepower for her size, capable of chastising the enemy in his own shallow waters. Unfortunately, while the Treasury approved of the use of small warships on distant stations because they were economic, it still imposed strict limits on the Naval Estimates and the Admiralty, forced to work within these constraints, was painfully slow to react.

It was the Crimean War which revealed that to produce tangible results the Navy needed gunboats that could carry the war to the enemy in the shallow waters of the Baltic and the Sea of Azov. The government of the day, flayed by the press and in Parliament for its bungling mismanagement of the war, was suddenly eager to make funds available. The Naval Expenditure for 1853, the last year before the war, amounted to £7 million. In 1854 it soared to £15 million and in 1855 to £19.6 million. Suddenly, far more gunboats were being built than the Navy could ever use. Many were never commissioned and rotted their lives away in reserve. Once this type of warship became a reality, however, it evolved by classes as did any other, beginning with the wooden *Gleaner* class of 1854 (216 tons, single screw 60 hp reciprocating engine producing a maximum speed of 8 knots, armament 1 × 68-pounder SBML, 1 × 32-pounder SBML and 2 × 24-pounder howitzers, complement 36 officers and ratings) to the steel *Cadmus* class of 1900 (1070 tons, twin-screw 1400 hp triple-expansion engine producing a maximum speed of 13 knots, armament 6 × 4-inch QF and 4 × 3-pounder guns, complement 120 officers and ratings). Strictly speaking, the evolutionary process also included gunvessels, which drew more water and were better suited to ocean work, and sloops, a term which was applied to smaller warships other than specialised craft. Nevertheless, as they were often required to perform the gunboat role, some of their activities have been included, where appropriate.

The layout of the gunboat was, of course, influenced by its shallow draught, which meant that much of the machinery and accommodation spaces lay above the waterline. The danger inherent in this was that boilers and steam pipes were vulnerable to enemy fire. Thus, not only was the vessel likely to be immobilised if the machinery spaces were penetrated, the engine room crew were at greater risk of being scalded to death than in any other type of steam-driven warship. In any sort of sea the gunboat's almost flat bottom ensured that it would roll horribly and, by its very nature, it was a very crowded little vessel in which officers and men lived on top of each other for months on end. In command was a junior officer whose powers of leadership had to be of a high order if morale was to be maintained. Often operating in isolation, he had to rely on his own judgement to restore a troubled situation, and sometimes he led landing parties in pursuit of his quarry. This was, perhaps, the last era in history when, unfettered by global communications, the junior naval officer could exercise his initiative to the full in the Hornblower tradition. Modern diplomats, profoundly expert in the art of polite inactivity, would be reduced to apoplectic incoherence by some of his activities, but the contemporary view was that results were what counted and the *fait accompli* was just that. There were, of course, dangers present in such a system and, as we shall see, it was inevitable that some individuals would overstep the mark.

Across the Atlantic, river gunboats played a most important if now largely forgotten part in securing a victory for the Union during the American Civil War. As control of the Mississippi and its tributaries formed an essential part of the strategy of both sides, North and South alike ingeniously converted side- and stern-wheel river steamers into protected gunboats. These not only engaged fortifications and troops ashore, but each other as well, fighting battles in which the ram sometimes proved to be an effective substitute for gunfire.

Under the command of British officers, a number of whom would achieve even greater fame in World War I, stern-wheel river gunboats also played an important, and sometimes hair-raising, role on the Nile during the Gordon Relief Expedition of 1885 and the reconquest of the Sudan 1896–8. Some of the gunboats were purpose-built for the latter campaign, being shipped from the United Kingdom in sections.

By the turn of the century the reasons which had brought the gunboat into being had largely vanished, save in China, where unsettled conditions and a degree of piracy still existed. Elsewhere, pirates had long since learned the folly of tangling with warships and were a dying breed. The slave trade, too, had nominally become a dead issue. In the colonies the rule of law had become firmly established. Where once gunboats ruled unchallenged, the colonial powers now preferred to demonstrate their status, as much for the benefit of other powers as for the indigenous population, by keeping much larger cruisers in the offing. It seemed as though the gunboats' work was done. Apparently there was no place for them in Admiral Sir John Fisher's modern Navy, with its big-gun battleships, powerful cruisers and flotillas of fast destroyers. Their numbers had been falling for some years and many of the survivors were now summoned home, sold, scrapped or reduced to mundane harbour duties, their crews dispersed among larger warships.

In fact, the gunboats' work was far from done. During World War I the German cruiser *Königsberg*, having taken refuge up the Rufiji River in German East Africa, was shelled to destruction by two river moni- tors, which were themselves an extension of the gunboat idea in that they were armed with battleship guns mounted on a shallow-draught hull. It was also in East Africa that one of the most remarkable gunboat adventures of all took place, providing C. S. Forester with the inspira- tion for his novel *The African Queen*. Lake Tanganyika was completely dominated by three German gunboats which exercised a paralysing effect on Allied troop movements in the area. The Navy's response was to ship two very small petrol-driven gunboats to Cape Town, whence they travelled 3000 miles by rail, along bush tracks hauled by traction engines or oxen, and down barely navigable rivers. Incredibly, their mission was a complete success, one of their opponents being captured, a second sunk and the third scuttled. The major part of gunboat activity during World War I, however, was undertaken by the new Insect class, which had been optimistically built for service on the Danube to support Serbian forces against the Austro-Hungarian Empire. In the event, they were employed in the Middle East where, on the Tigris, they experienced first remarkable success, then failure and frustration, and finally complete victory.

In the immediate aftermath of World War I, several Insects served with the Allied Intervention forces on north Russian rivers during the Civil War between the Whites and the Reds. Because of the unsettled state of central Europe, others patrolled the Danube, where one ferried the Austro-Hungarian Emperor Karl into exile following his abortive attempt to regain his throne in 1921. Others, again, went to China, where their traditional task of preserving order on the rivers was complicated by warlords who had seized local power following the overthrow of the Imperial dynasty. During the 1930s matters became even more compli- cated when the Japanese invaded. A British gunboat was damaged by shellfire and an American gunboat was sunk by air attack. The Japanese apologised, but their aggressive intentions were now apparent.

World War II saw the Insects in action in most theatres of war, but they were most successful serving with the Inshore Squadron which harassed the Axis armies in North Africa. Elsewhere in the Mediterranean they were present at the capture of Pantellaria and Elba as well as the invasion of southern France. On one occasion two of these now rather elderly warships emerged victorious from a sea battle with modern German corvettes.

It was the fall of Singapore in 1942 which destroyed the prestige of the colonial powers in the Far East. After the war ended, it quickly became apparent that the old days had gone forever. Symbolic of this, and an epic very much in the gunboat tradition, was the escape of the frigate *Amethyst* down the Yangtse in 1949, an incident which caused her would-be communist captors much loss of face. Yet far from leaving the stage of history quietly, the gunboat went on to achieve new levels of sophistication, for in riverine operations in southern Vietnam the Americans not only employed gunboats, monitors and troop carriers that bore a startling if superficial resemblance to those used on the Mississippi a century earlier, but also floating artillery platforms and air cushion vehicles capable of travelling across water, swamp or dry land.

My purpose, however, is not to trace the technical history of the gunboat, which has been set down very adequately elsewhere, as indeed has the political background to its uses. Nor is it to provide a complete chronicle of gunboat operations, for that would require several volumes. Rather it is to tell something of the story of those who served aboard these little ships and the manner in which they performed the various tasks they were set. Their actions demonstrated the qualities of high courage, leadership, self-sacrifice, independence, initiative, ingenuity and sometimes an astonishing impudence. Before he has penetrated very far into this somewhat neglected area of naval history the reader will probably share my conviction that fiction is seldom as remarkable, or as exciting and inspirational, as truth.

Bryan Perrett

1
LITTLE SHIPS, BIG WAR
Gunboat Operations During
the Crimean War, 1854–5

I n 1853 Tsar Nicholas I of Russia used the excuse of a brawl between Roman Catholic and Greek Orthodox monks in Bethlehem to proclaim himself the guardian of the Ottoman Empire's fourteen million Orthodox Christians. What he really wanted was Russian access to the Mediterranean through the Bosporus and the Dardanelles, and he was quite prepared to set about the virtual dismemberment of Turkey to achieve this. In his new-found capacity as religious champion, therefore, he demanded a number of concessions from the Sultan, knowing full well that their nature was such that no self-respecting sovereign could possibly grant them. Having, as anticipated, been rebuffed, in July he sent his troops to occupy Turkish provinces in Romania.

Unfortunately, he encountered unexpected opposition. France, now ruled by Napoleon III, regarded herself as the traditional protector of Roman Catholic interests in the Holy Land and was not prepared to have these ridden over by Russia. Simultaneously, Great Britain disliked the idea of the naval balance in the Mediterranean being disturbed by the intrusion of a Russian fleet. The despatch of British and French warships to Constantinople stiffened the Sultan's resolve and on 4 November he declared war on Russia.

On land, the Turks did unexpectedly well, but on 30 November the Russian fleet destroyed a Turkish squadron in Sinope harbour. In January 1854 the Anglo-French fleet entered the Black Sea to protect the Turkish coastline and on 28 March the Allies declared war on Russia. At this juncture the Tsar's adventure turned sour, for the following month Austria, with Prussian support, threatened to intervene unless he withdrew his troops from the Balkans. Reluctantly, he complied, but wrecked the ensuing peace talks by insisting on his right to pursue his bullying quarrel with Turkey. The Allies therefore decided to land an expeditionary force in the Crimea with the object of capturing and destroying the heavily fortified Russian naval base of Sevastopol.

The mismanagement of the British part of the land campaign, the blunderings of elderly or incompetent generals, the superlative courage of the troops and their terrible sufferings during the first winter of the war have all been so thoroughly covered elsewhere that there is no need to enlarge upon them here. Suffice it to say that while siege works were opened against the city and naval facilities of Sevastopol, lying on the southern side of a deep inlet, the term siege was not entirely appropriate as the inlet's northern shore remained in Russian hands. Consequently, reinforcements and supplies continued to pour across the harbour by a bridge of boats while, to make matters yet more difficult for the Allies, a large Russian field army hovered in the Crimea's hinterland.

The naval operations of what became known as the Crimean War were conducted in the Black Sea and the Baltic, with peripheral operations in the White Sea and the Far East. In some respects the Royal Navy was unprepared for a major war. Some of the admirals were as elderly and infirm of purpose as the generals, and so low were manning levels that ships of the Baltic Fleet were unable to complete their crews months after the war had begun. In the Black Sea, naval bombardment of Sevastopol's coastal forts produced inconclusive results. In the Baltic the Russians declined to come out and fight, and ice put an early end to operations. Thus, beyond imposing a blockade on an essentially self-sufficient land power and disrupting such sea-borne trade as it possessed, the naval operations of 1854 ended on a thoroughly unsatisfactory note.

The nub of the problem was that the line-of-battle ships, inhibited by large areas of shallow water in both the Black Sea and the Baltic, simply could not get close enough to do the enemy any real damage. What was needed were small, shallow-draught steam-propelled vessels with enough hitting power to hurt. As luck would have it, the Admiralty had already initiated a modest construction programme, intending to replace its sailing gun-brigs, the smallest ocean-going warships, with little screw steamers, and six such vessels, the *Arrow* class, were already in service. Recognising that these would be able to get within effective range of the Russian defences, the Admiralty also agreed that large numbers of such craft would be less vulnerable to return fire than larger ships. It was therefore decided to build four classes of what were called Crimean gunboats. The government, stung into action by press criticism of its handling of the war, willingly consented to a large construction programme; in fact, no less than 156 warships of this type were ordered, although some were completed too late to take part in the war and others, built hastily from green wood, were allowed to rot in an unfinished state.

The Crimean gunboats had a flat-bottomed hull and were powered by 20, 40 or 60 hp steam engines driving a single screw, giving a speed of between six and eight knots. The three gaff-rigged masts were stepped in tabernacles on the upper deck, through which protruded a tall, thin funnel. Armament consisted of two or three 68-pounder guns on slides, centrally mounted so that they could be moved over iron traversing rings to fire over either side. Later classes were armed with 32-pounder guns, also on slides, and 24-pounder howitzers on conventional trucks. Below decks, two-thirds of the available space was taken up by the engine, boiler, coal bunkers, water tanks, ration lockers and magazines. Fortunately, because of the simple sail plan and limited armament, only 35 men were required to handle the vessel. The men lived forward of the engine room and the two officers in a small space aft. Usually, a gunboat was a lieutenant's command but such was the rate of expansion during the war that some were commanded by masters, i.e. senior warrant officers.

The Baltic Fleet which returned to its station under Rear Admiral the Hon. Richard Dundas in May 1855 was very different from that which had gone out the previous year in that it consisted entirely of steam-driven vessels and contained numerous small craft suited to operations in cramped or shallow waters. These included seventeen mortar vessels and the gunboats *Gleaner, Pelter, Pincher, Ruby, Badger, Snapper, Biter, Dapper, Jackdaw, Magpie, Redwing, Skylark, Snap, Starling, Stork, Swinger, Thistle, Weazel* and *Lark.* The nature of their operations, however, continued much as before. The Russian Navy remained safe behind its massive defences in Kronstadt harbour, which, it was discovered, had been further protected with moored contact mines. In other respects, the Allied effort produced only the

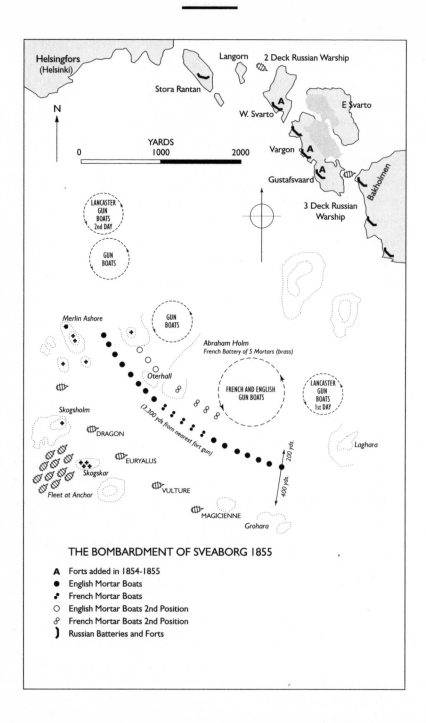

THE BOMBARDMENT OF SVEABORG 1855

A Forts added in 1854-1855
● English Mortar Boats
♪ French Mortar Boats
○ English Mortar Boats 2nd Position
♂ French Mortar Boats 2nd Position
) Russian Batteries and Forts

occupation of several islands, the elimination of a few batteries and the capture of some small vessels which had risked the blockade. Dundas and his French colleague, Rear Admiral Penaud, both came under pressure from home to produce more tangible results, but as an attack on Kronstadt was out of the question, their difficulty lay in choosing a suitable objective. Some officers were for bombarding the prosperous city of Helsingfors (Helsinki), the destruction of which would have a profound effect on public opinion in Russia. This idea was rejected in favour of a bombardment of the neighbouring fortress of Sveaborg, which was built on several interconnected islands including Vargon, Gustafsvaard, East Svarto, West Svarto and Lilla Svarto. The fortifications were of modern design, were fully manned and mounted over 800 guns. Channels to the north and south of the islands were blocked by two ships of the line, moored broadside on.

On the morning of 9 August the British and French mortar vessels formed a line approximately 3300 yards from the fortifications, opening fire at 07:00. The gunboats *Stork* and *Snapper*, armed with the new Lancaster guns, circling to the right of the line, concentrated their fire on the Russian warship blocking the southern channel. To their left *Starling, Thistle, Pelter, Biter* and *Badger* circled as they fired at the western batteries, while to their left the rest of the defences were engaged by circles containing *Vulture, Snap, Gleaner, Dapper* and *Redwing*. To the north, two more gunboats, *Magpie* and *Weazel*, exchanged fire with a detached battery on the island of Stora Rantan, covering the channel in which the second Russian warship was moored. The course of the action is described by Admiral Dundas in his despatch.

> A rapid fire of shot and shells was kept up from the fortress for the first few hours upon the gunboats, and the ranges of the heavy batteries extended completely beyond the mortar vessels; but the continued motion of the gunboats, and the able manner in which they were conducted by the officers who commanded them, enabled them to return the fire with great spirit, and almost with impunity throughout the day. About ten o'clock in the

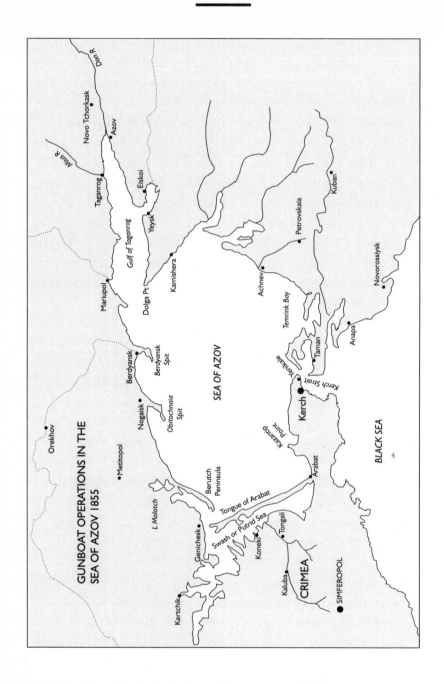

GUNBOAT OPERATIONS IN THE
SEA OF AZOV 1855

forenoon fires began first to be observed in the different buildings, and a heavy explosion took place on the island of Vargon, which was followed by a second about an hour afterwards on the island of Gustafsvaard, inflicting much damage upon the defences of the enemy, and tending greatly to slacken the fire from that direction. The advantage of the rapidity with which the fire from the mortars had been directed was apparent in the continued fresh conflagrations which spread extensively on the island of Vargon.

When the gunboats were recalled at sunset the fleet's boats took over, firing rockets which spread the blaze from Vargon to East Svarto. Dundas continues:

At daylight on the morning of the 10th, the position of several mortar vessels had been advanced within easier range, and the gunboats were again directed to engage. The three-decked ship which had been moored by the enemy to block and defend the channel between Gustafsvaard and Bakholmen, had been withdrawn during the night to a more secure position; but the fire from the batteries was increased, and the engagement was renewed with activity on both sides. Fires continued to burn without intermission within the fortress, and about noon a column of smoke, heavier and darker than any which had yet been observed, gave signs that the shells had reached combustible materials in the direction of the arsenal.

The bombardment continued for much of the night. A spy later reported that the dockyard had been wrecked, all government stores destroyed, the powder magazines blown up, 23 vessels burned and a further 18 seriously damaged, and 2000 men killed. This may well be an exaggeration of the true position although it was clear that extensive damage had been done. It is possible that the attack would have continued, but by the morning of the 11th the British mortars had been shot out to the extent that some had even split. As replacements would not reach the Baltic before the onset of winter, the mortar vessels were therefore sent home a month before the rest of the fleet. The gunboats, on the other hand, had proved themselves equal to the task for which they had been built, to the extent that Allied casualties amounted to just one man killed and several wounded. Nevertheless, it was to be with the Black Sea Fleet that their true potential was demonstrated.

The Black Sea Fleet, commanded by Vice Admiral James Dundas, was less troubled by winter than that commanded by his namesake in the Baltic, and in view of the stand-off at Sevastopol consideration had been given to ejecting the enemy by means of an indirect approach rather than head-on attack. Russian roads were primitive, difficult to use in winter and almost impossible during the *rasputitsa*, the spring thaw which turned them into mud wallows. Consequently, it was much easier for the Russians to supply their troops in the Crimea by means of water transport, using rivers and the Sea of Azov.

Disrupting this traffic had not been possible the previous year because the Allied navies lacked suitable warships capable of penetrating the shallow waters of the Azov. By the spring of 1855, however, this defect had been remedied, although before operations against the Russian supply line could commence it was necessary to secure control of the Straits of Kerch, which provided the only entrance to this otherwise landlocked sea. This was accomplished on 24 May by an Allied amphibious operation involving heavy and light squadrons plus landing forces consisting of 7000 French, 5000 Turkish and 3500 British troops as well as a Sardinian contingent. On both sides of the straits the enemy abandoned their positions with barely a token resistance, blew up their fortifications, abandoned about 100 guns, destroyed stores, provisions and ammunition, and burned such warships as were unable to make good their escape. In simply handing the Allies the keys of the Sea of Azov the Russians made their most critical mistake of the war.

The British light squadron, commanded by Captain Edmund Lyons, included several paddle-driven warships and the new screw gunboats *Wrangler*, *Viper*, *Lynx*, *Arrow*, *Snake* and *Beagle*. Even while operations were in progress to secure the straits, Lieutenant Henry McKillop, commanding the *Snake*, spotted a Russian warship of comparable size attempting to escape northwards. Ignoring the enemy fortifications, he promptly gave chase. No sooner had the two ships begun exchanging shots than two more Russian warships emerged to support their comrade, leaving *Snake* simultaneously engaged with three opponents. The gunboat, however, was extremely handy, and the Russians, no doubt expecting her to engage with conventionally mounted broadside guns, found themselves receiving fire from unexpected directions as the centrally mounted armament was heaved round to bear on each of them in turn. Several of their shots passed clean through *Snake*, fortunately without causing casualties or touching a vital area. On the other hand, taking a hit from one of the gunboat's 68-pounder shells was a serious matter for a small warship, leaving the Russians horrified that their apparently puny opponent could hit quite so hard. They had probably had enough by the time the six-gun paddler *Recruit*, followed by others, came thrashing her way towards the engagement, for they deliberately ran themselves aground and later set fire to their ships. The action took place within view of the Allied fleet, the French in particular being generous with their praise. McKillop was promoted commander as soon as he had completed his necessary period of sea time, with seniority from the date of his exploit.

Having been reinforced with several French ships, Lyons took his light squadron into the Sea of Azov the following day. As one contemporary observer, Hamilton Williams, wrote:

> It was like bursting into a vast treasure house, crammed with wealth of inestimable value. For miles along its shores stretched the countless storehouses packed with the accumulated harvests of the great corn provinces of Russia. From them the Russian armies in the field were fed; from them the beleaguered population of Sevastopol looked for preservation from the famine which already pressed hard upon them.

Furthermore, on the Kerch Straits themselves, the towns of Kerch and Yenikale contained coal stocks amounting to 12,000 tons, which would keep the Allied fleet going for a considerable period without recourse to its own colliers.

Lyons's ships proceeded to raise hell across the widest possible area. One was sent to cruise off the mouth of the Don, while two more were detached to Genichesk at the entrance to the Swash or Putrid Sea, a stretch of water separating the north-eastern coast of the Crimea from the Sea of Azov proper by a thin 70-mile-long spit of land known as the Tongue of Arabat. On 28 May the rest of the squadron bombarded Fort Arabat, situated at the mainland end of the Tongue. The engagement lasted some 90 minutes, at the end of which the defence works were wrecked by an internal explosion. Next day the squadron moved to Genichesk, where a landing party under Lieutenant Campbell Mackenzie set fire to storehouses and numerous ships in the harbour. A sudden change of wind direction would have reduced the amount of damage caused had not two officers, Lieutenants Cecil Buckley and Hugh Burgoyne, and Gunner John Roberts, returned ashore and started fresh fires where they would do most good, despite the presence of enemy troops and being beyond the gunfire support of their ships; all three were awarded the Victoria Cross.

Many Russian ships had fled from the Black Sea to the imagined security of the Azov as soon as the war had begun, and consequently the harbours of the latter were crowded. Just four days into his mission, Lyons was able to report that the enemy's losses thus far amounted to four naval steamers, no less than 246 merchant vessels of various types, plus supplies of corn and flour sufficient to feed 100,000 men for twelve weeks.

At the beginning of June the light squadron, reinforced with twelve launches armed with 24-pounder howitzers and rockets, began operating in the Gulf of Taganrog. When, on 3 June, the governor of Taganrog itself declined to surrender, some of the town's storehouses were set ablaze by fire from the boats. As this did not produce quite the desired result, Lieutenant Cecil Buckley and Boatswain Henry Cooper braved the fire of the 3500-strong Russian garrison to make repeated landings from a four-oared gig and start fresh blazes. By 15:00 the storehouses and most of the town were burning fiercely and the force withdrew. Boatswain Cooper received the Victoria Cross for his part in the action. On the 5th it was the turn of Mariupol and on the 6th Yeysk, all government stores in both places being destroyed. The situation now was that sea power was not simply disrupting the supplies of the Russian forces in the Crimea, but also those of the army fighting the Turks in the Caucasus as well. Having completed the first phase of its operations, the light squadron returned to Kerch where Lyons handed over to Commander Sherard Osborn. Sadly, on 17 June, Lyons received a mortal wound while taking part in a further bombardment of Sevastopol's sea forts.

Having replenished, the light squadron returned to its work of destruction. On 27 June a landing party destroyed a convoy of wagons near Genichesk, which was also the scene of a lively action on 3 July. On the latter occasion the gunboat *Beagle*, commanded by Lieutenant William Hewitt, attacked the floating bridge connecting the town with the northern extremity of the Tongue of Arabat, which provided a major supply route into the Crimea. While the gunboat gave covering fire, Hewitt sent two boats to cut the bridge's hawsers. With the Russians lining the beach only 80 yards distant, as well as shooting from nearby houses, this was a desperate business. Despite this, although the boats were riddled, only two men were wounded. The hawsers were cut under heavy fire by Seaman Joseph Trewavas, who received a minor wound while hacking at them. Trewavas was awarded the Victoria Cross. Simultaneously, the last remaining floating bridge between the Tongue of Arabat and the Crimea was burned by the paddle gunboat *Curlew*.

It was now apparent that the light squadron, and the new gunboats in particular, could go wherever they wanted and the Russians were powerless to stop them. Some extracts from Osborn's despatches convey the daily nature of operations.

Delayed by the weather, we did not reach Berdyansk until July 15th. I hoisted a flag of truce in order, if possible, to get the women and children removed from the town; but, as we met with no reply, and the surf rendered landing extremely hazardous, I hauled it down and the squadron commenced to fire over the town at the forage and corn-stacks behind it; and I soon had the satisfaction of seeing a fire break out exactly where it was wanted. It became necessary to move into deeper water for the night; and, from our distant anchorage, the fires were seen burning throughout the night.

On the 16th the Allied squadron proceeded to Fort Petrovski, between Berdyansk and Mariupol. At 9.30 a.m., all arrangements having been made, the squadron took up their positions, the light-draught gunboats taking up stations east and west of the fort, and enfilading the works front and rear, whilst the heavier vessels formed a semicircle round the fort. The heavy nature of our ordnance soon not only forced the garrison to retire from the trenches, but also kept at a respectable distance the reserve force, consisting of three strong battalions of infantry and two squadrons of cavalry. We then commenced to fire with carcasses (i.e. incendiary shells) but, although partially successful, I was obliged to send the light boats of the squadron to complete the destruction of the fort and batteries, a duty I entrusted to Lieutenant Hubert Campion. Although the enemy, from an earthwork to the rear, opened a sharp fire on our men, Lieutenant Campion completed this service in the most able manner. Leaving the *Swallow* to check any attempt of the enemy to reoccupy the fort, the rest of the squadron proceeded to destroy great quantities of forage, and some of the most extensive fisheries, situated upon the White House Spit.

On July 17th, in consequence of information received of extensive depots of corn and forage existing at a town called Glafirovka upon the Asiatic coast, near Yeysk, I proceeded there with the squadron. The *Vesuvius* and *Swallow* were obliged to anchor some distance offshore. I therefore sent Commander Rowley Lambert (*Curlew*) with the gunboats *Fancy, Grinder, Boxer, Cracker, Jasper, Wrangler* and the boats of *Vesuvius* and *Swallow.* He found Glafirovka and its neighbourhood swarming with cavalry and therefore very properly confined his operations to destroying some very extensive corn and fish stores.

I next proceeded to the Crooked Spit in the Gulf of Azov (Taganrog) on the 18th; and I immediately ordered Commander Craufurd, in the *Swallow*, supported by the gunboats *Grinder, Boxer* and *Cracker*, and the boats of *Vesuvius, Fancy* and *Curlew*, to clear the spit and destroy the great fishing establishments situated upon it. While this service was being executed, I reconnoitred the mouth of the river Mius, 15 miles west of Taganrog, in HMS *Jasper*. The shallow nature of the coast would not allow us to approach within a mile and three-quarters of Fort Temenos. I returned to the same place, accompanied by the boats of HMS *Vesuvius* and *Curlew*, and HM gunboats *Cracker, Boxer* and *Jasper*. When we got to Fort Temenos and the usual Cossack picket had been driven off, I and Commander Lambert proceeded at once with the light boats up the river. When immediately under Fort Temenos, which stands upon a steep escarp of 80 feet, we found ourselves looked down upon by a large body of both horse and foot, lining the ditch and parapet of the work. Landing on the opposite bank, at good rifle-shot distance, one boat's crew under Lieutenant Rowley was sent to destroy a collection of launches and a fishery, whilst a careful and steady fire of Minie rifles kept the Russians from advancing on us. We returned to the vessels, passing within pistol-shot of the Russian ambuscade.

On July 19th I reconnoitred Taganrog in the *Jasper* gunboat. A new battery was being constructed on the heights near the hospital, but, although two shots were thrown into it, it did not reply. To put a stop to all traffic and to harass the enemy in this neighbourhood, I ordered Commander Craufurd to remain in the Gulf with two gunboats.

A few days later the light squadron sustained its only serious loss of the campaign. The *Jasper*, commanded by Lieutenant Joseph Hudson, had silenced a Russian field battery. In an excess of enthusiasm, Hudson took the captured guns aboard as trophies, forgetting that the additional weight would result in the gunboat drawing more water. The ship ran aground and, although the guns were thrown over the side, she could not be got off. She was, therefore, abandoned and blown up – prematurely, some thought, in view of the small threat presented by the supine Russians. Despite this, during the weeks that followed, the light squadron continued to raid at will, to the point that repetition would become tedious. No sooner had the Russians brought forward fresh stores than they were destroyed long before they could reach the Crimea, either by gunfire or landing parties. In this way Genichesk, Beryansk, Taganrog, Mariupol, Arabat and other places on the Azov coast were all attacked regularly, in spite of strenuous Russian attempts to strengthen their defences.

Although the Russians were having much the worst of things in the Azov, their defence of Sevastopol was conducted with characteristic stubbornness. On 17–18 June Allied attempts to storm the Malakoff and the Redan, the garrison's two principal defence works, were repulsed with heavy loss. Nevertheless, the cutting of the Crimean supply route began to affect both Sevastopol's defenders and the Russian field army. On 16 August the latter made one last desperate attempt to dislodge the besiegers but were decisively defeated by the French and Sardinians on Traktir Ridge. As the fortress was now clearly doomed, the Russians began burning their remaining warships and made preparations to withdraw the garrison across the harbour. These were hastened when the French stormed the Malakoff on 8 September. That night the garrison withdrew after blowing up the rest of its fortifications, and the following morning the Allies occupied the city.

The fall of Sevastopol did not mean that the little ships' work had ended. On the eastern side of the Kerch Straits the enemy had begun assembling a small army at Taman and Fanagorinsk and it was thought that when the winter ice closed the straits, this might be used to cross it and recapture Kerch. On 24 September an Allied force including the gunboats *Lynx, Arrow* and *Snake*, plus eight French gunboats, ferried nine infantry companies to Taman and provided covering fire while the troops disembarked. Taman was hastily abandoned, as was

Fanogorinsk, where the fort and barracks were occupied and 62 guns rendered unserviceable. While this was taking place some 600 Cossacks appeared, only to be dispersed by the gunboats' fire. The force then burned the buildings and retired to Kerch with a quantity of useful stores.

In the Sea of Azov the light squadron continued its depredations. On 4 November it was the turn of Glafirovka, the defences of which had been considerably strengthened since the last visit in July. *Recruit, Grinder, Boxer* and *Cracker* first engaged the enemy trenches with shrapnel while *Clinker* was towing in the boats of the landing party, then set the corn stores ablaze with carcasses. The fight ended with a charge by Marines and cutlass-wielding seamen, led by Lieutenants Day and Campion, which drove the Russians out of their positions. Simultaneously, other ships raided Yeysk so that the day's operations left a two-mile stretch of coastline in flames. The last foray carried out by the gunboats and their landing parties penetrated the river Liman on 6 November, destroying stores piled along a four-mile frontage.

In the Caucasus, the Russians captured the Turkish fortress of Kars on 26 November, enabling the ministers of the new Tsar, Alexander II, to request peace negotiations with one success to their credit. The war had cost each side about a quarter of a million deaths, the majority caused by disease. Its results included the preservation of the Ottoman Empire's integrity and the Tsar's loss of his role as protector of the Sultan's Orthodox Christian subjects.

It would be simplistic to suggest that the light squadron's operations in the Sea of Azov were entirely responsible for the fall of Sevastopol. They did, however, make a considerable contribution to that end, and as far as resources and manpower were concerned, the light squadron was the most profit-bearing formation the Allies possessed. As Osborn commented in his despatch to his Commander-in-Chief:

I despair of being able to convey to you any idea of the extraordinary quantity of corn, rye, hay, wood and other supplies so necessary for the existence of the Russian armies, both in the Caucasus and the Crimea. During these proceedings we never had more than 200 men engaged.

Furthermore, at a trivial cost to itself, the squadron tied down tens of thousands of Russian troops across a wide area in an ineffective defence when they could have been more profitably employed elsewhere. In the subsequent honours and promotions Osborn became a Companion of the Bath and was promoted to captain; the rest of the squadron's commanders also received promotion to captain, and the majority of its lieutenants became commanders. Eight Victoria Crosses were awarded during the Kerch/Sea of Azov operations. To our eyes, used to the strict application of the modern regulations governing the supreme award for valour, this may seem a surprisingly high number. It must, however, be remembered that at the time the newly instituted Victoria Cross was the only medal that could be awarded to officers and men of *both* British armed services for acts of exceptional gallantry; again, few would be so mean-spirited as to argue that the instances quoted above were unworthy of recognition.

The operations in the Sea of Azov also convinced the Royal Navy that, with the bulk of the Fleet retained in home waters for the defence of the United Kingdom, the so-called Crimean gunboats provided an ideal and inexpensive means of policing the often troubled waters of a global empire that was still expanding.

2
CHINESE POISON
The Second Opium War, 1856–60

For the moment, Great Britain's position as the workshop of the world, producing everything from locomotives to dolls' eyes, remained unchallenged. Germany was still a geographical area embracing a number of autonomous states, the United States had yet to reach its full potential and was on the point of being torn apart by a tragic civil war, and Japan was still locked in her self-imposed medieval isolation. As trade was the lifeblood of the British economy, it was natural that her merchants and manufacturers should seek fresh markets and sources of raw materials wherever they could.

China, vast, mysterious and barely penetrated by Western commercial enterprise, offered such a market. Until 1834 British trade with China had been the monopoly of the Honourable East India Company but was restricted by the Chinese government to the port of Canton. After the monopoly ended, newcomers to the market found this restriction irksome in the light of the potentially vast rewards that would accrue from opening up the entire area to commercial activity. Unfortunately, in the Chinese scheme of things, merchants, and in particular foreign merchants, were regarded as being just one step up from soldiers and prostitutes, who were looked upon as the lowest of the low, but necessary evils withal. As if to emphasise the point, some merchants made a great deal of money by importing the drug opium from India and Burma. Opium was slowly destroying the moral fibre of the population in much the same way other drugs affect that of Western nations today. The Chinese declared the trade illegal but in 1839 their general heavy-handed treatment of British merchants, whether they were involved in the loathsome trade or not, resulted in the so-called First Opium War. This ended in 1842 with the Treaty of Nanking, as a result of which China ceded Hong Kong to Great Britain, opened the ports of Canton, Amoy, Foochow, Ningpo and Shanghai to British trade, paid an indemnity of £5 million, and granted British residents in China

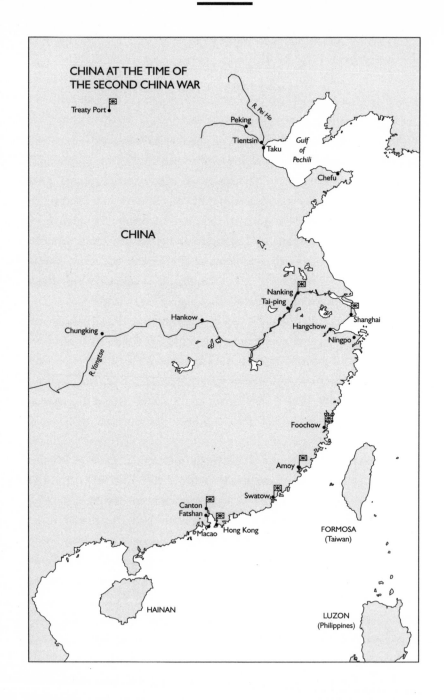

CHINA AT THE TIME OF
THE SECOND CHINA WAR

Treaty Port

R. Pei Ho

Peking

Tientsin
Taku

Gulf
of
Pechili

Chefu

CHINA

Nanking
Tai-ping

Hankow

Shanghai

Hangchow

Chungking

Ningpo

R. Yangtse

Foochow

Amoy

Swatow

Canton
Fatshan

Hong Kong

Macao

FORMOSA
(Taiwan)

LUZON
(Philippines)

HAINAN

rights which effectively placed them above the law. Naturally, this provoked considerable resentment among the Chinese, who deliberately chose to ignore many of the treaty's provisions. The harassment of British merchants continued, culminating in October 1856 with the arrest of the British schooner *Arrow* and the imprisonment of several members of her crew. The Royal Navy promptly bombarded Canton, the response of the local mandarin, Imperial High Commissioner Yeh, being to burn every British business in the area and offer a bounty of $30 for every British head received.

The Flag Officer East Indies and China Station was Rear Admiral Sir Michael Seymour, who had distinguished himself in the Baltic and lost the sight of his right eye while examining one of the Russian mines recovered off Kronstadt. Unable to maintain his position in the Canton River and its maze of creeks because of constant Chinese attacks, including the regular use of fireships, he retreated downstream to Macao, requesting reinforcement in the form of a squadron of gunboats and 5000 troops from India. The latter could not be despatched because of the outbreak of the Great Mutiny, but in May 1857 the gunboats *Haughty, Plover, Opossum, Bustard, Forester, Starling* and *Staunch* reached Hong Kong and it became possible to take the initiative again.

Seymour's first priority was to dispose of the mandarin fleet, which was well over 100 junks strong, each armed with a 32- or 24-pounder gun forward, plus four to six smaller guns elsewhere. The bulk of the fleet lay in Fatshan Creek, in the tangle of waterways south of Canton. Before he could tackle this, however, he had to secure his rear by eliminating a large detachment of junks lying in Escape Creek, a westerly branch of the Canton River. On 25 May, led by Commodore (later Admiral of the Fleet Sir Charles) Elliot aboard the tender *Hongkong* (sic), the gunboats *Bustard, Starling* and *Staunch* and the tender *Sir Charles Forbes*, all towing boats containing boarding parties contributed by larger warships, entered the creek and soon sighted 41 junks anchored across their path. The Chinese opened fire at once. Elliot's ships, also forming line-abreast, returned it, the big 68-pound rounds causing the splinters to fly. Yeh's men, used hitherto to firing at men in open boats in the confines of these tortuous, shallow waterways, had not expected this. They cut their cables, hoisted sail, broke out their sweeps and attempted to escape upstream. Drawing only three feet of water as they did, they probably felt secure but, to their horror, the gunboats followed them. The chase continued for several miles until, one by one, the gunboats grounded. Their crews tumbled into the pulling boats. Gradually, the gap began to close.

At this period, and indeed for many years after, British seamen were trained as a matter of course in the use of the cutlass, rifle and bayonet and other small arms. Those posted to the Far East, where piracy was a way of life for some, could expect to be engaged in hand-to-hand fighting, either while boarding or as part of a landing party. They were bigger and more aggressive than their opponents, who were usually reluctant to let matters come to close quarters. Such was the case now. Each junk kept up a barrage of grape and langridge until she was over-hauled, and was then hastily abandoned by her crew, who swam or waded ashore. Seventeen were taken in the main channel, a further ten

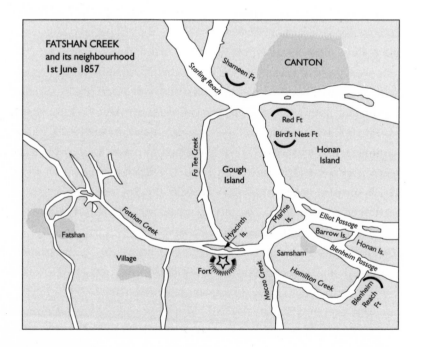

which turned off into a secondary creek being burned by their crews. Incredibly, only two casualties were sustained during the action although, such was the intense physical effort involved under a broiling sun, a number of men went down with heatstroke. The following day the pursuit continued as far as Tung Kwan, where the enemy abandoned their junks and a covering battery as soon as the boats opened fire. The force then itself came under fire from the houses along the waterfront, which had to be cleared by a landing party before the junks could be burned.

The way was now clear for Admiral Seymour to deal with the main body of the mandarin fleet in Fatshan Creek. The enemy junks were lying upstream of Hyacinth Island, a long, low feature dividing the river into two narrow channels. The southern channel was protected by a 19-gun fort on a hill, and the northern channel by a 6-gun battery. The position, therefore, was a strong one and, given the enemy's strength, quite capable of withstanding an attack by a force larger than that which Seymour had at his disposal.

Seymour led the attack personally aboard the two-gun paddle tender *Coromandel* (Lieutenant Sholto Douglas). The other vessels at his disposal were the *Hongkong* (Lieutenant James Goodenough) and the gunboats *Haughty* (Lieutenant Richard Hamilton), *Plover* (Lieutenant Keith Stewart), *Opossum* (Lieutenant Andrew Campbell), *Bustard* (Lieutenant Tathwell Collinson), *Forester* (Lieutenant Arthur Innes), *Starling* (Lieutenant Arthur Villiers) and *Staunch* (Lieutenant Leveson Wildman). In tow were boats containing seamen and Marines from the fleet's larger warships still lying off the mouth of the Canton River. Seymour's plan involved Commodore Elliot, with seamen and Marines from the *Coromandel, Haughty* and the boats they had in tow, capturing the 19-gun fort. While the fort was being attacked, Commodore the Hon. Henry Keppel, with the rest of the warships, was to pass Hyacinth Island and attack the mandarin junks. The attack took place on 1 June and is described by Seymour in his official despatch.

The flight of several signal rockets showed that the Chinese were fully alive to our proceedings. When within about 1000 yards of the fort, the *Coromandel* grounded on a barrier of sunken junks filled with stones, and the enemy opened fire. The leading party of seamen and Marines were immediately put in the boats and sent ahead; and under a very heavy fire of round (shot) and grape, in which the junk fleet joined, the fort was almost immediately in our possession, Commodore Elliot setting the good example of being one of the first into it. The landing was partially covered by the fire of the *Haughty*. One or two of the guns in the fort were immediately turned on the war junks. Happily, this important service was effected without loss.

The position was a remarkably strong one, and, defended by a body of resolute troops, might have bid defiance to any attack. The *Haughty*, having landed her party, went on with Commodore Elliot and the boats of the first division to co-operate with

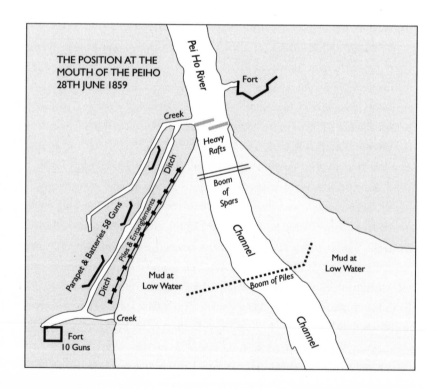

THE POSITION AT THE
MOUTH OF THE PEIHO
28TH JUNE 1859

Pei Ho River

Fort

Creek

Heavy
Rafts

Boom
of
Spars

Ditch

Parapet & Batteries 58 Guns

Piles & Entanglements

Channel

Ditch

Mud at
Low Water

Mud at
Low Water

Boom of Piles

Creek

Fort
10 Guns

Channel

Commodore Keppel. I ordered a portion of the Royal Marines, under Lieutenant and Adjutant Burton, to remain as a garrison in the fort, and sent Captain Boyle, RM, with the remainder, about 150 in number, to the scene of operations by land, to cut off the enemy retreating from the junks, and to prevent the advancing boats being annoyed by gingals (enormous muskets, usually fired from a wall) or matchlocks from a large village adjoining – a favourite tactic of the Chinese. One half of this force was ultimately sent back to the fort, and the remainder rejoined the squadron up the creek.

As soon as Commodore the Hon. H. Keppel perceived the men of the first division ascending the heights (to the fort), he advanced up the channel with the gun and other boats of the second, third and fourth divisions. With the exception of the *Haughty* and *Plover*, the gunboats soon grounded, but, agreeably to my instructions, the boats pushed ahead. The junks, which were admirably moored in position to enfilade the whole of the attacking force, soon opened a very heavy fire, keeping it up with great spirit, until our boats were close alongside, when the crews commenced abandoning their vessels, and to effect their escape across the paddy fields. The blowing up of one or two junks hastened the movement. In about twenty minutes we had possession of fifty junks.

Leaving the third and fourth divisions to secure the prizes, Commodore Keppel then proceeded about three miles further up the creek, where more mastheads were visible, and found twenty junks moored across the stream in a very strong position, which opened such a well-directed and destructive fire that he was obliged to retire and wait for reinforcements. The launch of the *Calcutta* was sunk by a round shot, the Commodore's galley had three round shot through her, and several other boats were much injured. On additional boats coming up, the Commodore shifted to the *Calcutta*'s black barge, and again advanced; and, after a severe action, the enemy gave way. They were pursued as far as Fatshan, a distance of seven miles, and seventeen of them (were) captured and burnt. In consequence of my orders not to molest this large and important city, the three junks which passed through the creek on which it is built effected their escape.

The result of this expedition was the capture of between seventy and eighty heavily-armed junks, mounting, on an average, from ten to fourteen guns (many of them long 32-pounders), nearly all of European manufacture. As no object would have been gained by removing the prizes, I caused them, with a few exceptions, to be burnt; and the flames and numerous heavy explosions must have been seen and heard far and wide.

This remarkable victory was gained at a cost of 13 killed and 44 wounded. Nevertheless, despite the loss of his fleet, Commissioner Yeh declined to negotiate, the reason being that British prestige in the Far East had been damaged first by the gross mismanagement of the early stages of the Crimean War, and then by the Great Mutiny in India, which was then at its height. It was as clear to Yeh as it was to Seymour that the British Army had its hands full and that, for the present, no troops could be spared for China. The Admiralty, however, did send out Captain Sherard Osborn, who had so distinguished himself in the Sea of Azov, with the gunboats *Algerine, Lee, Leven, Slaney, Banterer, Firm, Clown, Drake, Janus, Kestrel, Watchful* and *Woodcock*, together with three new gunvessels, *Cormorant, Surprise* and *Nimrod*, which were better suited to deep-water operations. France, too, was having her problems with China and in July Seymour was further reinforced with a French squadron under Rear Admiral Rigault de Genouilly.

Perhaps if the dispute had been confined to trade it could have been settled, despite the fact that the Peking government tended to regard the Cantonese as something of a law unto themselves and was itself distracted by risings and unrest in other parts of China. By now, an altogether new dimension had been introduced in that the Western powers, including Great Britain, France, Russia and the United States, were all demanding diplomatic accreditation to the Court of Peking. In the normal course of events, an ambassador presented his credentials directly to the monarch of the country to which he had been sent, but to the Chinese such a suggestion was outrageous. The fact was, that although they themselves would have been the first to agree that the Machu administration was rotten to the core, with 'squeeze' being extracted at every level, they venerated their Emperor as a god. The very geography of Peking, resembling a set of conjuror's puzzle boxes, confirmed this. Inside the walled Tartar City lay the walled Imperial City, inside which lay the walled Forbidden City, where the Emperor had his palace. Only the highest officials were permitted to approach him; to the rest of his subjects he remained unseen, remote and sublimely mysterious. The idea that barbarians from the outer edges of the world should be allowed to enter the Divine Presence was, therefore, completely unacceptable, and for that reason the British plenipotentiary, Lord Elgin, had been kept kicking his heels around the Far East to no purpose.

As the year drew to its close, Seymour felt strong enough to attack Canton itself. On 28 December, 32 Allied ships bombarded the city and its defences were stormed by landing parties. The Chinese requested and were granted a truce, but proved so unwilling to enter constructive negotiations that at dawn on 5 January 1858 the commander of the enemy's Tartar cavalry, General Muh, the governor of the city, Peh-Kwei, and High Commissioner Yeh himself, were all seized by what, today, would be called snatch squads. The first two were released to maintain order among the civil population, under the supervision of an international commission, but Yeh was shipped off to end his days in India.

Canton reopened for business on 10 February. The Imperial government, however, still refused to negotiate. At length Lord Elgin and the French plenipotentiary, Baron Gros, reached the conclusion that they would only get what they wanted in Peking itself. That would involve an overland march of 80 miles from Tientsin, lying at the junction of the Grand Canal with the Pei Ho River, 34 miles upstream from Taku, where the latter flowed between muddy banks into the Gulf of Chi-li. The Allied fleet arrived off the mouth of the river to find that the

Chinese, anticipating such a move, had begun fortifying the estuary. Seymour's despatch describes the defences:

> Earthworks, sandbag batteries and batteries for the heavy gingals have been erected on both sides for a distance of nearly a mile, upon which 87 guns in position were visible, and the whole shore had been lined with piles driven into the mud to oppose a landing. As the channel is only about 200 yards wide and runs within 400 yards of the shore, these defences presented a formidable appearance. Two strong mud batteries, mounting respectively 33 and 16 guns, had also been constructed about 1000 yards up the river, in a position to command our advance. In the rear several entrenched camps were visible, defended by flanking bastions.

On 20 May the local mandarin ignored Seymour's ultimatum to hand over the forts within two hours and at 10:00 the attack began. The North Forts were attacked by *Cormorant, Staunch, Bustard* and three French gunboats, and the South Forts by *Nimrod, Opossum, Leven, Firm* and two more French gunboats. In tow were the boats of the landing parties, numbering 1178 officers and men. *Cormorant*, under Commander Thomas Saumarez, went full ahead to smash her way through a boom of spars and chains. The forts themselves were quickly smothered by accurate fire from the gunboats and silenced. Proceeding upstream, the landing parties went ashore and took possession of the now-outflanked defence works. The Chinese responded with fire junks full of blazing straw, guided from the shore by ropes, but these burned themselves out harmlessly after *Bustard*, commanded by Lieutenant Frederick Hallowes, dispersed the handling parties with a few rounds. By 14:00 it was all over; the Allies sustained 87 casualties, all but 20 of them being French.

The gunboats proceeded up-river to Tientsin where, although brickbats were thrown at one or two officers who went ashore, most people were friendly and keen to supply the ships with fresh victuals. The Imperial government, now seriously alarmed and anxious that no further face should be lost, immediately despatched representatives to meet Lord Elgin. They willingly accepted every one of his demands, including the establishment of legations in Peking, the recognition of the legitimacy of the opium traffic, the opening of more ports to foreign trade, and co-operation in suppressing piracy. Understandably satisfied, the Allies withdrew.

Unfortunately, the Imperial government had no more intention of being bound by the Treaty of Tientsin than it had by the Treaty of Nanking. It temporised over matters of interpretation, declined to admit foreign diplomats to Peking, turned a blind eye to the renewed harassment of British merchants in Canton, closed the Yangtse and Pei Ho Rivers to British shipping, and began turning the coastal defences at Taku into formidable fortresses. In the spring of 1859 it was apparent that the Peking administration would have to be taught another sharp lesson. By then, Seymour had been relieved by Rear Admiral Sir James Hope, a man of undeniable courage, albeit one whose judgement had been questioned during the Crimean War. Nevertheless, in fairness to him, it must be said that once he had been ordered to force the mouth of the Pei Ho again, his options were limited, particularly as the depth of water above the bar at high tide was only 11 feet, thereby excluding warships larger than gunboats from the attack.

Again, the defences were infinitely stronger than they had been the previous year. It was said that the Chinese, impressed by the resistance offered by Sevastopol's coastal forts, had taken the advice of Russian military engineers. The Large South Fort now had ramparts half a mile long, with three commanding towers within the perimeter. A similar fortification had been built on the north bank and a little way upstream could be seen two smaller forts, one on each bank. The precise number of guns facing the attackers was concealed by matting hung from the walls. In addition, the navigable channel had been blocked by several formidable obstacles. At the river's mouth was a line of sharp iron stakes supported by tripods sunk into the mud, the intention being to tear the bottom out of any large craft which tried to pass over them; opposite the Large South Fort was a floating boom consisting of one stout hemp and two chain cables, supported by floating logs at 30-foot intervals; some 300 yards beyond the boom were two huge rafts, moored so as to leave only a narrow zig-zag channel between them; and beyond the rafts was another line of iron stakes.

In the third week of June 1860 Hope sent a message to the Chinese commander, demanding the removal of the obstacles. While his men continued to strengthen their defences, the latter replied that the barriers were there to keep out pirates and would be removed presently. On 21 June 1860 the admiral issued an ultimatum that if the obstacles had not been dismantled in three days' time, they would be removed by force. The answer he received was non-committal.

After dark on 24 June a reconnaissance party of three armed boats under Captain George Willes entered the river and examined the obstacles in turn. While the Chinese sentries paced the bank nearby, Willes crawled onto one of the rafts and reached the conclusion that it would withstand any amount of ramming by the small gunboats. Then, after exploding a demolition charge in the centre of the boom, the party retired, attracting several harmless cannon shots as it did so. The boom sustained little or no damage and was still firmly in place the following morning.

Having received Willes's report, a more cautious commander than Hope would have revised his plans. Hope, however, believed that he would experience no more difficulty than had Seymour the previous year, and decided to attack that very morning. His second mistake lay in timing the attack to coincide with high water at 11:30, for with every hour that passed the ebbing tide would expose an ever-expanding expanse of clinging mud, two feet deep and intersected by creeks, which the landing parties would have to cross in the teeth of the enemy's fire.

Hope elected to lead the attack aboard Lieutenant Hector Rason's gunboat *Plover*. The other vessels participating in the attack were the gunboats *Opossum* (Lieutenant Charles Balfour), with Captain Willes aboard, *Starling* (Lieutenant Arthur Villiers), *Janus* (Lieutenant Herbert Knevitt), *Lee* (Lieutenant William Jones), *Kestrel* (Lieutenant George Bevan), *Banterer* (Lieutenant John Jenkins) and *Haughty* (Lieutenant George Broad), the gunvessel *Cormorant* (Commander Armine Woodhouse) and the sloop *Nimrod* (Acting Commander James Wynniat). Although the *Cormorant* and the *Nimrod* mounted four and six guns respectively, the gunboats were each armed with one 68- and one 32-pounder gun, plus, in some cases, two howitzers. This seems little enough to pit against the 600 guns which later events revealed were contained in the two South Forts alone. Hope could not possibly have known this, but the extensive work carried out on the enemy fortifications should have suggested to him that he was badly out-gunned from the start. His plan, in fact, was based on wishful thinking, in that nine of the gunboats would be required to anchor below the outer barrier of iron stakes and cover the forts while two more broke through each of the obstacles in turn, clearing the way upstream. If the Chinese resisted, their guns would be silenced and the forts stormed by a 500-strong landing party of sailors and Marines provided by the larger warships anchored beyond the bar, carried ashore in steam pinnaces, ships' boats and junks.

The operation got off to an ominously bad start. Navigational difficulties prevented the gunboats getting into position until well after the appointed time and two of them, *Banterer* and *Starling*, stuck fast on mud banks in positions which prevented all their guns from bearing. At 14:00 *Opossum*'s crew passed a cable round one of the outer stakes and the gunboat went full astern, but so well had it been secured that 30 minutes of hard pulling were required before it was wrenched free. *Plover*, followed by *Oppossum,* passed through the gap and closed in on the floating boom.

For the moment, the forts had remained silent, but now they hoisted flags, unmasked a frightening array of embrasures, and opened a tremendous fire, the accuracy of which clearly indicated that the Chinese had been training hard. The gunboats, just 200 yards abeam of the Large South Fort and with the Large North Fort 400 yards off the starboard bow, returned this. From time to time they had the satisfaction of dismounting a Chinese gun, but it was quickly replaced, as were the men who had been killed around it. By 15:00 both gunboats had been seriously knocked about. Aboard *Plover,* Rason had been cut in two by a round shot, as had Captain McKenna of Hope's staff, and only nine of the 40-strong crew remained alive and uninjured. Hope's thigh was torn open by a splinter, but he refused to leave the deck. Also aboard *Plover* was a young midshipman undergoing his baptism of fire. His name was John Fisher and, as First Sea Lord many years later, he would lead the Royal Navy into the 20th century and be responsible for introducing the dreadnought battleship. Whatever he may have thought previously, the sights and sounds he witnessed off the Taku Forts that day disabused any idea that war was a glamorous occupation.

At this point, something remarkable happened. Anchored outside the bar was the flagship of the US Navy's Asiatic Squadron, commanded by Flag Officer (Commodore) Josiah Tattnall. During the War of 1812 he had fought against the British as a midshipman, but that lay in the past and he was not enjoying the spectacle of two of their gunboats being knocked apart. Calling away his steam launch, he disregarded the Chinese fire and came alongside the stricken *Plover.* Climbing aboard, he suggested to Hope that his launch should be used to evacuate the wounded, an offer the admiral gratefully accepted. Tattnall returned to his boat to find the crew missing. Presently they appeared from forward, sweating, powder-stained and grinning sheepishly.

'What have you been doing, you rascals?' he shouted. 'Don't you know we're neutrals?'

'Beg pardon, sir,' said one of the men, 'they were a bit short-handed on the bow gun and we thought it no harm to give them a hand while we were waiting.'

Turning to Hope, Tattnall could only shrug and comment, 'I guess blood must be thicker than water!' It was a remark that would be long remembered by both navies.

At 15:00 Hope gave permission for *Plover*, now virtually reduced to wreckage, to retire. Calling forward *Lee* and *Haughty*, he had himself transferred to *Opossum,* which was in little better state, with barely enough men to keep the guns firing and none to deal with a fire on her stern. Hardly had the admiral established himself aboard than he was felled by a tangle of falling rigging. Despite the acute pain caused by three cracked ribs, he had himself strapped up and insisted on being lifted into a boat to visit *Lee* and *Haughty* while *Opossum* also dropped downstream. *Lee* received such a battering below the water-line that her pumps could no longer cope. Lieutenant Jones, her commander, was reluctant to order a man over the side to plug the holes because the current would probably sweep him into the churning propeller. Boatswain Woods, however, declaring that for the moment it didn't seem to matter much where he was killed, went over with a line round his waist and a supply of plugs. He managed to plug several holes, but the ship was filling too quickly and had to be run aground to prevent her sinking. *Haughty* was also knocked about and retired when her place was taken by *Cormorant* and *Kestrel*. Aboard *Cormorant*, Hope had himself placed in a chair on deck until, having lost consciousness once, he allowed himself to be taken out to the hospital ship at the bar, handing over command of the operation to Captain Charles Shadwell of the frigate *Highflyer*. At about 17:30 *Kestrel*, riddled and with only three of her crew unwounded, went to the bottom.

The enemy fire slackened, as well it might, given that the gunboats were either sunk, disabled or aground. Unfortunately, Shadwell took this development to mean that the Chinese had had enough and decided to launch the landing party against the Large South Fort, irrespective of the fact that it would have to wade across 500 yards of tidal mud before it reached the ramparts. Predictably, the result was a disaster. The Chinese opened up with cannon, gingals, muskets, stink bombs filled with burning sulphur, and even arrows. Only 50 men, their paper cartridges wet through, reached the walls and they were repulsed with ease. The party floundered back to the shoreline, where some of its boats had sunk. The last of them, up to their necks in the rising tide, were not taken off until 01:00 next morning. Of the 500 men who had landed, 68 were killed and nearly 300 wounded.

The same tide lifted *Kestrel* and brought her downstream, bottom upwards. *Lee* was adjudged a total loss and was burned next day. *Plover* had gone aground while coming out of action; *Cormorant* was sent to get her off but the Chinese battered both ships until they sank. Casualties among the gunboat crews amounted to 25 killed and 93 wounded. It was the worst reverse in the entire history of gunboat warfare. Hope commended many individuals in his despatch, but because the engagement ended in defeat no decorations or promotions were awarded, despite the exemplary courage displayed by the crews in attempting to fulfil an impossible task.

At home the news of the reverse was received with outrage, although Hope retained his command as the public was impressed by the courage he had shown under fire. In March 1860 the Imperial government was sent an ultimatum demanding ratification of the Treaty of Tientsin, an apology for firing on Hope's ships and compensation for the losses incurred. A reply was neither expected nor forthcoming and, as the mutiny in India had been quelled, an expeditionary force was assembled. Consisting of 11,000 British and Indian troops under Lieutenant General Sir James Hope Grant and 6700 French under Lieutenant General Cousin-Montauban, this landed at Peh-tang, several miles north of the Pei Ho estuary, on 30 July. On 21 August, while Admiral Hope's ships again bombarded the Large North and South Forts, the troops stormed the Small North Fort in a dashing attack from the rear. The Small South Fort was immediately abandoned by the enemy. The commander of the Large North Fort blustered briefly, then allowed the French to take possession without a shot being fired. Within were several guns taken from the gunboats lost the previous year. The 2000-strong garrison, expecting to be massacred, were simply disarmed and sent home. Across the river, Hang Foo, the mandarin commanding the now isolated Large South Fort, surrendered next day.

The Allies advanced up-river to Tientsin and then began marching on Peking, defeating a Chinese field army in two engagements. The Imperial government indicated its willingness to talk, but then behaved with crass stupidity by kidnapping the Allied negotiators and holding them to ransom against a further advance. When the advance was resumed the captives were savagely tortured to the extent that over half of them died. Grant was preparing to storm Peking when, on 13 October, the Imperial government capitulated, agreeing to every one of the Allied demands, including the surrender of Kowloon on the mainland opposite Hong Kong, the payment of a substantial indemnity and ratification of the various treaties. In reprisal for the atrocities committed, the Imperial Summer Palace was looted and the Yuen-Ming-Yuen, a group of palaces set in beautiful gardens, was burned to the ground.

Apart from a brief undeclared war with France in the 1880s, the Imperial government avoided conflict with the Western powers for the next 40 years, when it provided unofficial support for the Boxer Rising of 1900. The reaction to this would involve warships and troops from many nations and, once again, the Taku Forts were stormed prior to an advance on Peking to relieve the embattled Legation Quarter. Many of the minor characters in this drama would achieve fame later in life. For example, the young American engineer who laid out the defences of the International Settlement at Tientsin was named Herbert Hoover and one day he would become President of the United States. Serving on the staff of Vice-Admiral Sir Edward Seymour, whose uncle had effected the first capture of the Forts, was Captain John Jellicoe, who would command the Grand Fleet at the Battle of Jutland. Also present was another future commander of the Grand Fleet, Commander David Beatty, who we shall meet again commanding a gunboat at the Battle of Omdurman; and, commanding the destroyer *Fame* in the Gulf of Chi-li, was Lieutenant Roger Keyes, who was to lead the Zeebrugge Raid in 1918 and become Chief of Combined Operations in the World War II.

As for the crumbling Manchu dynasty, it was to be held together by the iron will of the Dowager Empress Tzu Hsi until 1908, when she and the Emperor Kuang Hsu, who was little more than a figurehead, died mysteriously within a day of each other. The new Emperor, Pu Yi, ascended the throne of his ancestors at the age of two, but reigned only until the revolution of 1911, after which China became a republic, an event which solved few of the country's problems.

3
THE DEMISE OF JOLLY ROGER
The Suppression of Piracy in the East Indies
and the South China Sea, 1855–69

As trade between Europe and the Far East developed, so did piracy, on a scale that dwarfed the activities of the Caribbean buccaneers of the previous century. It has been suggested that the pirates of the East Indies, now Malaysia and Indonesia, and of the South China Sea, were simply fishermen impelled by hardship to seek a dishonest living. An examination of the facts, unfortunately, suggests that fishing was a last resort when their activities brought commerce to a standstill. The truth was that in both areas pirates operated in fleets large enough to intimidate the local authorities and were just as much a menace to their own people as they were to European traders.

In the East Indies the pirates' favourite vessel was the rakish flying-prahu, 50 feet long and with a 14-foot beam. The prahu had a high poop and a long bowsprit, and was steered by two oars, one on each quarter. The bipod mast, mounted well forward, carried a jib and a lug-lateen mainsail, with a similar but smaller sail being carried by a mizzen. Usually, one or two heavy swivel guns were mounted fore-and-aft. While this does not seem particularly dangerous, the prahu was the fastest thing afloat and, acting with others in a pack, could easily run down a merchant vessel or escape from a pursuing warship. The pirates of the Indies were a notably savage lot who would willingly slaughter everyone aboard any vessel that offered the slightest resistance, regardless of age or sex.

Small wonder, then, that the appearance of prahu sails struck terror into every merchantman sailing the waters of the Indies. The Dutch, having extensive possessions in the area, strove to contain the menace, as did the Sea Service of the Honourable East India Company in its time, and, of course, the Royal Navy. The pirates quickly learned that even if they felt strong enough to challenge small warships their prahus were soon knocked to pieces by the dozen, with heavy loss of life, so they avoided direct contact as much as possible. The difficulty lay in getting at them, for their lairs lay in fortified villages up rivers too shallow for conventional warships to navigate. Naval landing parties therefore had to proceed upstream in the pulling boats, being sniped at from the jungle-covered banks the while, and sometimes being treated to a dose of grape or langridge from a cannon sited in a cleared fire-lane. As they approached the village, they might find the channel closed with piles and have to proceed on foot. Finally, they would have to storm the stockades of the village itself, supported by nothing heavier than the boat guns. This could involve heavy hand-to-hand fighting against invariably superior numbers. Generally, however, the pirates, more used to butchering helpless victims than confronting disciplined aggression, disliked the experience and took to their heels. Their village was then burned, as were their prahus, and their guns were taken out to sea and dropped into deep water, beyond hope of recovery.

While such punitive raids would put a pirate community out of business for a considerable time, other communities would gladly cash in on the vacuum so created, until they in turn were neutralised. Furthermore, it was inevitable that the landing parties would incur unwelcome casualties. However, the arrival of Crimean gunboats in the area accelerated the rate at which law and order could be imposed, as they could not only proceed further up rivers than conventional warships, but their impressive firepower often broke the enemy's will before the landing parties could launch their attack.

As might be expected, piracy in the South China Sea was even more of a menace and much better organised. It was, in fact, very big business with long-term financial strategies and entire fleets at its disposal. During the early years of the 19th century a widow named Ching Shih became the most powerful pirate leader ever, having at her disposal no less than 800 junks, about 1000 smaller craft and some 70,000 men, organised efficiently into six squadrons which operated in designated areas. She was quite beyond Imperial control, any naval mandarin who fell into her hands being roasted alive or treated to the Death of One Thousand Cuts. In due course her squadron commanders fell out and came to blows. One, having offered himself and his ships to the Imperial government, was rewarded with the rank of naval mandarin. Others, including Ching Shih, seeing which way the wind was blowing, did likewise, until all the more prominent pirates became nominal members of the Imperial Navy.

That did not mean the end of piracy. Ching Shih's fleet had simply outgrown itself to the point that it could no longer be sustained with adequate plunder or even sufficient rations. Thereafter, pirates continued to operate in smaller, more manageable numbers. Unlike their brethren in the East Indies, who sought immediate gain, the Chinese preferred to maintain the flow of commerce, charging junk owners protection money or impounding ships, cargoes and important passengers until they were ransomed. The difficulty facing the Royal Navy was that, initially at least, it was unable to engage even the most obvious pirate junk unless it was caught in the act of interfering with British shipping; nor could it mount punitive raids into sovereign Chinese territory in time of peace, despite the wishes of the local population and the mandarins' inability or deliberate reluctance to tackle the problem themselves. The despatch of Commander E. W. Vansittart of the sloop *Bittern*, written off the mouth of the River Min on 1 March 1855, illustrates the point perfectly:

The neighbourhood seems infested with pirates; miserably poor boats followed the brig begging assistance; one village sent me a well drawn up petition; another a present of waste paper and joss sticks; fishermen, and passage boats, small traders, all telling the same pitiable story. Landing on Hootow, I was quickly surrounded by peasantry. Desiring the interpreter to ask them why so many fine looking fellows permitted strangers to molest them, they declared it was useless to resist pirates, and so whenever pirates came they, the villagers, 'hid themselves and cried'. I could not offer any direct support, but trust good may arise indirectly. At various points along the coast we sighted small knots of piratical craft, but without information against them of their interference with our Flag, I could not act.

Having run up the river to within eight miles of the city of Wanchow, I learnt that a portion of the West Coast Pirate Squadron that had detained the English schooner *Zephyr* was still higher up. I detached the Second Lieutenant with four boats and a strong party to push past them with the flood tide in the grey of the morning, bringing them between the boats and the ship until I communicated with the mandarins. This was fortunate (as) the pirates were thrown off their guard although found with guns crammed and matches lighted. Three were captured without resistance; two escaped inland (i.e. up-river); the five or six others had put to sea shortly before our arrival. The Chief and many of the crews got away, but the 64 remaining Canton men were secured and will be delivered up to the authorities here. The Toutai and Chinese admiral at Wanchow were evidently so powerless that it appeared useless to remonstrate on the permitted outrage against a British vessel almost under their walls, but I thought it well to bring the point forward and was met with pretty sayings and civilities. They informed me that they had lately entered into engagements with these very pirates, on which I offered to hand them over. This the mandarins declined, saying it would be better to carry them to Foochow, and thanked me for taking them.

Given the Imperial authorities' apparent impotence, much of which can be attributed to piratical threats or bribes, it is hardly surprising that warship captains, free from immediate political restraint, began to take the law into their own hands. On 20 October 1858 Admiral Seymour received the following despatch from Captain Nicholas Vansittart of the *Magicienne,* following her return to Hong Kong:

I have the honour to inform your Excellency that I arrived at the port and anchored off the town of Swatow in HM ship under my command, on the 13th inst, finding there HMS *Fury.* Commander Leckie having informed me that he was in communication with the Chinese authorities, with Mr Barton,

Agent to Messrs Dent, and Mr Sullivan, Agent to Messrs Jardine & Matheson, concerning 2200 bags of sugar that had been piratically seized on or about the 21st ult from the English brig *Pantaloon* by a large force from the town of Sow-ah-pow, a well-known piratical town some miles up the narrow channel on the opposite side of the town of Swatow, I requested Commander Leckie (as I was under medical treatment) to continue his inquiries and exertions towards the recovery of the sugar and that I would remain there in case it should be necessary to use force.

On the 15th inst the mandarin of the village near Sow-ah-pow having informed Commander Leckie that the pirates refused to give up the sugar and that he was unable to force them, on the next morning the 16th inst, the Marines and boats of this ship, with those of the *Fury*, started soon after daylight for Sow-ah-pow, but, although I went myself, I left command of the expedition under Commander Leckie as originally arranged.

Upon our arriving off Sow-ah-pow shortly after 8 a.m., not only was there no mandarin to receive us (information having been given that the boats were coming up to inquire into the transaction), but many hundreds of men, armed chiefly with matchlocks and some gingals, had come down near the water at Sow-ah-pow, which was 1200 yards inland, the men all in good position on the heights, under the lee of the dikes of the water courses, and in among the sugar cane. They immediately opened fire on us and jeered us to come on. The boats returning the fire for some minutes, orders were given by Commander Leckie for the Marines and a party of seamen to land, when the pirates kept up a continual fire, retreating and taking up other positions as they went.

Having taken possession of the heights, the other positions, and advanced to within 50 yards of the town, driving the enemy before us into the said place, Commander Leckie, Messrs Barton and Sullivan and also myself were of the opinion that a good bombardment, from the boats, would be more advisable and more likely to be the means of recovering the sugar than if we went in and set fire to the town. Orders were sent down to that effect, the force that was landing taking up a commanding position at 100 yards from the town. The bombardment was most successful, the shell firing from the boats being perfect, as was also the rocket practice. Another letter having been forwarded to demand the sugar, stating that if they still refused, a second visit would be paid and the town not spared, the expedition returned to their respective ships the same afternoon. The casualties on our side were two severely wounded, both belonging to HMS *Magicienne*.

Having remained at anchor off Swatow, until their answer should arrive, which I am happy to say is to the effect that they are willing to hand over the sugar and come to any settlement, I left the said anchorage on the 19th inst, leaving the further arrangements to Commander Leckie.

It took the British authorities in Hong Kong some time to discover that the proximate cause of much piratical activity lay right under their noses. One of the biggest of the Mr Bigs in the business ran a successful barber's shop in the mercantile quarter of the city. There he picked up information regarding the sailings of valuable cargoes and their destinations, which he supplied to the pirates at a price. Other sources of income included protection, extortion and blackmail. It was difficult for Europeans to penetrate the local community, and informers from the latter, if discovered, received short shrift from the triads, the Chinese secret societies that existed to protect and advance sectional interests. To some extent, British registered shipping could be protected by sailing in escorted convoys, although the Royal Navy could not be everywhere at once. The pirate barber, however, was playing a dangerous game in which it was inevitable that he made enemies, and in due course he was obliged to leave the colony for the good of his health.

Rear Admiral Hope relieved Seymour in April 1859 and on 11 March of that year issued an order for a sweep against the pirates. The results of this were recorded by the senior officer involved, Captain Colville of the *Niger*, in his despatch of 16 March:

Acting on information received at Macao, the whole of the 12th inst was spent in searching for a fleet of piratical vessels cruising in the vicinity of the Tang Rocks, but failing to discover them I weighed towards evening and anchored late off Koolan, with the intention of visiting Tsu-chung, under whose batteries a formidable fleet of piratical junks was known to be lying, the depradators of several valuable cargoes, an owner and Master of two of the captured junks acting as pilots under the able and effective assistance of Mr Caldwell, Register-General.

Accordingly, at seven on the morning of the 13th, I proceeded with the boats in tow of the gunboats *Clown* and *Janus* and after a run of 14 miles came within sight of a large flotilla of heavily armed junks and row-boats hauled under the protection of what we subsequently discovered to be regular defences consisting of a water stockade with a double ditch and high stockaded embankment armed with 36 guns protecting the whole sea face of and flanks of Tsu-chung.

Directing Lieutenant Wells in the ten-oared cutter to examine a suspicious junk to windward whilst the *Janus* overhauled two others to leeward, I took the remaining boats directly in towards the central force of junks, leaving the *Clown* to cover our movements but with peremptory orders to fire only in case the shore batteries opened on the boats.

However, it soon became evident that the enemy were prepared for a determined resistance; the crews of the junks joined the villagers, who with violent ejaculations and waving white flags on which the character 'Hoong-Kin-Wong' (a triad king) was prominent, invited us on, at the same time a heavy fire of round and grape opened on our advance. Forming behind a knoll of land, insulated by 500 yards of shallow water from the left extreme of the stockade, leaving the pinnace to cover the landing, and much assisted by the very excellent shell practice of the gunboats, the storming party dashed waist deep at the stockade and receiving a fire of grape entered the embrasures of an eight-gun battery, bayoneting the defenders who crowded the inner ditch and appeared paralysed by the vigour of the proceedings! After a short hand-to-hand encounter they retired precipitately, and now was seen the extraordinary sight of sixty bluejackets and Marines chasing 500 armed men through brakes and narrow acclivities for nearly two miles in the rear of the works! In this movement great numbers of the enemy were killed and it had the effect of turning the sea defences thus rendered comparatively harmless.

The storming party were now joined by the men under Lieutenants Blake and Wells, who by a judicious detour to the right had materially assisted to the discomfiture of the pirates. Every house in the town was a magazine in which large quantities of arms and munitions were stored. I consequently directed the village to be burned, eight large piratical fighting junks and eleven fast boats shared a similar fate, their guns having previously been sunk in deep water. The thirty-six guns of the land defences were also destroyed. Considerable resistance was offered by two of the junks, the boats being repeatedly hulled.

When I bring to Your Excellency's notice the very large force of men consisting of at least 1300 effectively armed, with a necessary perfect knowledge of locale and the determination they evinced in opposing our landing, I cannot but feel astonished at our good fortune – not a casualty occurred whereas the loss to the enemy could not have been under 180 men. After communicating with a mandarin junk force just arrived from Macao with the information that seven pirate junks were at anchor off Li-wan-mun opposite Moto, the boats returned to the ship at Koolan.

On the 14th, having despatched the *Niger* to await my arrival at Macao, I proceeded with the whole boat force to examine the numerous crannies to the west of Broadway *en route* to Li-wan-mun. In Sykee, a bay opposite Koolan, four piratical junks, with guns numerically formidable, were driven on shore and burnt by Lieutenant Villiers. In the largest an English Red Ensign was found. In a deep inlet to the north of Soochow three others were captured and destroyed.

Arriving at Li-wan-mun, I was informed that seven junks had slipped a few hours previously and run higher up the creek. The villagers in pointing out their position were graphic in their account of the barbarities they were committing and hailed our arrival with the most enthusiastic rejoicings. A hamlet had been sacked and a passage boat taken that very morning. Advancing until dusk, I anchored and prepared, by getting pilots, for prosecuting my search in the morning.

On the 15th we weighed at daylight and piloted by boatmen who had been robbed by these pirates on the evening of our visit, threaded the remainder of the tortuous reach connecting Broadway with a river running in a parallel direction. The piratical squadron were shortly discovered ahead using every effort to escape. When the sternmost mounting 24 guns was brought to, she proved to have been a rice boat captured in January from the Hong Kong Chinese merchant who accompanied Mr Caldwell. I caused her, therefore, having previously removed the guns, to be restored. Seven large passage boats were likewise released.

The gunboats were now unfortunately taking the ground. I despatched the boats to capture the remainder, a service I am bound to add most ably executed, the pinnace under Mr Blake, the senior lieutenant present, after a running fight of one hour and a quarter driving one of nine guns on shore, her crew being immediately pounced upon by mandarin soldiers. Another junk of 12 guns, after a vigorous resistance in which two stink-pots were thrown into the boats of *Janus* under Lieutenant Knevitt, was carried by boarding, and three others mounting respectively seven, nine and 22 guns were captured and burnt by Lieutenant Villiers with the two cutters in co-operation with the *Clown*.

Exclusive of the crew who fell into the hands of the mandarins, 21 pirates were killed on this occasion by the fire of the boats, and the guns, mostly 18- and 24-pounders of American manufacture, were sunk beyond means of recovery. I then returned to the ship at Macao, arriving at midnight, from whence I proceeded this morning to join your flag.

Given repeated hammerings such as this, the pirate menace would probably have been solved even earlier than it was, save that the débâcle at the Pei Ho River a few months later not only reduced the number of gunboats available but also demonstrated that the Royal Navy was fallible. The losses, however, were quickly made good. The replacements had conventionally shaped hulls and were thus less lively in heavy weather. They included several slightly larger barque-rigged gunvessels, up to 185 feet long with proper holds and improved accommodation, armed with one 68-pounder rifled muzzle-loader and four 24-pounder howitzers.

Once a gunboat had been sent to the Far East it was Admiralty policy that she should end her days there, with any necessary repairs being carried out at Hong Kong. Commissions lasted between three and four years, with replacement crews being sent out aboard transports or troopships. Service aboard gunboats was uncomfortable and so cramped that tall officers shaved with their heads through the skylight and their mirrors propped up on deck. The food was dreadful and the ships themselves notoriously bug-ridden. Nevertheless, the service was popular. It provided junior officers with a real chance to distinguish themselves, and it gave the crews a far more interesting life than they would ever have had aboard the spit-and-polish battleships of the Home Fleet. It did not matter whether a man was serving aboard a gunboat, a gunvessel or a sloop – being a gunboat man indicated a special state of mind involving the use of personal initiative and action, and that set him apart from the rest of the Navy.

Gunboat service could also be lucrative. Long before, the Admiralty had introduced an incentive known as Head Money, awarded as a bounty to crews in proportion to the number of slaves freed from captured slavers, and pirates killed or captured. For example, the crews of *Niger, Clown* and *Janus* shared £1600 for the actions of March 1859 described above. Once the Second Opium War was over, the gunboats returned to the suppression of piracy with a will. *Kestrel*, repaired after her battering at the Taku Forts, received £1400 for actions on 23 and 25 July 1860 and 18 November 1861. The gunboat squadron's biggest earner was undoubtedly *Opossum*, whose crew received £1000 for nine actions between 29 October 1864 and 17 October 1865; £1000 for two actions in February 1866; shared £2000 with *Osprey* for an action on 18 July 1866; shared £1715 with *Cockchafer, Haughty* and *Algerine* for various actions between October 1863 and March 1868; and shared £2500 with *Janus, Bouncer, Leven* and *Haughty* for actions between May 1865 and June 1869. As a commander earned £301 per annum, a lieutenant £200, a mate or sub-lieutenant £66, a midshipman £31, and an ordinary seaman £23, these figures are impressive, especially when one takes into account the small size of a gunboat's crew. Altogether, a total of £56,238 was paid in such bounties between 1851 and 1869, indicating the scale of the problem, the principal beneficiary being the sloop *Bittern* which, prior to the arrival of the Crimean gunboats, earned £10,000 between June 1854 and March 1856. Complaints that the system was open to abuse by the over-enthusiastic may have been justified in some cases, but it produced results. By 1869 coastal piracy was all but dead, leaving the gunboats free to concentrate on maintaining order on China's rivers, along which trade was steadily expanding inland.

Pirates were not the only problem facing the gunboats. Quite apart from its troubles with foreign powers, the Chinese Imperial government was engaged in a protracted and bloody civil war with the Taiping rebels, who wished to place their own candidate on the throne. Officially, the United Kingdom played no part in the conflict, but when British interests in Shanghai were threatened by the Taipings, Admiral Hope threw the Royal Navy's weight behind the Peking authorities. On 10 May 1862 the Imperial army launched an attack on Ningpo, off which was anchored a small Allied naval force under Captain Roderick Dew of the sloop *Encounter*. Several Imperial junks deliberately placed themselves close to the Allied ships, so that the latter were also treated to some of the defenders' fire. Dew, a fire-eater, promptly retaliated by ordering all his ships, including the gunvessel *Ringdove*, the gunboats *Hardy* and *Kestrel* and the French gunboats *Etoile* and *Confucius*, to open fire on the walls of the city, which were then stormed by the grateful Imperial faction. Taking the *Hardy* and *Confucius* with him, Dew proceeded up the Yangtse and began interpreting neutrality in his own fashion, forming a naval brigade which assisted an Imperial force in the capture of Kahding on 24 October 1862. For Whitehall, already embroiled in a dispute with the United States over the British-built and crewed commerce raider *Alabama*, this was one exercise in personal initiative too many, and Dew was recalled early the following year. Curiously, command of the rag-bag Chinese force, designated the Ever Victorious Army by Peking, was given to a seconded officer of the Royal Engineers, Major Charles Gordon, who we shall meet again.

No summary of gunboat operations in Chinese waters would be complete without mention of an unusual squadron known as The Vampire Fleet. This was nominally part of the Imperial Navy and consisted of seven former British ships, including the gunvessel *Mohawk* and the gunboat *Jasper*. The Vampires were commanded by Captain Sherard Osborn, now a Chinese admiral, but soon established a reputation for doing just as they pleased, which sometimes lay well beyond any recognised definition of law and order. One of his subordinates, Captain Hugh Burgoyne, VC, another veteran of the Azov Flotilla, went off to become a blockade runner for the Confederacy; returning to the Royal Navy, he lost his life when his ship, the experimental battleship *Captain*, capsized while on manoeuvres with the Channel Fleet on 7 September 1870. Osborn resigned command of the Vampires when Peking suggested his ships be placed under the control of local mandarins, believing that the latter would simply use them in their own petty squabbles. To prevent their falling into pirate or Taiping hands, the British insisted that they were sold outside China.

As has already been mentioned, the wooden Crimean gunboats had been rushed into service and obviously they would not last forever. Their bigger replacements, of composite iron and wood construction, began entering service in 1867. They had a barquentine rig and, depending upon their class, were driven by either single or twin screws at a speed of nine or ten knots. Armament consisted of two 64-pounder muzzle-loaders and two 20-pounder Armstrong breech-loaders; in the 1880s some were rearmed with 4-inch and 5-inch breech-loaders. New gunvessels also began entering service in 1870. Some, with twin screws, were designed specifically for work in Chinese rivers; others, with a single screw, were intended for ocean-going service. Their common armament was one 7-inch rifled muzzle-loader between the funnel and the mainmast, and two 68-pounder muzzle-loaders or two 64-pounder breech-loaders, one at the bow and the other at the stern.

In 1860 there were 24 gunboats and six gunvessels serving on the China Station. Thirteen years later there were only three gunboats and eleven gunvessels present, proof enough that the Chinese equivalent of the Jolly Roger had been driven from the seas, although the great rivers of China could never be regarded as being completely safe from gentlemen of fortune. They required constant patrolling by the gunboats of the Western nations but, by and large, a form of stability had been imposed that would last until the ancient empire was swept away by revolution.

4

GUNFIRE ON THE MISSISSIPPI

Federal and Confederate Gunboats in Action, 1862–3

To most people, the American Civil War consisted of a series of land campaigns in which naval activity played but a peripheral part. Yet this was far from being the case. In 1861, Lieutenant General Winfield Scott, the US Army's then General in Chief, devised what became known as the Anaconda Plan. This involved raising a strong army which would advance down the Mississippi to the Gulf of Mexico while the US Navy imposed a blockade on the Southern ports. The effect of this, he argued, would be to cut the Confederacy in two and squeeze the major part of it into submission. Aged 74, Scott retired before the year was out, chagrined to see his advice ignored by Washington politicians who sought to impose solutions of their own. The predictable result of their amateur meddling was that the Union made little or no headway against the Confederacy and the war was inevitably prolonged. In the end, the North only began to make real progress when Scott's strategy was implemented.

The Mississippi is one of the world's great rivers, providing not simply a vital artery of trade but also a great strategic barrier. Rising in the far north, it is joined during its long journey to the Gulf of Mexico by many other important rivers. It has its flood season, during which widespread inundations take place, and carries so great a volume of water that its course can change dramatically. Low water, too, can produce its own problems, as sand and mudbanks may appear and disappear without warning, making navigation a matter for experts. For these reasons, most of the river's commerce during the years immediately prior to the war was carried in flat-bottomed steamers driven by stern or side paddle wheels.

From the outset, both sides were conscious that most of Louisiana, and the whole of Arkansas and Texas, lay on the right or western bank of the Mississippi. They were not the most powerful of the Southern states, but they were capable of shipping men and supplies across the

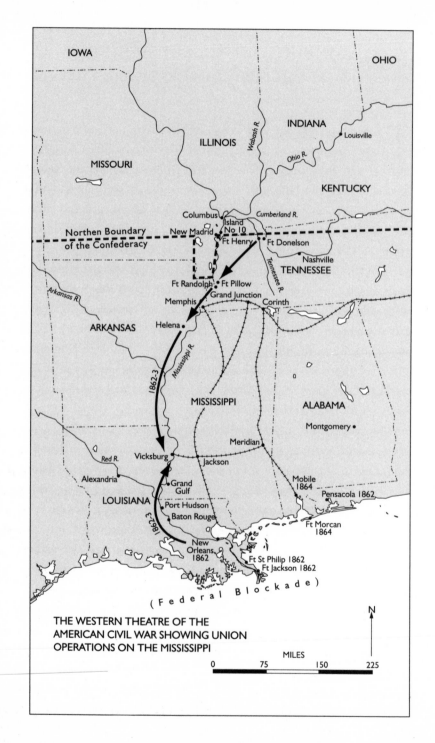

IOWA

OHIO

ILLINOIS

INDIANA

Louisville

MISSOURI

Wabash R.

Ohio R.

KENTUCKY

Columbus

Cumberland R.

Northen Boundary
of the Confederacy

New Madrid

Island
No 10

Ft Henry

Ft Donelson

Nashville

Tennessee R.

TENNESSEE

Ft Randolph

Ft Pillow

Arkansas R.

Memphis

Grand Junction

Corinth

ARKANSAS

Helena

1862-3

Mississippi R.

MISSISSIPPI

ALABAMA

Montgomery

Red R.

Vicksburg

Meridian

Alexandria

Jackson

LOUISIANA

Grand
Gulf

Mobile
1864

Pensacola 1862

1862-3

Port Hudson

Baton Rouge

Ft Morcan
1864

New
Orleans
1862

Ft St Philip 1862

Ft Jackson 1862

(F e d e r a l   B l o c k a d e)

N

THE WESTERN THEATRE OF THE
AMERICAN CIVIL WAR SHOWING UNION
OPERATIONS ON THE MISSISSIPPI

MILES

0   75   150   225

river to the main body of the Confederacy, where the most important campaigns were being fought. As long as the Confederates retained control of the river, such support would continue; if, however, the Federals were to wrest control from them, not only would that support be reduced to a trickle, the heartland of the Confederacy would be open to invasion from the west as well as from the north.

There was, therefore, much at stake. On the outbreak of war Federals and Confederates alike set about converting river steamers into gunboats. This was done by constructing a protected casemate containing an enclosed gun deck on the original hull, and providing protection for the side or stern wheels and the upper pilot house. In this context it should be mentioned that contemporary references to the wheelhouse refer not to the pilot house, which contained the wheel by which the ship was steered, but to the structure built around the side- or stern-wheel.

It was appreciated that the gunboats would often be subjected to heavy, close-range fire from shore batteries or fortifications. The case- mates were therefore constructed from heavy balks of timber laid back at an angle to provide better protection and sheathed in sheet iron, sometimes with a thick layer of compressed cotton between. Cotton, in fact, was to play an important part in this brown-water war. At the beginning of the war the Confederate government had banned the export of cotton in the mistaken belief that the ensuing world shortage would induce recognition of the new nation by industrialised countries, principally Great Britain and France. Consequently, cotton began to pile up all over the South. Thus, when the Federals captured supplies they either put it to their own industrial use or exported it to pay for the war effort. Baled cotton was also proof against small-arms fire and was used by both sides to protect their more improvised gunboats, as were bales of hay. According to the nature of their protection, gunboats were referred to as 'iron-clads', 'cotton-clads' or 'hay clads'.

Within the casemate, most guns were mounted broadside, with up to five pointing ahead, the same number pointing astern if the vessel was a side-wheeler, but only two aft if it happened to be a stern-wheeler. The nature of the armament varied considerably, most gunboats being equipped with whatever heavy weapons were to hand; the Confederates, having no cannon foundries of their own, employed ordnance captured at the Norfolk Navy Yard in Virginia. The gun crews shared the casemate with the vessel's engine and boilers. In action the only ventilation for this overheated environment came through the gun ports; furthermore, if the casemate was penetrated there was a high risk that men would be scalded to death when boilers or steam pipes were ruptured. It was anticipated that when engaged with their own kind, gunboats would inevitably come to close quarters and for that reason the bows of many were strengthened for ramming.

The first major operations in which the Federal gunboats were engaged was the capture of Forts Henry and Donelson, situated respectively on the Tennessee and Cumberland Rivers on the border between Kentucky and Tennessee. Both rivers flowed northwards to join the Ohio, which in turn flowed west into the Mississippi. It can be seen, therefore, that the Federals could not begin their advance down the Mississippi without subduing this threat to their flank and rear.

In February 1862 the then Major General Ulysses S. Grant advanced against the two forts from Cairo, Illinois, accompanied by a flotilla of gunboats under the command of Commodore Andrew Foote. Four of these, *Cincinnati, Carondelet, St Louis* and *Essex,* were purpose-built 'tin-clads' as described above, but a further three, *Taylor, Lexington* and *Conestoga,* were simply converted wooden steamers.

It was decided to tackle Fort Henry first and, heading south up the Tennessee, the gunboats began exchanging fire with the defences during the afternoon of 5 February. Foote reminded his gun crews that their primary targets were the enemy's guns, adding that each shot cost the government $8.00 and that value for money was what he was after. Bad weather held up Grant's troops during the night, but shortly after 11:00 the following morning the gunboats had begun to close in on the fort, the armoured vessels leading and opening the engagement with their bow guns.

The *Essex,* under Commander William Porter, son of the American naval hero of the War of 1812, scored first, a shell from her No. 2 gun, laid by a seaman named Jack Matthews, who had served in both the

Royal and United States Navies, bursting fair and square within an embrasure. The fort itself was now a blaze of gunfire and the gunboats were firing steadily. As the wind was brisk, the powder smoke was dispersed quickly, giving both sides a clear view of their targets. *Essex* had fired 72 rounds when a shell smashed through a gun port on the port side, bursting a boiler and severing steam lines. The interior of the forward gun deck was immediately filled with scalding steam in which several men died a horrible death. The survivors, including Porter, went over the side through the gun ports. In the water, Porter was supported by a seaman named John Walker, who also assisted him on to the rubbing strake, enabling him to re-enter the vessel through one of the after ports; had Porter been in the pilot house, as might be expected, he would not have survived as both its occupants were scalded to death. Her power gone, *Essex* began to drift downstream, having sustained the loss of ten killed, 23 scalded and five missing, presumed drowned; eight of the worst scalding cases did not survive.

Elsewhere, the battle had gone the Federals' way, with comparatively few casualties. *Cincinnati, Carondelet* and *St Louis* continued to close the range until they were level with the fort. Unable to withstand the sustained battering, its commander ordered a white flag to be hoisted and came off in a small boat to conclude the surrender details with Commodore Foote. Commander Henry Walke of the *Carondelet*, placed in command of the fort until relieved by Grant's troops, has left vivid picture of its interior:

The first glance over the fort silenced all jubilant expressions of the victors. On every side lay the lifeless bodies of the victims, in reckless confusion, intermingled with shattered implements of war. The largest gun of the fort was disabled, being filled with earth by one of our shells striking the parapet near its muzzle; the muzzle of another was broken by our shell; a third, with broken carriage and two dead men, was almost buried under heaps of earth; a fourth burst, scattering the mangled gunners into the water and in all directions, scarcely one of them escaping. The scene was one which robbed us of all feelings of exultation. Some of our shells had pierced entirely through the breastwork, throwing tons of earth over the prostrate gunners, and then plunging ten feet into the earth beyond, or through the cabins in the rear, afterwards setting fire to them by their explosions.

Grant immediately decided to march on Fort Donelson, lying just ten miles across country on the parallel Cumberland River. For Foote's gunboats this meant retracing their steps down the Tennessee to the Ohio, then heading up the Cumberland. On 12 February the *Carondelet* arrived ahead of the flotilla and at about midday began firing at the fort in the hope that by replying the enemy would disclose the position of his batteries. When no response was forthcoming the engagement was broken off, but it was immediately apparent that taking Fort Donelson would be a much tougher proposition than Fort Henry had been, for not only had it been constructed on higher ground, it was also manned by a much stronger garrison.

Grant had three divisions with him and more troops were on their way. Having all but encircled the fort, on the following morning he wrote to Walke of the *Carondelet*:

Most of our batteries are established and the remainder soon will be. If you advance with your gunboat at 10 o'clock a.m., we will be ready to take advantage of every diversion in our favour.

Walke co-operated willingly and began bombarding the fortifications, simultaneously becoming the target of every rebel gun that would bear. At 11:30 a heavy calibre round smashed its way through the forward port corner of the casemate and skipped over the protective barrier in front of the boilers. It then passed over the steam drum, struck the beams of the upper deck, carried away the railing around the engine room and burst the steam-heater, and, glancing back into the engine room, 'seemed to bound after the men,' as one of the engineers said, 'like a wild beast pursuing its prey'. When it burst through the side, it knocked down and wounded a dozen men, seven of them severely. An immense quantity of splinters were blown through the vessel. Some of them, fine as needles, shot through the clothes of the men like arrows.

The *Carondelet* withdrew temporarily to transfer her wounded to a transport, effect repairs and send her hands to dinner. She then resumed the bombardment until most of the ammunition for her heavy weapons had been expended. Walke retained the offending cannon ball as a souvenir of the battle.

During the night Foote, now flying his flag aboard the *St Louis*, arrived with the armoured *Louisville* and *Pittsburg* as well as the wooden *Taylor* and *Conestoga*. The following afternoon the four protected gunboats, in line abreast, approached the fort and for the next two-and-a-half hours engaged in a murderous firefight with the Confederate batteries. In turn, the *St Louis*, with a badly wounded Foote aboard, the *Louisville* and the *Pittsburg*, sustained such serious damage that they were compelled to drop back out of the fight; the last, in doing so, collided with the stern of the *Carondelet*, smashing her starboard rudder. All the *Carondelet's* boats were shot away, as was her anchor and flagstaffs, her funnel was riddled and torn, and, in Walke's words, the iron plate armour was ripped off 'as lightning tears the bark from a tree'. Inside the casemate several men were beheaded by shots coming through the gunports and a hastily loaded gun exploded. Given the volume of fire to which the gunboats were exposed, the overall Federal loss of only 12 killed and 42 wounded was testimony to the efficiency of their makeshift armour. Nevertheless, the fact was that on this occasion their bombardment had failed.

Naturally, the Confederate artillerymen were jubilant. Unfortunately for them, Fort Donelson was not provisioned for a siege and, with the exception of Lieutenant Colonel Nathan Bedford Forrest, commanding the garrison's cavalry element, the senior officers present were of mixed quality. Nevertheless, on 15 February the fort's commander, Brigadier General Gideon Pillow, decided that his troops would break out of their encirclement and join the nearest Confederate field army. In the circumstances this was probably the correct decision, even if it meant abandoning the fortifications. His troops fought well and by evening had all but broken through the Federal cordon. At this point Pillow lost his nerve, ordering them to back to their own positions. During the night a council of war decided that surrender was the only alternative. Forrest and his cavalrymen successfully escaped to fight another day, but on 16 February some 9000 Confederate soldiers became prisoners of war.

The loss of Forts Henry and Donelson was a serious blow for the South, compelling the withdrawal of Confederate forces from most of Kentucky and western Tennessee. Nine days after Donelson had fallen, Grant entered Nashville. Continuing his advance up the Tennessee, he fought and won the bloody two-day Battle of Shiloh, during which he received support at a critical period from the wooden gunboats *Taylor* and *Lexington*.

In the meantime, Foote's flotilla had commenced operations on the Mississippi itself. Here the situation was that the way south was blocked by the heavily fortified Island No. 10, so called because it was the tenth island south of the Ohio's confluence with the Mississippi. Island No. 10 lay in an angle of a sharp S bend and its guns were capable of firing over both the penisulas formed by the S. It was, furthermore, supported by Confederate batteries on the left bank of the river. Foote's gunboats had exchanged shots with it and reached the conclusion that it was too tough a nut to crack, particularly as they were now fighting downstream and, if disabled, would drift directly under the enemy guns and on towards the waiting rebel vessels to the south. There was, however, another consideration. A Federal army under Major General John Pope had marched down the right bank of the river and set up its headquarters at New Madrid, Missouri, at the downstream end of the S. Pope wanted to ferry his troops across the river, thereby isolating those rebels still holding positions on the left bank above Island No. 10. He could not do so because of the Confederate gunboats and, though fully aware of the risks involved, requested urgent assistance from Foote.

At length Captain Walke of the *Carondelet* volunteered to run the gauntlet under cover of darkness. Few gave much for his chances of success, but every precaution was taken. The exhaust steam was re-routed to vent into the wheelhouse so that the enemy would not be alerted by its puffing. Additional protection was provided by timber balks and bales of hay. The boiler was surrounded by stacked cordwood.

To protect the vessel against the worst effects of the fire from the left bank batteries, a barge containing coal and hay was lashed to her port side. Finally, a company of infantry came aboard as a defence against possible boarders.

The *Carondelet* left her moorings at 22:00 on the night on 4 April. A heavy thunderstorm was raging as she disappeared into the rain-lashed darkness. From time to time she was brilliantly illuminated by lighting flashes. After half a mile had been covered without attracting the enemy's attention, those aboard began to relax, believing that they would complete the entire passage unobserved. At this point the funnel soot, deprived of the exhaust steam's dampening effect, caught fire. Flames shot high in the air until the engineer opened the flue caps. The rebel sentries must have been sheltering from the torrential rain for, incredibly, there was no response.

A few minutes later the funnels began belching flames again. This time the *Carondelet* was spotted. The enemy response began with a few musket shots and then their guns opened fire. Walke ordered full speed ahead. For the next half hour the gunboat was engaged continuously by the left bank batteries and then the defences of Island No. 10. The air seemed thick with flying shot and bullets but it was all passing overhead. Realising that the enemy could only see their target during the intermittent lightning flashes, Walke declined to give them any assistance by opening fire himself. The island was passed, leaving the only opposition an armed dry dock moored three miles downstream. The few shots fired by this caused neither casualties nor damage. Prearranged gun signals were used to warn the troops in New Madrid of the gunboat's approach, then, two hours after setting off, the *Carondelet* quite suddenly found herself in safe waters again. Wilfully disregarding the standing regulations of the 'dry' US Navy, Walke gave instructions for the mainbrace to be spliced. Next morning he received personal visits from General Pope and Mr Scott, the Assistant Secretary of War, and numerous army officers came aboard to offer their congratulations.

Two nights later the *Pittsburg* also made the passage under cover of another thunderstorm. Pope now had the protection he needed to ferry his men across and put his plans into immediate effect. The Confederates holding Island No. 10 and the left bank, now cut off from their own people, surrendered on 7 April, yielding 7000 prisoners, the dry dock, numerous guns, large quantities of stores and ammunition, and several vessels.

Following the fall of Island No. 10, Foote proceeded down-river with his flotilla until he was confronted by Fort Pillow on the left bank, surmounting Chickasaw Bluffs. As most of Pope's troops were required elsewhere, there was no prospect of repeating the recent success. The flotilla based itself at Plum Point, some five miles above the fort, which was bombarded by mortar vessels.

On the night of 23–24 April, far to the south, a large Federal naval force under the command of Commodore David Farragut had entered the mouth of the Mississippi, fought its way past Forts St Philip and Jackson, and captured New Orleans, sinking several Confederate gunboats in the process. After these recent reverses, the Confederate States Navy badly needed a victory to shore up its morale. A gunboat squadron was therefore assembled below Fort Pillow with the object of mounting a surprise attack on Foote's ships.

Foote had never recovered from the wound he had received at Fort Donelson and on 9 May he was relieved by Captain Charles H. Davis. It was the custom for one of the Federal gunboats to stand overnight guard beside the mortar vessel which was doing most of the bombarding, three miles below the main anchorage. That night it was the turn of Commander Stembel's *Cincinnati*. Nothing untoward was expected and by dawn her steam pressure had dropped so far as barely to give her steerage way. Suddenly, to his horror, Stembel saw the funnel smoke of six Confederate gunboats rounding the bend towards him.

All hands rushed to quarters while the engineers hurled oil into the furnaces in a desperate attempt to raise steam. The CSS *General Bragg*, leading the enemy squadron, was closing in at speed with the clear object of ramming the *Cincinnati* amidships. Stembel put a broadside into his opponent and managed to turn his ship until she was almost bows on to avoid the worst of the impact. Even so, the *General Bragg* tore a gash in her side measuring twelve feet long by six deep, flooding the magazine. The *Cincinnati* fired another broadside and the *General Bragg* drifted off, badly holed herself. Next came the CSS *Sumter* which, having absorbed a couple of shots from the *Cincinnati's* stern guns, rammed Stembel's ship to a depth of three feet, destroying the steering gear and rudders as well as opening her hull. Minutes later the CSS *General Lovell* rammed the *Cincinnati* in the bows. The ship settled in shallow water and the crew, having fired a last few defiant rounds, took refuge on the upper deck, which remained above water. Here Stembel was shot in the jaw by a sniper.

Led by Davis in the *Benton*, the Federal gunboats were coming down river as soon as they could raise steam. A confused mêlée ensued in which the USS *Mound City* was badly holed forward and just managed to reach the bank in a sinking condition. Then, having achieved what it set out to do, the Confederate squadron retired whence it had come, showing varying degrees of damage. Although both the *Cincinnati* and the *Mound City* were raised and back in commission the following month, the almost bloodless affair at Plum Point was an undoubted Confederate success, albeit one from which no dividends would be drawn.

Nevertheless, in the western theatre of war the Confederacy was engaged in a strategic withdrawal. On 4 June it was discovered that Fort Pillow had been abandoned, as had Fort Randolph some distance downstream. Davis immediately took his squadron down to Memphis, where he was joined by several army-manned rams under Colonel Charles Ellet, Jr. The sole purpose of these latter vessels was ramming and, while their boilers and other vital areas were protected, they carried no armament save small arms.

At Memphis, Davis found the entire Confederate River Defense Fleet drawn up to receive him and on the morning of 6 June a battle took place, witnessed by the entire population of Memphis from the high bluffs upstream of the city. Unfortunately for them, as neither the armament of the Confederate ships, nor their protection, matched that of the Federal opponents, the result amounted to a massacre.

In line abreast, the two squadrons surged towards each other. In the centre, Ellet's ram *Queen of the West* smashed into side of the *General Lovell*, which sank immediately. On the Federal right another ram, the

Monarch, carved her way through the starboard wheel of the CSS *General Price*, which made her way to the Arkansas shore in a sinking condition.

The *Queen of the West* now found herself under attack from two rebel ships, the *Beauregard* on one side and the *Sumter* on the other. She managed to slip between them, one of her wheels being disabled in the process, and her two opponents collided. Colonel Ellet, who had received a wound that was to prove mortal, headed his ship for the Arkansas bank where he sent an officer and a squad of men to receive the surrender of the *General Price*'s crew.

The fight had now drifted below the city and at this point the outnumbered and outgunned Confederates attempted to make good their escape. The *Monarch*, in hot pursuit, rammed the *Beauregard* and left her sinking. She then pursued the enemy flagship, the *Little Rebel*, which had already sustained such damage at the hands of Davis's gunboats that she, too, was making for the Arkansas shore. She arrived first, her crew running off into the woods, and the *Monarch* gave her a nudge that put her hard aground.

Of the remaining enemy vessels, the *General Bragg*, *Sumter* and *Jeff Thompson* surrendered, the last being blown apart when fire reached her magazine. Only the *Van Doorn* escaped, to be burned at Liverpool Landing in the Yazoo River to prevent her capture. As Walke of the *Carondelet* wrote:

> The die was cast, and the crowd of mourning spectators melted away, in unutterable sadness for loved ones lost, and their sanguine hopes of victory forever gone. The spectacle was one which subdued all feelings of resentment on the part of the victors, and awakened a natural sympathy towards the vanquished – their fellow countrymen – on shore. The general grief and the weight of woe inflicted, on some of the spectators, was such as could arise only from a civil war, like that in which we were then engaged.

Memphis surrendered and, apparently, the Mississippi had now been cleared of Confederate warships. The only remaining obstacle to complete Federal domination of the river was the fortress of Vicksburg, Mississippi, and thither Davis took his squadron, anchoring above the town. To emphasise the fact of Union strangulation, Farragut brought his warships up from New Orleans, running past the Vicksburg batteries to reinforce Davis.

There were ample grounds for satisfaction that the war in the west was proceeding according to plan, but, mixed as had been the fortunes of the Confederate States Navy on the Mississippi, it still had an ace up its sleeve. This was the CSS *Arkansas*, part ram and part gunboat, which was nearing completion in rebel-controlled territory, far up the tributary Yazoo River, which entered the Mississippi north of Vicksburg.

The *Arkansas* differed from other gunboats in that her low-pressure engines provided power for twin screws. The details of her armour and armament are provided by Lieutenant Isaac N. Brown, CSN, who was to take her into action:

> The straight sides of the box (casemate), a foot in thickness, had over them one layer of railway iron (rails); the ends closed by timber one foot square, planked across by six-inch strips of oak, were then covered by one course of railway iron laid up and down at an angle of 35 degrees. These ends deflected overhead all missiles striking at short range, but would have been of little security under a plunging fire. This shield, flat on top, covered with plank and half-inch iron, was pierced for ten guns – three in each broadside and two forward and aft. The large smoke-stack came through the top of the shield, and the pilot house was raised about one foot above the shield level. Through the latter led a small tin tube by which to convey orders to the pilot. The battery was respectable for that period of the war: two 8-inch 64-pounders at the bows; two rifled 32-pounders (old smooth-bores banded and rifled) astern; and two 100-pounder Columbiads and a 6-inch naval gun in each broadside – ten guns in all, which, under officers formerly of the United States service, could be relied upon for good work, if we could find the men to load and fire.

Brown's crew eventually included over 100 men of the former River Defense Fleet, supplemented by some 60 artillerymen provided by General Jeff Thompson. The mission which Brown had been set was wildly ambitious, involving as it did having to fight his way to Vicksburg, where he would re-coal, then fighting his way down-river through New Orleans and past the lower Mississippi forts to the Gulf of Mexico, and finally heading east along the coast to join the Confederate naval force at Mobile, regardless of whatever blockading warships might be present.

On 12 July 1862 the *Arkansas* completed fitting out and took her contingent of soldiers aboard. Two days later she began dropping down the Yazoo towards the Mississippi, her engineers struggling with machinery that even at this stage was beginning to give trouble. During the night two of her crew deserted and reached the gunboat *Essex*, warning the Federals of the impending attack. Both Farragut and Davis were aware that the Confederates were up to something but neither believed that they possessed the technology to produce the sort of war vessel described. Nevertheless, they decided to send three of their own ships up the Yazoo to discover the truth.

By dawn on the 15th the three ships, the *Carondolet*, the wooden gunboat *Taylor* and the army ram *Queen of the West*, had reached Old River, an expanse of water where the Yazoo flowed through an earlier course of the Mississippi. Quite suddenly they sighted a large, brown-coloured warship bearing down on them, belching smoke from her single funnel. At this stage she was flying no flag, but there could be no mistaking her intentions.

The crews of all four ships went to quarters. Lieutenant Joseph Ford, commanding the *Queen of the West*, recognised that going against the current his ship could not develop enough speed to damage his heavily armoured opponent, and, having no armament save her ram, he reversed course. Captain Walke of the *Carondelet* and Lieutenant Commander Gwin of the *Taylor* simultaneously reached the conclusion that by doing likewise they could engage the *Arkansas* with their stern armament and draw her into an engagement with the Federal fleet, which would be alerted by the sound of gunfire.

A round from the *Taylor* penetrated the *Arkansas's* pilot house, mortally wounding the chief pilot. Shortly after, a spent bullet from the same source struck Brown on the temple, knocking him unconscious and sending him tumbling through the hatch on to the gundeck below. When he came to, he found himself being laid out in a row of dead and wounded. Returning to the pilot house, he saw that the *Taylor* was drawing steadily ahead of her consort and therefore decided to make the *Carondelet* his principal target.

His problem was that one of his big forward guns had dismounted itself when first fired, so he steered a zig-zag course to bring his broadside guns into action. After an hour the *Carondelet*'s steering gear had been disabled and she ran aground. As the *Arkansas* steamed past she gave her a broadside which shattered boats, pumps, steam lines and steering gear and penetrated her hull. While steam belched from every gunport and aperture, her survivors leapt from her decks to swim ashore. During the engagement four of her crew were killed, 15 were wounded and a further 16 were reported as missing. Although Walke managed to refloat and repair his ship later in the day, there could be no doubt that for once the *Carondelet* had met her match; nor was she to be alone in this. It was another of many such coincidences in this sad conflict that Walke and Brown were good friends who had served together in the pre-war Navy.

As the ships reached the bar of the Yazoo, turning south towards Vicksburg, Brown concentrated his fire on the *Taylor*. For the next hour the latter received such a battering that 25 of her crew, including four officers, were killed or wounded. The *Arkansas*, however, also sustained her share of damage. Her funnel was holed repeatedly, thereby reducing the up-draught through the furnaces; several connected steam pipes were severed, causing the boiler pressure to fall by no less than 100 pounds within minutes. The temperature in the engine room soared to 130 degrees, so that the staff had to be relieved every quarter of an hour; on the airless gundeck men were forced to strip to the bare minimum as the heat soared to 120 degrees.

If Walke and Gwin had thought that the sound of the guns would alert the fleet they were sadly mistaken. Most officers in the anchorage simply believed that the gunboats were having a brush with Confederate troops. Even when the *Taylor* and the *Queen of the West* hove into view someone remarked that the former seemed to be bringing in a prize. Only when Gwin's ship was seen to be in action with something astern was the alarm raised.

For his part, Brown was now confronted by some 30 enemy vessels. These included four army rams, eight ocean-going warships of Farragut's squadron, and three of Davis's gunboats, the rest being either mortar vessels which had been bombarding the fortress, or transports. Some were already at quarters, others were going to quarters, some were raising steam and others had it raised. Whatever degree of surprise the scene presented, Brown was faced with impossible odds. With only 20 pounds of pressure left in the boilers, he lacked the power to retire upstream without being overhauled and battered to wreckage. The only alternative was for the *Arkansas*, her propellors turning slowly, to run the gauntlet and ride the current downstream to Vicksburg.

'Brady,' he said to the replacement pilot, 'shave that line of men-of-war as close as you can, so that the rams will not have room to gather headway in coming out to strike us.'

The ordeal lasted for 30 minutes, during which the *Arkansas* became the target of every Federal warship as well as the troops ashore. In return she inflicted casualties and damage on every ship she passed. The scene within the casemate is described by one of Brown's officers, Lieutenant George W. Grift:

An 11-inch shell broke through immediately above the port, bringing with it a shower of iron and wooden splinters which struck down every man at the gun. My Master's Mate, Mr Wilson, was painfully wounded in the nose, and I had my left arm smashed. Curtis was the only sound man in the division when we mustered the crew at quarters, at Vicksburg. Nor did the mischief of the last shot end with my poor gun's crew. It passed across the deck, through the smoke-stack, and killed eight and wounded seven men at Scales's gun. Fortunately, he was

untouched himself, and afterward did excellent service at Grim-
ball's Columbiad.

Brown had ordered the Confederate colours to be hoisted before this
action. Inevitably, they were shot away in the tempest of shot and shell
directed at the vessel. Replaced at great risk by Midshipman Dabney
Scales, they were shot away again; Scales was for trying to replace
them once more, but was prevented from doing so by Brown. The last
ship to be encountered was Davis's *Benton*, lying directly across the
Arkansas's bows. Brown wrote:

> Though we had but little headway, his beam was exposed, and
> I ordered the pilot to strike him amidships. He avoided this by
> steaming ahead, and, passing under his stern, nearly touching,
> we gave him our starboard broadside, which probably went
> through him from rudder to prow. This was our last shot, and
> we received none in return.

The *Arkansas* was cheered into Vicksburg by a crowd estimated to
number 20,000. As Grift relates, her victory had its price:

> We got through, hammered and battered, though. Our smoke-
> stack resembled an immense nutmeg grater, so often had it been
> struck, and the sides of the ship were as spotted as if she had
> been peppered. A shot had broken our cast-iron ram. Another
> had demolished a hawse-pipe. Our boats were shot away and
> dragging. But all this was to be expected and could be repaired.
> Not so on the inside. A great heap of mangled and ghastly slain
> lay on the gundeck, with rivulets of blood running away from
> them. There was a poor fellow torn asunder, another mashed flat,
> whilst in the 'slaughter house' brains, hair and blood were all
> about. Down below 50 or 60 wounded were groaning and
> complaining, or courageously bearing their ills without a
> murmur. All the army stood on the hills to see us round the point.
> The flag had been put on a temporary pole, and we went out to

return the cheers of the soldiers as we passed. The Generals came on board to embrace our Captain, bloody yet game.

In fact, the *Arkansas's* losses were not quite as serious as Grift thought, amounting to 12 killed, three seriously wounded and a further 15 with lesser wounds. During her run she had disabled the *Carondelet* and the *Taylor*, burst the boiler of the ram *Lancaster*, inflicted varying degrees of damage on numerous other vessels and caused her opponents casualties totalling 42 killed and 69 wounded. Brown received immediate promotion to commander in recognition of his remarkable achievement. Having transferred his wounded ashore, he moved the *Arkansas* to the coaling berth and began the more urgent repairs. The artillerymen who had temporarily joined his crew returned to the army. A request for replacements met with a ready response until the volunteers went aboard, where they saw the interior walls of the casemate 'besmeared with brains and blood, as though it had been thrown by hand from a sausage mill'; after that their enthusiasm cooled somewhat.

Farragut, who had earned the right to judge, described the *Arkansas's* passage as a 'a bold thing'. In his report to Secretary of the Navy Gideon Welles he expressed 'deep mortification' at the surprise inflicted on the entire Federal fleet. Welles, almost incoherent with rage, described the incident as being 'the most disreputable naval affair of the war', adding that the destruction of the *Arkansas* had become 'an absolute necessity'.

Farragut was already taking what he believed to be appropriate steps. That very night he had a light fixed on the right bank, opposite the *Arkansas's* anchorage. This was to serve as a firing indicator while his ships dropped below Vicksburg, braving the fire of the shore batteries as they did so. Suspecting the purpose of the light, Brown simply shifted his position several hundred yards downstream. As a result, the *Arkansas* sustained only one hit, the rest of the Federals' fire being wasted. More casualties were caused among Farragut's crews and the gunboat *Winona* was so badly damaged by the shore batteries that she had to be run aground.

During the next week the Federals tried hitting the *Arkansas* with their mortar craft. As their target's rust-brown sides, almost invisible against Vicksburg's clay bluffs, made her difficult to spot, she sustained no damage. On 22 July, Farragut and Davis mounted a fresh attack. With only a small crew aboard, the *Arkansas* beat off Commander William Porter's *Essex* in a point-blank gunnery duel. She was then faced with the *Queen of the West*, clearly intent on ramming. Brown turned his bows towards her and the blow was a glancing one. Receiving the *Arkansas*'s broadside as she slid past, the *Queen* ran aground, although she later managed to get herself off. Two days later, Farragut, worried by the falling level of the river, took his deep-water ships south again, and shortly after Davis withdrew his gunboats to Helena, Arkansas.

For a while, the *Arkansas* was left unmolested. Brown went on sick leave, his place being taken by his executive officer, Lieutenant Stevens. At this juncture Confederate plans in the west included the recapture of Baton Rouge, Louisiana, by a force under General Breckenridge. It was decided that while the attack was in progress the *Arkansas* would deal with the Federal gunboats lying offshore. Stevens protested that his ship had not yet been returned to a battle-worthy condition, and that in particular the engines were giving serious trouble. General Van Dorn, commanding at Vicksburg, obtained orders over-ruling him. On 3 August the *Arkansas* left on her last voyage.

During the early hours of 4 August Stevens stopped just short of the confluence of the Red River so that his chief engineer could check over the engines. At 08:00 he started downstream again. After 20 miles of trouble-free running he was within sight of Baton Rouge and the sounds of fighting were clearly audible. He sent the crew to stations but at that point the starboard engine gave up. It took until dusk to repair it. Stevens called at a convenient coal yard to refuel, only to have the engine fail again. This time it took all night to forge a replacement crank pin. By 09:00 on 5 August, however, the *Arkansas* was within sight of the Federal gunboats. Both sides opened fire and at this point the port engine failed, followed a minute later by the starboard. When the chief engineer reported the situation as hopeless, Stevens had no alternative but to drift to the bank, disembark his crew and prepare the *Arkansas* for scuttling. Her guns loaded and run out, she was set ablaze and allowed to drift down on the enemy. From time to time one of her guns fired defiantly. Finally the flames reached her magazine and she was blown to pieces. Stevens found himself weeping unashamedly. It mattered not that Breckenridge had taken Baton Rouge, for he lacked the strength to hold it.

Perhaps the *Arkansas's* achievements have been somewhat eclipsed by the duel earlier in the year between the CSS *Virginia* (formerly USS *Merrimack*), which was of similar but superior construction, and John Ericsson's revolutionary turret vessel USS *Monitor* in Hampton Roads, as well as the cruise of commerce raiding CSS *Alabama*; there can be doubt, however, that they earned a most honourable place in the short history of the Confederacy.

With the *Arkansas* gone, Federal domination of the Mississippi was almost complete, although Vicksburg continued to offer stubborn resistance. In November 1862 Davis handed over command of his gunboat squadron to Rear Admiral David Dixon Porter. The following January the squadron sailed up the Arkansas River and bombarded Fort Hindman. In March, with the level of the Mississippi risen some 17 feet above normal, it outflanked the Confederate defences of the Yazoo, which included minefields, by penetrating the swollen bayous to the north of the latter. Here the strange sight could be seen not only of gunboats passing through forests, but also travelling simultaneously north, south, east and west as they followed the serpentine wanderings of the waterways. This operation also served to divert attention from the fact that Grant's army was being ferried from the right bank of the Mississippi to the left at Bruinsburg, below Vicksburg.

The Confederates would enjoy some further minor successes on the Mississippi and the Red River, but in strategic terms they had already lost the campaign. Closing in from the east, Grant placed Vicksburg under close siege and on 4 July 1863 the fortress surrendered; this was the second hammer blow the South would endure within 24 hours, for the previous day General Robert E. Lee had been decisively repulsed at Gettysburg with heavy loss.

From this point on, the Confederacy was on the defensive. No matter how many gallant rearguard actions it fought, it was systematically dismembered as Sherman swept in from the west and Grant brought overwhelming force to bear from the north. It finally surrendered in April 1865.

For many former career officers who, because of their convictions, had fought for the South, life became very hard as it would be many years before such men would be permitted to re-enter the armed services of the United States. One such was Commodore Josiah Tattnall, who, it will be recalled, had passed the famous comment to his British counterpart that blood was thicker than water during the action off the Taku Forts in 1859. Unhappy with life in the defeated South, he had moved to Halifax, Nova Scotia, where his circumstances had deteriorated to the point that he was described as living in absolute penury. Hearing of this, a group of British naval officers, including some who had known him in China, opened a subscription which rescued him from his plight. Nor, as we shall see, was this by any means the last occasion when John Bull and Cousin Jonathan exchanged favours.

5
THE WORLD'S POLICEMEN
Gunboats and the *Pax Britannica*, 1865–90

Although the principal area of the Royal Navy's gunboat operations remained China, gunboats were employed across the world in a wide variety of environments on innumerable tasks. These included containing the Fenian threat on the Great Lakes of North America, destroying the slave trade off East Africa and in the Persian Gulf, punitive expeditions up West African rivers, police actions in the Caribbean and the Pacific, surveying and generally showing the flag. So numerous were the actions in which they were involved that here it is only possible to describe a representative handful.

The least creditable of these was the so-called Jamaica Rebellion of 1865. Slavery itself had been abolished in the British West Indies over a generation earlier, and many former slaves had taken to cultivating their own land, growing the staple crop of sugar. Unfortunately, the combination of drought and a depressed world sugar market created severe hardship and a degree of discontent. On 7 October the magistrate at Morant Bay imposed a fine of four shillings on a minor offender. This was considered outrageous and the crowd, led by a man named Bogle, rescued a voluble protester who was about to be arrested by the court officials. Three days later a small police party was sent to arrest Bogle but was overpowered by a 300-strong armed mob. The mob went on to burn down the courthouse, which was defended to the death by the magistrate, some Volunteers and a few civilians.

Governor Eyre had already despatched the sloop *Wolverine* with troops aboard and summoned the two small Crimean gunboats *Nettle* and *Onyx* from Bermuda. By the time they reached Morant Bay much of the heat had gone out of the situation. The warships fired a few shells and the soldiers combed the countryside, burning the houses of known malefactors. Unproven atrocity stories about the rebels abounded and, with the recent and terrible events of the Indian Mutiny in the forefront of his mind, Eyre over-reacted badly. He decided not only to arrest a local mulatto politician, George Gordon, on a charge of sedition, but also to try him and everyone else involved in the attack on the courthouse by court martial, which was itself illegal under British law.

Appointed president of one of the courts martial was Lieutenant Herbert Charles Alexander Brand, commander of the *Onyx*, a man whose type was mercifully the exception rather than the rule in the service. Once a bumptious, bullying midshipman, he had in his twenties developed sadistic tendencies. His court sentenced 122 men and four women to hang, and 33 men received between 50 and 100 lashes; if any of the latter retained signs of an independent spirit after their flogging, they received a further 25 lashes for their trouble. Among those hung were Grant and Bogle. On the scaffold Brand snatched Gordon's glasses from his face; Gordon's dignified response was to request that his friends in London be informed of the facts. Several cat-o'-nine-tails were made aboard the *Onyx*. Rumour had it that they incorporated wire strands for better effect, but Brand denied this and no proof exists. At the beginning of November Colonel Lewis of the Militia assumed presidency of the court and satisfied himself with hanging a further 50 men. He was succeeded by Lieutenant Oxley of the *Wolverine*, who hung one man and flogged two more. On 4 November the remaining prisoners, 99 men and 40 women, were released, most of the men being sent on their way with a flogging.

As the avowed attitude of Victorian Britain to its colonial subjects was one of benevolent paternalism, the affair generated outrage at home. Governor Eyre, a Brigadier-General Nelson and Brand all faced criminal proceedings for wilful murder, but were acquitted. Brand and Oxley were censured by the Admiralty because of irregularities in the manner in which they had conducted their courts martial. Brand remained in the Navy until 1883 and the fact that he did not rise beyond the rank of commander suggests that the affair had done him no good. The principal lesson for colonial governors and their military subordinates, not least young gunboat commanders required to exercise keen personal judgement at short notice, was that the general public would not tolerate the needless application of ruthless force against subject peoples.

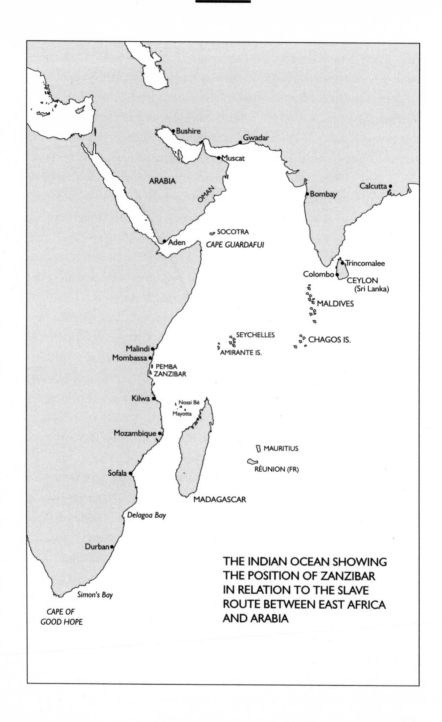

THE INDIAN OCEAN SHOWING
THE POSITION OF ZANZIBAR
IN RELATION TO THE SLAVE
ROUTE BETWEEN EAST AFRICA
AND ARABIA

Unfortunately, not all the subject peoples were inclined to recipro-
cate these sentiments. This was especially true of some Pacific islanders,
among whom cannibalism was still common. On 17 September 1874
the schooner *Sandfly*, commanded by Lieutenant William Nowell, paid
a routine visit to Edgecumbe Island in the Santa Cruz group. She was
immediately subjected to an unprovoked attack, which was beaten off.
In retaliation, Nowell burned the two offending villages and destroyed
20 canoes. Three days later the *Sandfly* was anchored off Santa Cruz
Island. The natives, apparently friendly, swarmed aboard, then attacked
the crew. Grabbing their weapons, the seamen fought back, killing some
30 of them. Nowell pursued the survivors ashore in his boats,
destroying their abandoned canoes and setting fire to two villages.
During the next three days it became necessary to protect the ship's
water parties with rifle fire and an occasional shell from the schooner's
gun. Continuing her cruise, the *Sandfly* arrived off Api Island in the
New Hebrides group, where she shelled a village, the inhabitants of
which were known to have murdered and eaten a boat's crew from a
merchant vessel, the *Zephyr*.

The following year Captain James Goodenough, Commodore of
the Australian Station, paid another visit to the Santa Cruz group in
the *Pearl*, armed with 17 guns. When he went ashore in Carlisle Bay on
12 August he was received in a friendly manner and even invited into
the village. However, no sooner had the British been put at their ease
than the natives began shooting arrows at them. Goodenough and six
of his men were hit but managed to reach their boats. Four boats were
sent in to burn the village in reprisal, with strict instructions from
Goodenough that no lives were to be taken. This act of clemency was
not deserved as the arrows were poisoned; within ten days the
commodore and two seamen were dead. By a strange irony, Goodenough's last official act before leaving New South Wales had been to
unveil a statue of the great explorer Captain James Cook, who had met
his death in very similar circumstances.

The trade in slaves between East Africa and Arabia continued long
after this infamous traffic had been stamped out elsewhere, for despite
the Royal Navy's continued efforts to eliminate it, the slavers believed

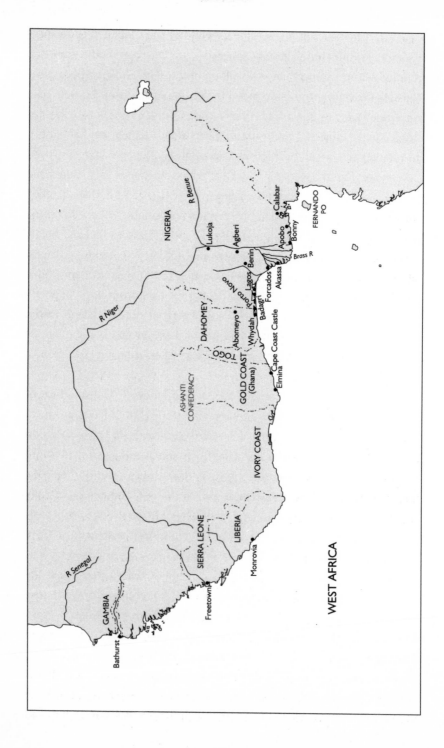

WEST AFRICA

that the rich rewards justified the risks. By the end of the 1860s, however, the situation had begun to change. For example, during five months of 1869 the screw gunboat *Nymphe*, under Commander Edward Meara, took no less than 19 slave dhows, while other warships achieved comparable success. On 13 March 1874 the *Daphne*, under Commander Charles Foot, captured a 200-ton dhow with 230 slaves aboard off Madagascar; tragically, before they could be landed, 40 of the slaves perished during a cyclone.

Between October 1874 and April 1876 the boats of the guard-ship *London*, based at Zanzibar, captured 39 dhows. This was due in part to the fact that during this period the ship was commanded in succession by Captains George Sulivan and Thomas Sulivan, both of whom were widely experienced in dealing with slavers and knew just where to look for their quarry. Another factor in the Royal Navy's continued success was the recent supply of steam pinnaces to warships. This came as an unpleasant surprise to dhow captains, who had sometimes been able to outrun pulling or sailing boats. One of the more interesting captures was made by three members of the *London*'s crew, Boatswain Richard Trigger and Gunners Stephen Quint and Stephen Hopes, while sailing in the guard-ship's yacht *Victoria* during their spare time. Spotting a dhow becalmed some seven miles distant, they pulled towards it for two hours in the yacht's dinghy. The dhow's crew were hostile but, cutlass in teeth, Trigger boarded the vessel over the bows and cowed the opposition. Quint and Hopes, finding the hold full of slaves, knocked down the Arab master, tied him up and dumped him in the dinghy. At the first breath of wind, the seamen made sail on the dhow and, with the dinghy in tow, picked up the *Victoria* and rejoined their parent ship.

In late 1874 a rebel named Abdallah and his band seized the old Portuguese fort at Mombasa, then a possession of the Sultan of Zanzibar, and declared themselves independent. In January the following year the Sultan, learning that the rebels had also burned the town, requested British assistance in restoring order. Accompanied by the British consul, Captain George Sulivan set off at once with 100 bluejackets and Marines aboard the four-gun survey vessel *Nassau* (Lieutenant Francis

Grey) and the gunboat *Rifleman* (Commander Stratford Tuke). On 19 January the rebels were driven out of the fort by a five-hour bombardment during which they lost 17 killed and 51 wounded. The boats were then sent in to take possession of the fort, which was handed back to the Sultan's representative. There were no British casualties. The *Rifleman*, it should be added, was also very active during this period in preserving law and order in the Gulf of Oman and the Persian Gulf.

Yet, for all the risks, the Arab slavers were not inclined to give up their lucrative trade without a fight. On 3 December 1881, off Pemba Island, Captain Charles Brownrigg, who had been appointed to the *London* the previous year, ran alongside a dhow flying French colours in his steam pinnace. The dhow's crew, 25 strong, fired a volley and boarded the pinnace, overwhelming the eleven men aboard. Brownrigg and three of his men were killed and three more were wounded before the Arabs made off, having also sustained some loss. The dhow was subsequently found abandoned. On 30 May 1887 an almost identical incident occurred in the same area. Lieutenant Frederick Fegen of the sloop *Turquoise* intercepted a dhow in his pinnace. The dhow opened a sharp musketry fire to which the pinnace replied with her 9-pounder. Unexpectedly, the dhow then bore down and boarded. Fegen shot two of the Arabs with his revolver and ran through a third with his sword. He was, however, on the point of being speared when Able Seaman Pearson disposed of this fourth assailant with his cutlass. During the mêlée Fegen was wounded in the right arm but continued to fire his revolver with his left hand. Eventually, nine of the 13 boarders were disposed of and the rest, scuttling back aboard their own craft, sheered off. Fegen gave chase and was rewarded when a rifle shot killed the enemy's helmsman. The dhow ran ashore and partially capsized. At this point more Arabs appeared on the shoreline, opening fire on the pinnace to cover the escape of their friends. Fegen dispersed them with several 9-pounder shells, then went on to rescue 53 slaves from the wreck, a further 12 having been drowned during the capsize. Of the eight men aboard the pinnace, four were wounded in the fighting, one of them mortally. Fegen was invalided home but was promoted to commander in recognition of his action.

The East African slave trade was finally strangled by an international blockade of the Zanzibar littoral, mounted for several months in 1889–90 by the navies of those powers with interests in the area, including Great Britain, Germany, Italy and Portugal, under the direction of Rear Admiral the Hon. Edmund Fremantle.

The West African coast, in particular the equatorial regions where the slave trade to the Americas and the Caribbean had its roots, presented problems of its own for gunboat captains. This horribly hot and humid zone was still no healthier than it had been when it was called The White Man's Grave. The colonies there were of little financial value, being maintained largely to prevent other powers extending their influence in Africa. The former slave catchers, having been deprived of their traditional occupation, turned to local piracy and general harassment of those attempting to conduct legitimate business, while jealous inland tribes eagerly sought opportunities to enrich themselves with the wealth created by the latter. Consequently, gunboats acted in much the same punitive role as they did in the East Indies, penetrating rivers to eliminate the malefactors' strongholds. Sometimes the disturbances were of such a scale, notably in the areas of the Niger and Congo Rivers, as to justify a reaction by several vessels. Often, access to secondary waterways was choked by tropical growth, giving the criminal element which had retired to their upper reaches a sense of security. This proved to be illusory as, inexorably, the gunboats, pinnaces and ships' boats cut their way slowly but steadily through the tangle. Then, a few shells would set the stockaded village alight and, with the sun glinting on Marine bayonets and the cutlasses of the bluejackets, the place would be stormed. Such measures generally brought order to the coast within a few years, although in the Gold Coast the powerful Ashanti nation posed such a threat that campaigns involving substantial land forces had to be mounted against them in 1873, 1896 and 1900.

On the other side of the world the Royal Navy's Pacific Squadron moved its base from Valparaiso, Chile, to Esquimault, Vancouver Island, in 1870. Early in 1879 Rear Admiral Algernon de Horsey, the senior naval officer at Esquimault, received a frantic request for assistance from the citizens of Sitka, Alaska, who believed that the local Indian tribes were about to rise and massacre them. This placed him in a somewhat difficult position as Sitka lay in American territory, the United States having purchased Alaska from Russia in 1867. On the other hand, the Sitkans said that requests to their own government for help had gone unanswered, and there could be no denying that the US Army had removed its own tiny garrison from Sitka two years earlier, leaving Alaska denuded of troops. De Horsey therefore despatched the gun vessel *Osprey*, commanded by Commander the Hon. Henry a'Court. On arrival, a'Court contacted the Indians, who were indeed in a belligerent mood, and was told by them that whatever he might do, they could take the US revenue steamer *Oliver Wolcott*, then lying in the harbour, whenever they wanted. With the permission of the latter's skipper, a'Court put a party of bluejackets and a Gatling machine gun aboard the little steamer to reinforce her own crew, enabling her to intercept some war canoes belonging to the rebellious chiefs. This seemed to induce a more reflective mood among the Indians and prevented what could have become a very ugly incident. As soon as she had been relieved by an American corvette, the *Osprey* returned to Esquimault.

During these years, vessels serving on the West Indies Station could expect to be involved in one sort of excitement or another. While those areas under colonial administration remained quiet enough, parts of the Caribbean and some Central and South American states remained congenitally unstable. Revolutions were commonplace, dictators being installed or ejected with bewildering frequency, usually in the name of 'the people'. In many cases the only people whose opinions counted were those with access to guns, the situation being aggravated by filibusters who supplied arms or served as mercenaries for profit.

In 1865 a politician named Sylvestre Salnave attempted forcibly to depose the president of the Haitian Republic, Fabre Geffrard, and seized the fortified harbour of Cap Haitien. On 22 October the six-gun paddle sloop *Bulldog*, commanded by Captain Charles Wake, was cruising off Acul when she came across the Salnavist steamer *Valorogue*, firing into a British Jamaica packet vessel. Bearing down, Wake warned the *Valorogue*'s captain that unless he desisted immediately his ship would be sunk under him. The rebel complied, taking his ship into Cap Haitien. There he presented Salnave with his version of events and the latter, enraged by this apparent insult to his prestige, attacked the British consulate, where a number of refugees from the coup had sought safety.

Early next morning the *Bulldog*, in company with several small government warships, was lying off the mouth of the harbour. The consul came off in a boat to inform Wake that the refugees had been shot, the consulate wrecked and the flag insulted. Wake's demand for an apology and the promise of compensation was met with a derisory response. He therefore cleared for action and, opening fire on the outermost fort at 08:45, began fighting his way into the harbour in the teeth of the coastal batteries' gunfire. Spotting the *Valorogue*, which had been the proximate cause of all the trouble, lying at anchor, Wake made straight for her. Unfortunately, he was unfamiliar with the harbour, as was his newly joined navigating officer, and the *Bulldog* ran fast aground on an unsuspected reef, not only within point-blank range of a shore battery, but also within musket shot of the *Valorogue*.

For the rest of the day Wake and his men fought the fight of their lives. By 09:45 the *Valorogue* had been sent to the bottom, and 20 minutes later she was joined by the largest schooner in Salnave's fleet. Not content with that, *Bulldog* blew up a powder magazine on shore, set the town ablaze and dispersed enemy riflemen with blasts of grape and canister. At 11:30 Wake, feeling it was time to go, sent a message to the American warship *De Soto*, requesting her to tow him off. The *De Soto*'s captain, Lieutenant Commander Howell, USN, willingly did his best and when the *Bulldog* refused to budge he offered to take her wounded aboard. The fight raged on until, at dusk, the sloop had expended most of her ammunition. Determined that she should not fall into enemy hands, Wake transferred some of her wounded to the *De Soto* and then, having set her ablaze, went aboard the government steamer *Vingt-Deux Decembre*. Finally, the flames reached the *Bulldog*'s magazine and she blew herself apart. Given the ferocity of the fighting, casualties among her 175-strong crew were remarkably low – just three men killed and ten wounded. Retribution was swift. On 9 November the 26-gun screw frigate *Galatea* and the gunboat *Lily* subjected the Cap Haitien batteries to a nine-hour bombardment. As each fell silent they were occupied by government troops.

Wake was court-martialled and severely reprimanded for hazarding and prematurely abandoning his ship. The Admiralty, however, assured him that the sentence cast no imputation on his honour or courage; nor did it affect his career, for in due course he attained the rank of vice-admiral. At the time of his trial he received tremendous support from the public and *Punch* even published a poem on the subject:

Then here's three cheers for Captain Wake; and while we sail the sea,
May British Bulldogs always find Captains as stout as he,
That's all for biting when they bite, and none for bark and brag,
And thinks less about court-martials than the honour of the flag.

One officer who fitted *Punch's* requirements to a tee was Commander Sir Lambton Loraine, commander of the 16-gun screw sloop *Niobe*. Loraine was extremely direct in his manner, was no respecter of persons, possessed a somewhat awkward turn of phrase, and produced results very quickly. Early in 1873 his ship had arrived in Puerto Plata, on the northern coast of San Domingo, known today as the Dominican Republic, to find that three refugees from political violence had been forcibly removed from the British consulate by the authorities and were lying fettered in prison. Loraine promptly made it clear to the governor that there would be truly unpleasant consequences if he did not personally unshackle the prisoners and deliver them aboard the *Niobe*, after which San Domingo troops would replace the Union Flag that had been removed from the consulate and salute it with 21 guns. Recognising a man who obviously meant business, the governor complied to the letter.

In June the same year, Vice-Admiral Edward Fanshawe, commanding the West Indies Station, despatched the *Niobe* to the Central American isthmus, where a British-financed railway was being built from Puerto Cortez on the Atlantic to the Pacific. Both the railway and its staff, it seemed, were being threatened by a local political upheaval. The root of the problem was that President Medina of Honduras had been overthrown by a Señor Arias. Neither the Hondurans nor their neighbours in Guatemala had much time for Arias and troops from both nations began assembling under General Palacios with a view to restoring Medina to office. Unfortunately, close to Puerto Cortez lay the town of Omoa, containing the old Spanish fort of San Fernando, and this was in the possession of a General Streber, who supported Arias. Streber, who considered himself to be something of a warlord, had already made exactions from the railway company and tried to force its employees to join his army. At this point in the tangled story, the *Niobe* arrived. Loraine issued a sharp warning to Streber, who seemed to take it seriously, then continued on his way to Belize in British Honduras, where he hoped to obtain a balanced picture of the overall situation.

In Belize he met Mr Debrot, the British vice-consul at Omoa, who, with the Spanish and Portuguese consuls, had been forced to flee the town because of the threat of violence from Streber's men. They had taken refuge on Zapotillo Cays, a group of small islands which were dependencies of British Honduras. Streber had sent troops after them and, handcuffed, they were being shipped back to Omoa when they were rescued by a steamer belonging to General Palacios of the pro-Medina faction.

Returning to Omoa, Loraine learned from Palacios that his troops had not only secured Puerto Cortez, but also cut off Streber's contact with the interior. As luck would have it, the *Niobe* had yellow fever aboard and was forced to cruise off the coast while the outbreak was brought under control. Seeing this, Streber assumed that Loraine lacked either the means or the will to enforce his threats. His men ransacked Mr Debrot's premises, tore down the Union Flag, fired on General Palacios's troops under a flag of truce, looted the town, causing £20,000 worth of damage to the property of foreign nationals in the process, and flung four British nationals in gaol after flogging one of them.

Learning of this as soon as conditions aboard permitted him to return to the coast, Loraine brought the *Niobe* to anchor off Fort San

Fernando on 18 August. The next morning he gave Streber several hours to explain his conduct, release the prisoners and consider his proposals for reparation. No satisfactory reply having been received, at 14:30 *Niobe* began a four-hour bombardment of the ancient walls with her 7-inch and 40-pounder guns. Streber's men responded with ill-aimed rifle fire. The bombardment was renewed at 01:00 on 20 August and maintained until 04:00. Streber, rapidly losing face with his followers, displayed a white flag at 09:00 and sent off his adjutant in a boat to request a 72-hour truce. Loraine remarked that the *Niobe* had no need of a truce and would commence firing again at 14:30, although he subsequently sanctioned a further delay. The following morning Streber agreed unconditionally to meet all of Loraine's demands, including the release of the prisoners, reparation and return of the stolen goods. By now, with his men deserting in droves, it was beyond his power to make full restitution, although the prisoners were set free. On 10 September Loraine sent a party ashore to close up the plundered houses and nail a flag above the vice-consulate. Three days later, having satisfied himself that British interests in the area were secure, he sailed for Jamaica. In fact, both he and *Niobe* were on the eve of their greatest adventure.

Cuba, still a Spanish colony, was torn by a revolt against her mother country, which was itself in the throes of a constitutional crisis. Nowhere was support for the Cuban rebels stronger or more active than in the United States. On 23 October the American steamer *Virginius*, a former Confederate blockade runner, left Kingston, Jamaica, ostensibly bound for Port Limon in Costa Rica. Of the 103 passengers aboard, 32 were British subjects, 14 were citizens of the United States and the rest were mostly Cubans. The British authorities in Jamaica were deeply suspicious of the *Virginius*, and rightly so, as her Cuban passengers included four prominent *insurrectos*. Shortly after leaving Kingston, the captain claimed that she had developed a leak and anchored off the Haitian coast, ostensibly to complete repairs. While these were in progress, a cargo of arms and ammunition was brought aboard. When the voyage was resumed, the dismayed passengers were informed that their destination was Cuba rather than Costa Rica.

op: Because of the shallow waters of the Baltic, often
nly small warships could get within effective range of
he Russian coast defence batteries. The scene shows
hree paddle sloops engaging the fortifications at
Hango Head, Finland. *Anne S.K. Brown Military
Collection, Brown University Library*

lbove: The situation improved with the arrival of
urpose built, shallow-draught gunboats with real
itting power, similar to that shown on the left in this
print of the attack on Bomarsund in the Aland Islands.
*Anne S.K. Brown Military Collection, Brown University
Library*

Below: The Allied bombardment of Sveaborg fortress.
Although the artist has not quite captured the tactics
used by the gunboats and mortar vessels, his depiction of
the defences and the Russian blockships is accurate.
Helsingfors (Helsinki) lies in the left background. *Anne
S.K. Brown Military Collection, Brown University Library*

Above: Allied gunboats batter the defences of Arabat in the Sea of Azov. Lyons' flagship *Miranda* is in the right foreground. *Anne S.K. Brown Military Collection, Brown University Library*

Left: Captain Sherard Osborn, RN, was responsible for Allied gunboat operations in the Sea of Azov during the final months of the Crimean War, causing damage and destruction out of all proportion to the size of the force employed. He also saw much active service in China and at one stage was seconded to the Imperial Chinese Navy as an admiral, commanding the notorious Vampire Squadron. He was also involved with polar exploration. *National Maritime Museum Neg No A1308*

Top: An 'on the spot' sketch showing the gunboat *Naughty,* followed by ships' boats, leading the attack on Chinese war junks in Fatshan Creek, 1 June 1857. *National Maritime Museum Neg No PW2415*

Above: Admiral Seymour's British and French gunboats in action against the Taku Forts on 20 May 1858. The easy victory gained encouraged Admiral Hope to mount a similar attack the following year. However, by then the fortifications had been greatly strengthened. *National Maritime Museum Neg No A 7544*

Below: The Hon East India Company's paddle sloop *Nemesis* puts paid to a flotilla of pirate junks in Anson's Bay, 7 January 1841. *National Maritime Museum Neg No 792*

Above: Commodore Foote's Federal gunboat squadron captures Fort Henry, Tennessee, 6 February 1862. *Anne S. K. Brown Military Collection, Brown University Library*

Below: On the morning of 10 May 1862 the Federal squadron, now commanded by Commodore Davis, was surprised by its Confederate opponents at Plum Point Bend. The battle was not quite the Union victory suggested by the print, for although several Confederate ships sustained damage, the Federal *Cincinnati* was sunk in shallow water and the *Mound City* only saved herself by running aground. *Anne S.K. Brown Military Collection, Brown University Library*

Above: Officially classed as a small masted cruiser,
HMS *Algerine* nevertheless owed much to earlier
gunboat designs, despite being somewhat larger. She
was launched in 1895, by which time warships of this
type were steadily replacing gunboats around the
world. Her armament consisted of six 4-inch quick
firing and four 3-pdr guns and her engines could
produce a maximum speed of 13 knots. The simple rig
emphasises the declining importance of sail. *Imperial
War Museum Neg No Q43260*

Below: HMS *Alarm,* launched in 1892, was another
interim design and was classed as a torpedo-gunboat.
Armament consisted of two 4.7-inch and four 3-pdr
guns plus five or eight torpedo tubes; she was capable
of a maximum speed of 20 knots. She is seen here in
her smart Victorian livery of lined black hull, white
upperworks and buff funnels and ventilators. Many of
the new torpedo-boat destroyers carried the names of
the old Crimean gunboats. *Imperial War Museum Neg
No Q38073*

LORD CHARLES BERESFORD R.N.C.B.
CONDOR

Left: A patriotic montage including a photograph of Lord Charles Beresford and an artist's impression of the gunboat *Condor* tackling Fort Marabut, Alexandria. *National Maritime Museum Neg No X 391.*

Right: The gunboat *Sultan* dispersing dervishes with her Maxim machine guns at Omdurman. In the background is the Mahdi's tomb, damaged by shellfire. *Sultan* was commanded by the then Lieutenant Walter Cowan, RN, whose active service career continued well into World War II. *National Army Museum*

Below: The hull of a new gunboat being shipped forward in sections along Kitchener's Desert Railway. On arrival at Abadiya the gunboats were assembled and launched for the final phase of the advance on Omdurman. *Museum of Army Transport*

Above: The monitor *Mersey* which, together with her sister ship *Severn,* destroyed the German cruiser *Königsberg* in the Rufiji river. This class of monitor was armed with three 6-inch guns and two 4.7-inch howitzers. *Imperial War Museum Neg No SP 84*

Below: The wreck of the *Königsberg.* Despite her destruction, the Germans stripped out her 4.1-inch guns, which were used during General von Lettow Vorbeck's brilliant campaign in East Africa. *Imperial War Museum Neg No Q49499*

Top: Another view of the wrecked *Königsberg. Imperial War Museum Neg No Q45678*

Below: The impossible takes a little longer … A traction engine hauls one of Spicer Simson's gunboats over an improvised river crossing. *Imperial War Museum Neg No Q67645*

bove: Journey's end. *Mimi* is edged towards her
unching site. Imperial War Museum Neg No Q67680

elow: Mimi and *Tou Tou* photographed shortly before
eir engagement with the German *Kingani.* Although

they were the smallest gunboats ever built, their
success altered the whole strategic balance in the area
of Lake Tanganyika. The figure in the 'skirt', centre
right, is Commander Spicer-Simson. *Imperial War
Museum Neg No Q67687*

Above: Insect Class gunboat *Gnat* proceeding up-river on the Tigris. *Imperial War Museum Neg No HU 65303*

Bottom: An un-named Insect Class gunboat pegged down to the bank and providing fire support for ground troops on the Tigris. Main armament consists of two 6-inch guns, supplemented by two 12-pdr guns. *Imperial War Museum Neg No Q24829*

Opposite page, top: Fly Class gunboat *Sedgefly* engaging targets ashore. Armed with one 4-inch and one 12-pdr gun, the Flies were classed as Small China Gunboats and shipped out in parts to Abadan for assembly on

the spot. A range finder can be seen in use above the circular 12-pdr mounting. The local Arabs would murder stragglers and wounded without a second thought, but were in awe of the gunboats. *Imperial War Museum Neg No Q24817*

Opposite page, bottom: Mantis with the recaptured *Firefly* lashed alongside. *Firefly* was lost during the retreat from Ctesiphon in 1915 and was known as *Suleiman Pak* in Turkish service. The White Ensign can be seen flying from her mast above the Turkish flag. *Imperial War Museum Neg Q67790*

Left: A Bolshevik shell explodes alongside the gunboat *Glowworm* in the River Dvina, North Russia. *Imperial War Museum Neg No SP 2325*

Below: The wreck of the submarine depot ship *Pamiat Azova,* one of several Soviet warships sunk during the coastal motor boat attack on Kronstadt naval base. She held dismal memories for British submariners un-fortunate enough to be based aboard her during World War I. *Imperial War Museum Neg No Q69746*

Right: Following conversion in 1922, *Bee* became the flagship of the Rear Admiral commanding the gunboats on the Yangtse. She was scrapped at Shanghai in 1939. *Imperial War Museum Neg No HU 73414*

Below: Chinese river pirates under the guard of a naval boarding party. During this period pirates often mingled with the passengers of merchant vessels, which responded by fortifying their bridge and engine room spaces. *Imperial War Museum Neg No HU 42744*

Above: On 12 December 1937 Japanese artillery opened fire on *Ladybird,* causing casualties and damage, some of which is seen here. Note the tarpaulin covering a hole below the waterline. The Japanese apologised, but almost immediately sank the American gunboat *Panay.* *Imperial War Museum Neg No NYP 57281*

Left: On the night of 16/17 December 1940 *Aphis* penetrated the fortified harbour of Bardia, sank three Italian supply ships and caused an enormous amount of damage ashore before making good her escape. She is seen here at Sollum a little later in the campaign. When they were not actually fighting, the Insects of the Inshore Squadron acted as supply carriers for Wavell's advancing troops, delivering 100 tons of drinking water daily for a period, ferrying in reinforcements and shipping out prisoners. *Imperial War Museum Neg No E 1430*

bove: Ladybird was sunk by air attack in Tobruk
arbour but one of her 3-inch guns remained above
ater and, manned by gunners of the Royal Artillery,
ontinued to play an active part in the anti-aircraft
efence of the fortress. *Imperial War Museum Neg No E
848*

Below: Damage sustained by *Amethyst*'s bridge and
director tower when communist artillery deliberately
opened fire on her in the Yangtse on 20 April 1949.
Imperial War Museum Neg No HU 45374

Above: The Chinese communists sustained a serious loss of face because of the *Amethyst*'s dramatic escape. Her damage repaired and spruce in a fresh coat of paint, *Amethyst* is seen here on her way home from the Far East to receive a hero's welcome. *Imperial War Museum Neg No HU 45389*

Below: Armoured Troop Carriers and Monitors of Naval Task Force 117, Mobile Riverine Force, leaving their base at the start of an operation. My Tho River, Vietnam, 26 September 1967. *US Army*

On 31 October the *Virginius* was intercepted by the Spanish warship *Tornado* some 20 miles off the Cuban coast. Turning away towards Jamaica, she dumped the arms and ammunition but was overhauled, arrested, and taken into Santiago de Cuba. There, the governor, Brigadier General Don Juan Burriel y Lynch, promptly flung all aboard into gaol, declaring that they were pirates and would be tried accordingly. The four *insurrecto* leaders were shot out of hand. On 6 November 37 members of the crew, including eight American and 19 innocent British subjects who had been employed as firemen, cooks and stewards were tried and convicted by a naval court martial. They were messily shot against the wall of the town's slaughter-house the following morning, amid wild cheering from Santiago's loyalist population. On 8 November another 12 prisoners shared the same fate.

Burriel was acting entirely on his own initiative, claiming that telegraphic communication with Spain and with the Captain General of Cuba in Havana, hundreds of miles to the west, had broken down. Unfortunately for him, there was still contact with Jamaica, whence the angry British authorities had despatched the *Niobe* on the evening of 6 November. She reached Santiago two days later, just too late to prevent the second batch of killings. Accompanied by Mr Theodore Brooks, the British vice-consul, Loraine immediately made for the governor's palace to demand an end to the executions. Burriel sneeringly objected to his interference and promised nothing save access to the British prisoners in gaol. Furious, Loraine gave the consulate permission to spread word that if more innocent blood was shed he would sink the Spanish warship lying closest to the *Niobe*. This amounted to a virtual declaration of war, no mean feat for a mere commander, but it did the trick. There were no more executions and Burriel, having agreed to refer the matter to the Captain General, made himself scarce, leaving his unfortunate deputy governor, Morales, to handle an extremely hot potato.

The affair had now entered the diplomatic level. Spain had ceased to be a major naval power at Trafalgar and, with troubles enough of her own, she simply could not afford to be drawn into actual hostilities. On 15 November instructions were issued to the Santiago authorities to terminate their high-handed actions. The *Virginius*, escorted by two

Spanish warships, had already been despatched to Havana. By the end of the month American and French warships had arrived off Santiago. Deputy governor Morales, wishing to be relieved of the problem, clandestinely removed the prisoners from gaol during the night of 3 December and sent them to Havana aboard one of his gun vessels. Learning of this, Loraine gave chase with the *Niobe* and, having banged the Captain General's table, obtained orders for the Spanish captain to return to Santiago with the prisoners. Unable to withstand the diplomatic pressure, Spain handed back the *Virginius* on 15 December; she sank off Florida while being towed to New York. Three days later the surviving prisoners, 102 in number, were surrendered to the American corvette *Juniatta* under the supervision of the *Niobe*. All that remained was the question of compensation, which was settled between the governments concerned.

Loraine became the hero of the hour, receiving not only the thanks of both Houses of Parliament, but of the French government as well. His most enthusiastic, grateful and generous admirers, however, were American. In April 1874 the Common Council of New York awarded him the Freedom of the City, a most remarkable distinction for a comparatively junior officer of the Royal Navy. He paid a private visit to receive the honour, during which he was lionised, shown round the public institutions, attended a reception in his honour at the Army and Navy Club, and even paid a midnight visit to the Fire Department. Asked whether he would like a public reception, he modestly declined, but got one just the same, at which he was presented with the Council's beautifully illuminated resolutions. In reply to Mayor Havemeyer, he said:

> I have to thank your Honor once more for your kind expressions. I really am getting nervous and tired, almost, in returning thanks for the excessive kindness which I have met at the hands of the citizens of New York. I am proud if any efforts of mine have tended to save the lives of Americans. After all, blood is thicker than water and the people of England have a strong affection for their American citizens.

Notwithstanding his having apparently forgotten the rather important matter of American Independence, this response, according to the *New York Times*, 'elicited applause from all present'. His visit was undoubtedly a success and, shortly after he had left he received the present of a silver brick from American well-wishers.

By the late 1880s large areas of the world had come under the control of the European powers and the immense potential industrial, economic, naval and military power of the United States was beginning to emerge. By and large, order now existed in what had once been troubled areas. The situations which required gunboats to act as international policemen were fast disappearing. Cruisers, with their gleaming white tropical awnings and glinting brasswork, were now used by the great powers to impress the natives and each other in place of the hardworking little gunboats and gunvessels that had borne the brunt of global expansion. The Royal Navy, furthermore, was on the eve of a great modernisation programme which concentrated on the development of large warships. By the score, the gunboats were withdrawn from active service to be sold or scrapped, although a few continued to be built for service on the world's great rivers. Perversely, no matter how mighty battlefleets might become, it was the gunboat that continued to make history.

6
DEATH ON THE NILE
Egypt, 1882 and the Gordon
Relief Expedition, 1884–5

During the 19th century the Ottoman Empire, unable either to defend itself adequately or exercise effective rule throughout its sprawling Middle Eastern and Mediterranean territories, declined from the status of a major power to the extent that it became known as The Sick Man of Europe. Egypt, for example, while nominally a province of the empire, had long attained virtual independence under its own Khedive or Viceroy.

The Khedive Ismail made strenuous efforts to modernise Egypt but in doing so he incurred huge foreign debts which the country was unable to support. As a consequence of this, British and French financial advisers became virtual controllers of the Egyptian economy and the British government purchased Ismail's shares in the recently completed Suez Canal at a moderate price. In 1879 Ismail was deposed and replaced by his son Tewfik. Naturally, many Egyptians resented the growing foreign influence in their affairs and in September 1881 their rumbling discontent finally erupted under the leadership of Colonel Achmet Arabi Pasha, who enjoyed widespread support throughout the army. By the end of May 1882 the authority of the Khedive had been repudiated and Arabi had become a virtual dictator. The following month serious rioting took place in Alexandria during which some 50 Europeans, including the British consul and three Royal Navy seamen, were killed. At about the same time Arabi began strengthening the forts covering the seaward approaches to the harbour. As Great Britain and France possessed considerable financial interests in Egypt, warships from both nations converged on Alexandria with a view to restoring law and order. On 10 July the commander of the British fleet, Admiral Sir Beauchamp Seymour, informed Arabi that unless the new fortifications were surrendered immediately they would be destroyed by naval bombardment. This was too much for the French who, for reasons of their own, promptly took themselves off to Port Said; it was a decision which France was to regret, for from this point onwards it would be the British influence which would predominate in Egypt. Doubtless encouraged by their departure, Arabi rejected Seymour's ultimatum.

Seymour had at his disposal the battleships *Inflexible, Monarch, Temeraire, Alexandra, Sultan, Invincible, Superb* and *Penelope,* the gunboats *Beacon, Bittern, Condor, Cygnet* and *Decoy,* the paddle despatch vessel *Helicon* and the ammunition depot ship *Hecla.* These would be engaging 13 forts and coastal batteries, many of which were either badly constructed or in a ramshackle state. Furthermore, the Egyptians could only oppose 44 heavy rifled guns against the British 97, the rest of their 249 guns being either smoothbore antiques or mortars.

The engagement began at 07:00 on 11 July. The battleships opened fire at ranges between 1000 and 3750 yards, closing in as the day wore on. The overmatched Egyptians fought back bravely but were gradually driven from their guns not only by the fire of the battleships' heavy weapons but also by rockets and Gatling and Nordenfeldt machine guns. By 17:00 the last of their guns had been silenced. Their casualties were estimated as being 150 killed and 400 wounded out of a total of approximately 2000 men manning the defences. British casualties amounted to five killed and 28 wounded. Little serious damage was done to the ships. *Superb* had a hole measuring ten by four feet blown in her hull just above the waterline, plus two smaller holes fore and aft. *Alexandra* sustained 60 hits, of which 24 were outside her armour. Her casualties and damage would have been greater had not Gunner Israel Harding picked up an enemy shell with a burning fuse and dumped it in a water tub, an act which earned him promotion and the Victoria Cross. *Inflexible*, too, had a lucky escape, thanks to something of a ballistic freak. She was struck below the waterline by a 10-inch Palliser shell which ricocheted upwards through the deck, killing one man and mortally wounding another, then wrecked the captain's cabin, all without exploding; during the course of its flight, while travelling base first, it impressed its manufacturer's name into an iron bollard which it struck.

The bombardment of Alexandria was not, therefore, the most notable of naval engagements, but it does provide an opportunity to introduce Commander Lord Charles Beresford, commander of the

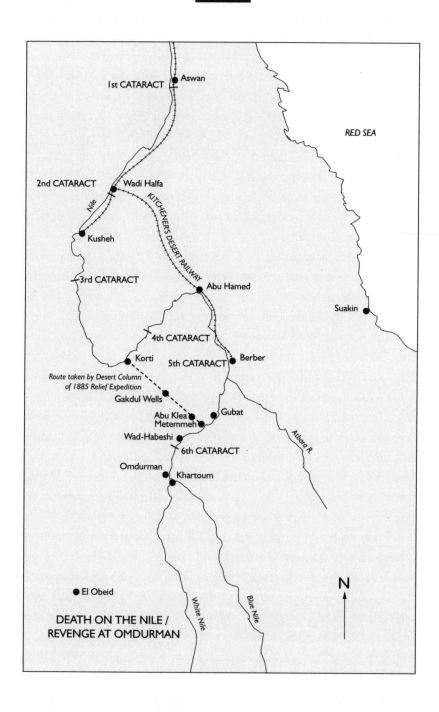

DEATH ON THE NILE /
REVENGE AT OMDURMAN

gunboat *Condor*. The unarmoured gunboats had been ordered to stay out of harm's way but this did not suit Beresford's temperament at all. At 08:30, observing that Fort Marabout, at the western end of the defences, had opened fire on the battleships without itself becoming a target, he closed in with *Condor* and engaged it himself with his one 7-inch and two 64-pounder guns. At length he dropped anchor so close to the fort that its guns could not be depressed sufficiently to return the fire, while by warping to and fro he was able to batter all the enemy's gun positions. At 10:00 the remaining gunboats were ordered to his assistance. As the last of the fort's guns fell silent a great cheer went up from the fleet and Admiral Seymour signalled 'Well done, *Condor*!'

The withdrawal of Arabi and his troops provided the city's criminal element with a golden opportunity for looting and arson. On 13 July detachments of bluejackets and Royal Marines were put ashore to restore order, bringing with them their Gatling guns on field carriages. It took several days' sustained effort, involving the use of machine guns, rifle and bayonet and even fists, to bring the rioters under control. On 15 July Captain John Fisher of the *Inflexible*, in overall command of operations ashore, was reinforced by a party of US Marines, who, together with the British naval police, were placed under Beresford and performed sterling service. 'The Americans,' noted William Clowes, 'co-operated in the most loyal and friendly fashion with the British. In consequence, apparently, of the example set by them, the senior naval officers of one or two other nationalities also offered to land men, and their offers were gratefully accepted.'

The events at Alexandria led to a number of promotions being made, including that of Beresford to captain.

Nevertheless, despite having sustained a serious reverse, Arabi remained intransigent and continued to enjoy the support of the army. As an unstable Egypt presented an obvious threat to the Suez Canal, now Great Britain's principal sea route to her imperial possessions in the Far East, a 25,000-strong army under Lieutenant-General Sir Garnet Wolseley was put ashore at Ismailia, within the canal itself, with the object of restoring a more acceptable regime. Having been worsted in a series of skirmishes at Kassassin, Arabi withdrew his troops to a well-constructed line of entrenchments at Tel-el-Kebir, blocking further progress towards Cairo. During the night of 12/13 September 1882 Wolseley's army executed a brilliant approach march and drove the Egyptians from their trenches in a dawn attack. Arabi surrendered the following day when the British cavalry reached Cairo and was sent into exile in Ceylon. The campaign marked the beginning of 70 years of continuous British presence in Egypt. At the time there was no thought of so continuous a commitment, but a succession of necessities would ensure that it was maintained. Of these, the first was the troubled state of the Sudan, where a rebellion had broken out in 1881.

The leader of the rebellion was a devout ascetic named Mohammed Ahmed, better known to history as the Mahdi or Expected Guide. The Mahdi preached a return to the purest values of Islam and the over-throw of Egyptian rule in the Sudan, which had been marked by exploitation, corruption, slavery and casual indifference to the needs of its inhabitants. The revolt attracted widespread support and soon the dervishes, as the Mahdi's followers were known, were in control of whole provinces, having eliminated numerous Egyptian garrisons and field forces in the process. The last straw came in November 1883 when a 7000-strong Egyptian army commanded by a British officer, Colonel William Hicks, was annihilated by 20,000 dervishes near El Obeid. As a result of their successes, the dervishes had become a formidable force, equipped with modern artillery, machine guns and rifles taken from their former rulers.

In Cairo, the British government's senior representative, Sir Evelyn Baring, formed the opinion that further attempts to recover the Sudan would simply be a waste of military and economic resources. The Egyp-tians agreed, but were anxious to secure the safe evacuation of their remaining garrisons and the survivors of their civil administration. After some debate, they accepted the offer of Major-General Charles Gordon's services to achieve this end. Gordon had enjoyed a distin-guished career in China and, from 1877 to 1879, he had held the post of governor general of the Sudan, where his incorruptibility had earned widespread respect. He was the Victorian ideal of a Christian gentleman who devoted all his spare time and considerable energy to charitable works; he was also that nightmare of politicians, an honest man of principle with a will of iron.

Gordon was the first to admit that the Sudan he returned to in February 1884 was a very different place from that which he had left in 1879. Whether he could have initiated an evacuation is open to debate. What is clear is that shortly after his arrival in Khartoum he decided to stay put, driven by a sense of honour that would not allow him to desert those placed in his charge. Every one of his requests for assistance was denied by Prime Minister William Gladstone's philanthropic Liberal administration. By the end of May Khartoum was besieged by 60,000 well-armed dervishes. Believing that, sooner or later, a relief column would appear, Gordon fought the battle of his life. He used all his skills as a professional military engineer to strengthen the fortifications, strung barbed wire and laid mines; he mounted regular destructive sorties on the enemy's positions; and, with such protection as could be afforded by timber balks and sandbags, he converted his few small river steamers, none of them larger than a modern tug, into makeshift gunboats which were used to raid deep into dervish-controlled territory.

Gordon also had a powerful ally in the British public, whose sense of fair play was outraged by the government's failure to help him. Together, the Conservative opposition and the press waded into Gladstone at every opportunity. A motion of censure in the Commons was narrowly defeated. Gladstone, fearing electoral disaster for his party, gave way in August, sanctioning the despatch of a relief force of 10,000 men to be selected from the entire army, plus a small naval contingent. In command would be Sir Garnet Wolseley, by now the government's favourite military trouble-shooter.

Quite apart from whatever action the enemy might take, the physical difficulties involved in getting to Khartoum were immense. Two routes were possible, of which the shorter began at the port of Suakin on the Red Sea, crossed the Desert of the Belly of Stones to Berber on the Nile, then followed the river upstream. This was considered impractical not only because dervish tribes were in virtual control of the Suakin hinterland, but also because there were too few wells along the desert route. The longer Nile alternative would permit use of river steamers and the Egyptian railway system as far as Wadi Halfa on the Sudan border. Against this, the journey would be made at the time of year when the river was falling, exposing the series of rapids known as cataracts, of which six existed between Aswan and Khartoum. Passage of these would be both time-consuming and dangerous, but not for nothing had Wolseley built up a reputation for meticulous planning. He had encountered similar difficulties during the Red River expedition in Canada and ordered some 800 boats to be shipped out from England immediately, including a large number of specially constructed Canadian *bateaux* with flat bottoms which drew little water and were therefore suited to the passage of the cataracts. To man them he recruited 300 Canadian *voyageurs,* some of whom were of the opinion that Khartoum lay within the Arctic Circle and arrived in Egypt dressed accordingly.

Gradually, the relief force assembled at Korti. On 17 November Wolseley received a message from Gordon to the effect that he doubted whether he could hold out more than another month. Wolseley was therefore faced with the most difficult problem of his career. Upstream of Korti was the Great Bend of the Nile, in negotiating which the obstacles posed by the Fourth, Fifth and Sixth Cataracts would have to be overcome before Khartoum was reached. However, a track through the Bayuda Desert cut across the arc of the bend, connecting Korti with Gubat, only 96 miles from Khartoum, and along this were just sufficient wells to support a small force. Wolseley therefore adopted a daring and extremely dangerous plan in which the main body of the expedition would continue up-river while a flying column was sent across the desert to Gubat, where arrangements would be made for Gordon's gunboats to be waiting. The object of the operation was not so much Gordon's relief but the reinforcement of his garrison so that, hopefully, it would be able to hold on until the spring when the Nile began to rise and Wolseley would be able to complete his task.

The Desert Column, commanded by Brigadier-General Sir Herbert Stewart, consisted of just 2000 men; cynics might argue that there was no point in risking more in what seemed to be a suicidal venture. It contained four camel regiments, a cavalry squadron, a half-battery of Royal Artillery with three 2.5-inch mountain guns, a Royal Engineer detachment, a Royal Navy detachment, a portable field hospital and transport details. The Naval Brigade, commanded by Lord Charles Beresford, was raised from ships of the Mediterranean Fleet and consisted of two divisions. Only the First Division, with six officers, 51 petty-officers and seamen and one Gardner machine gun, had reached Korti in time to leave with the Desert Column; the Second Division, similarly constituted, would follow on as soon as it arrived.

The seamen thoroughly enjoyed the novel experience of 'playing soldier'. Invariably good-humoured, they displayed a higher level of personal initiative than the more formally disciplined troops. They tackled their tasks with gusto, causing their camel-riding instructors much amusement as they applied the language of the sea to the ships of the desert. 'Mind your helm, Jack, or you'll run me aboard!' they would shout, or 'Steer small, Bill – she won't go astern!'

On 31 December another message was received from Gordon. It had been written two weeks earlier and the messenger also delivered a verbal request that Wolseley should come quickly. The main body of the Desert Column set off during the night of 9 January 1885, its pace restricted to the camel's plodding two-and-three-quarter miles per hour. Save at Gakdul, the supply of water from the wells was inadequate and the march was a hard one. As there were no secrets in the Sudan, the Mahdi was well aware of what was happening. He detached no less than 12,000 men to fall on Stewart, with orders to let him advance to a point from which there could be no escape once he had been defeated. After that, Gordon would be provided with physical proof that the Desert Column had been destroyed and, recognising that his last hope had vanished, he would cease his futile resistance.

For his part, Stewart prudently dropped off parties to secure his line of communications, although this reduced his fighting strength. On 15 January he learned that the enemy were holding his next objective, the wells at Abu Klea, and formed a zareba for the night. The following morning, leaving sufficient men to hold the zareba, he formed a square, this being the usual tactic in desert warfare when the enemy's superior numbers would enable him to turn the flanks of any other formation. With the square went the three mountain guns, the naval detachment with its Gardner and, in the centre, camels carrying water, ammunition and medical supplies.

Stewart had decided that if the dervishes would not attack him, he would attack them. When the square had reached a point approximately 500 yards from the line of dervish banners, some 5000 of the enemy surged forward, provoked beyond endurance by the sight of a mere 1500 men advancing confidently towards them. The mountain guns went into action and volley firing commenced. Within 100 yards of the square the dervish dead and wounded began to pile up. The enemy changed the direction of his attack, streaming past the square with the clear intention of smashing through its left-rear corner. To meet the threat, the naval detachment was pushed out with the Gardner and the square closed behind them.

The Gardner was a manually operated weapon with five barrels mounted side by side, served in turn by a crank-operated sliding feed block, and it had performed extremely well during Admiralty trials. It fired about 40 rounds, which Beresford perceived were flying too high. The lay was adjusted and the gun fired a further 30 rounds, cutting a swathe through the running figures. Then it jammed. The fault lay not in the weapon but in the ammunition, for as the extractor pulled the head of an expended case free, the rest of it split in the chamber, so preventing the loading of further rounds. Beresford tells us what happened next:

The captain of the gun, Will Rhoods, Chief Boatswain's Mate, and myself unscrewed the plate to clear the barrel, or take the lock of the jammed barrel out, when the enemy were upon us. Rhoods was killed with a spear. Walter Miller, armourer, I also saw killed with a spear at the same moment on my left. I was knocked down in the rear of the gun, but uninjured, except for a small spear scratch on my left hand. The crowd and crush of the enemy was very great at this point and, as I struggled up I was carried against the face of the square, which was literally pushed back by sheer weight of numbers about twelve paces from the position of the gun. The crush was so great that at the moment few on either side were killed, but fortunately this flank of the square had been forced up a very steep little mound, which enabled the rear rank to open a tremendous fire over the heads of the front rank men. This relieved the pressure and enabled the front rank to bayonet or shoot those of the enemy nearest them.

Nearby, savage hand-to-hand fighting was taking place. Led by a mounted emir, a number of dervishes smashed through the ranks into the interior of the square. They lived for only a few seconds, most being killed by fire from the rear rank of the opposite face, which had turned about. At the same time, Stewart's second-in-command, Colonel Fred Burnaby, was killed when he charged out of the square at the enemy; he was a noted traveller and sportsman who was said to have a death wish.

The close-quarter fighting lasted for five minutes, at the end of which the dervishes simply turned and walked away, pausing now and then to shout insults. The square replied with a derisive cheer, several rounds of case shot from the mountain guns, and a few volleys. Beresford and his men went out and cleared the Gardner's stoppage, exacting their revenge until the enemy disappeared. About 1100 of the dervishes had been killed, and probably a larger number were wounded. The Desert Column's losses amounted to nine officers and 65 other ranks killed, plus nine officers and 85 other ranks wounded. In defending the Gardner the naval detachment lost eight killed, including two officers, and seven wounded.

The wells at Abu Klea were occupied and, leaving its wounded under guard, the Desert Column resumed its march during the afternoon of 18 January. It continued throughout the night until, shortly after dawn, the cavalry reported that the Nile was just five miles further on but that between it and the column was an even larger dervish force than had been encountered at Abu Klea. Stewart decided to rest his weary men and constructed a zareba near the village of Abu Kru, together with a redoubt for the mountain guns and the Gardner. 'We shall first have breakfast,' he said, 'then go out and fight.'

In the meantime the enemy occupied a gravel ridge and pushed out riflemen who sniped continually at the zareba from unseen positions. Casualties began to mount. Stewart was himself hit in the groin and the wound proved mortal. Assuming command, Colonel Sir Charles Wilson decided to persevere with his plan. Leaving some 300 men, a quarter of his entire strength, to guard the zareba and the redoubt under Beresford's command, he formed his square at 10:00. His advance was supported by the mountain guns and when dervish cavalry began hovering menacingly on the left they were dispersed by the naval detachment's Gardner. Suddenly the enemy began swarming off the ridge, coming on at a steady run. Volley firing started at once but, seeing that it was having little effect, Wilson ordered his bugler to sound Cease Firing. Save for quietly spoken orders to lower sights, the square waited in disciplined silence as the dervishes came on. Not until they were within 300 yards was Commence Firing sounded. The volleys blasted out, followed by rapid independent firing. Their experience at Abu Klea had taught the men to shoot deliberately, aiming low and to kill. 'All the leaders and their fluttering banners went down,' wrote Wilson. 'No one got within 50 yards of the square. It only lasted a few minutes; the whole of their front ranks were swept away and then we saw a wild backward movement, followed by the rapid disappearance of the Arabs in front of and all round us. We had won and gave three ringing cheers.' The dervishes fled in the direction of Metemmeh, leaving hundreds of their dead strewing the ground. The Battle of Abu Kru cost the Desert Column one officer and 22 other ranks killed, and eight officers and 90 other ranks wounded.

The square marched on to the Nile where it drank its reward. The following day it returned to pick up those at the zareba and its redoubt, then established a fortified base at the village of Gubat, a few miles upstream from Metemmeh. Having crossed 176 miles of desert and fought two major engagements, the Desert Column, by now reduced to about 1000 effectives, was completely exhausted and in dire need of rest; some of the horses had had no water for two days and most of the camels none for five days.

On 21 January smudges of smoke coming downstream announced the arrival of Gordon's four little gunboats, the *Bordein, Safieh, Tewfikieh* and *Talahawiyeh.* They confirmed that Gordon was still holding out and reported that another large body of besiegers had been detached to intercept the Desert Column. All the naval detachment's commissioned officers save Beresford were either dead or incapacitated by wounds, and although he was himself so seriously ill that he could barely walk, he had the vessels ready for the return voyage within 24 hours. Wilson, however, concentrated on the necessary task of consolidating his position and it was not until 24 January that he set off personally with the *Bordein* and the *Talahawiyeh*, determined to break through to Khartoum. Apart from putting an engine room artificer aboard each of them, he left the Egyptian crews in charge of their vessels. He did, however, take with him 20 men of the Royal Sussex Regiment in scarlet tunics borrowed from the Guards, remembering that Gordon had once said that the sight of a few red coats would convince the Mahdi that Great Britain meant business.

The brave but hopeless venture deserved a better ending. The *Bordein* ran aground on the 25th; she did so again the following day and it took 24 hours to get her off. On the 28th the gunboats began passing through the besiegers' lines, exchanging fire with them as they had done on so many occasions. This time there was a difference as fire was also opened on them from Khartoum's defences, where the red flag of Egypt with its sickle moon and star no longer flew above the governor general's palace. Khartoum was now in enemy hands. With a heavy heart Wilson recognised that there was no more to be done. He gave the order to reverse course and began fighting his way downstream.

The reality was that the city had been at the Mahdi's mercy for some time. There has been much speculation as to why a decisive assault was not launched earlier. The Mahdi seems to have respected Gordon as an honourable man whose piety equalled his own. He even offered to let him depart without so much as a ransom, but Charles Gordon was not the man even to consider such an offer while others depended upon him. For a while the Mahdi was content to allow Khartoum to starve itself into surrender. It was the arrival of the Desert Column at Gubat that changed his mind. Abu Klea and Abu Kru had cost him the lives of 2000 of his followers, including numerous emirs, and many more would never recover from their wounds. Some of the *Ansar*, his most trusted warriors, were said to be nervous of these few but terrible soldiers who feared nothing but dealt death so swiftly. With the British now less than 100 miles from Khartoum he was not prepared to risk further blows to his prestige. Khartoum was to be stormed immediately, although Gordon's life would be spared. The Nile, which served as the city's moat, was now at its lowest, leaving the defences exposed. When, during the early hours of 26 January, the dervishes swarmed over them, the half-starved garrison was in no condition to offer serious resistance and was massacred. Seeking the Mahdi's favour, some of his followers brought him Gordon's head. The story has it that he was unable to meet the unflinching stare of the hooded blue eyes; doubtless, as an absolute ruler who brooked no disobedience, he gave short shrift to those who had deliberately defied his orders.

Filled with sad thoughts, Wilson and his men continued downstream in their gunboats. Fate, however, had not finished with them yet. On the 29th the *Talahawiyeh* ran aground and could not be got off. While her crew, guns and ammunition were being transferred to a local *nuggar* some of the Mahdi's men appeared, shouting for the Sudanese aboard to give themselves up. The latter, while thoroughly demoralised, were suspicious and asked for a safe conduct to be sent to the dervish fort at Wad-Habeshi, about 30 miles south of Gubat, held by 3000 men. Wilson continued downstream but on the 31st disaster struck again when, thanks to the low water, the *Bordein* was wrecked off the island of Mernat, just above Wad-Habeshi. Everyone got ashore, bringing with them such weapons, ammunition and food as they could, and threw up a tiny fort for themselves. Wilson recognised that, for the moment, they would have to stay where they were; it was one thing for the entire Desert Column to march through enemy territory, and quite another for Wilson, with barely a platoon, to try to reach home through country swarming with dervishes.

However, a rowing boat was to hand, and, after dark, Lieutenant E. J. Stuart-Montagu-Wortley of the King's Royal Rifle Corps set off in this to summon help. Sliding silently past Wad-Habeshi on the current, he reached Gubat early the following morning.

Meanwhile, Wolseley had despatched Colonel Redvers Buller across the Bayuda Desert to take command of the Desert Column. With him Buller brought such reinforcements as could be spared, amounting to three more mountain guns and the Second Division of the Naval Brigade, consisting of seven officers and 50 seamen with another Gardner machine gun. One of the officers, Chief Engineer Henry Benbow, had burdened himself with a complete toolkit, an iron plate and a bag of nuts and bolts. Buller thought this was extremely funny and asked Benbow whether he intended to repair camels with it; within days, he was to eat his words.

With the new arrivals, Beresford, now recovered somewhat, had been able to put the *Safieh* into fighting trim. She was, in his own words, 'a penny steamer in a packing case', driven by paddles and with a large boiler that protruded above deck level. Her armament consisted of two mountain guns, protected by railway sleepers and boiler plate fore and aft, and the two Gardners positioned to fire over the bulwarks amid-ships. By the time Stuart-Montagu-Wortley arrived with his grim news, the *Safieh* had spent several days raising hell locally, raiding villages, capturing livestock and supplies and bombarding a fort.

With men from both his detachments, reinforced by 20 infantry marksmen, Beresford immediately set out in the *Safieh* to rescue Wilson. Pushing against the current, the little steamer could only manage two-and-a-half knots, but by 07:00 on 2 February the enemy fort was in sight. As the channel would take the gunboat within 80 yards of its guns, Beresford ordered his machine gunners to concentrate on the embrasures, which they did to such good effect that not a shot was fired until she was 200 yards upstream of the position. At this point the Gardners would no longer bear and the enemy fired a round which penetrated the boiler. All the engine room staff were scalded by escaping steam, two of them badly. With power lost, the *Safieh* drifted in to the opposite bank, 500 yards above the fort. A fierce firefight developed during which the efforts of the 20 marksmen, supplemented by 14 bluejackets, only began to take effect when one of the Gardners was moved to a platform aft, one officer being wounded and a petty officer being killed during the exchange. Thereafter, no dervish dared show himself at the embrasures.

After shot-holes in the hull had been plugged, it was the turn of Henry Benbow, who had a three-inch hole in the boiler to repair. The boiler did not cool sufficiently until 11:00 for work to begin. Then, because the engine room staff had been incapacitated, he worked almost alone for the next ten hours, shaping his 14- by 16-inch plate and boring holes in it and the boiler. The one task he could not perform by himself was to pass the bolts through both from the inside. He flushed the boiler regularly with cold water but by early evening the temperature within was still unbearable. A negro boy, whose name has sadly been lost, was offered a large sum of money to go in. Smothered in protective grease, he was lowered inside, only to shoot out as though he had been fired from a circus cannon. He bravely tried again, and this time managed to get the bolts through. The plate was calked, the nuts tightened down and the *Safieh* was ready to raise steam again.

In the meantime, Wilson and his men, alerted by the firing, had arrived in their *nuggar*. Together, Beresford and Wilson devised a plan. During the night the *nuggar*, with the wounded and injured aboard, would be allowed to drift past the fort, so giving the enemy the impression that the gunboat had been abandoned. Simultaneously, Wilson and the rest of his party would make their way stealthily along the friendly bank to a point downstream of the fort. The *Safieh* would raise steam quietly before dawn, then turn and dash past the fort to pick up the *nuggar* and Wilson's party.

At first all went well. The party on foot disappeared into the darkness. The *nuggar* slipped past the fort, attracting some inaccurate fire. The dervish gunners also opened fire on the gunboat, but as Beresford had forbidden any return and everyone was concealed from view, they soon desisted, believing that she was a deserted hulk. At 05:00 the fires were lit. Some 50 minutes later an Arab stoker opened the draught plates on his own initiative, producing a blast of flame and sparks from the funnel. Yells of fury came from the fort, but before the enemy could man his guns Beresford had weighed anchor and was proceeding upstream and out of range. After he had travelled three-quarters of a mile he turned and came surging back with the current behind him. As the *Safieh* passed the fort she gave it a hammering with her guns, machine guns and rifles. Some distance beyond, however, she came upon the *nuggar*, hard aground and still within range of the enemy. While the gunboat stood by and gave covering fire, a party under Sub-Lieutenant Colin Keppel was sent across in a boat. Keppel was wounded but after a while he managed to lighten the craft sufficiently to float her. Together, the *Safieh* and the *nuggar* moved downstream to the point where Wilson and his party were waiting. They were picked up and at 17:45 that evening reached the camp at Gubat.

It is some measure of the intensity of the fighting at Wad-Habeshi that the mountain guns fired 126 rounds, the machine guns 5400 and the rifles 2150. Without Henry Benbow's 'camel repair kit' the story would undoubtedly have had a different ending. Beresford did not recommend him for the Victoria Cross because he believed that the deed itself had to be performed in arms, a mistake which he always regretted. Nevertheless, Benbow did receive the personal thanks of Lord Wolseley, who gave him a silver cigarette case, promotion to Inspector of Machinery and, when the Distinguished Service Order was instituted the following year, he was one of its first recipients. Beresford became a Commander of the Bath. The boy who entered the boiler was happy with his reward, which made him a rich man by local standards.

Elsewhere, the River Column defeated a dervish force at Kirbekan on 10 February, but with the death of Gordon and the fall of Khartoum the entire purpose of Wolseley's expedition had been removed. Taking advantage of renewed Russian interest in Afghanistan, the Gladstone administration made it clear that beyond the defence of the Egyptian frontier and Suakin on the Red Sea, there would be no further direct British involvement in the Sudan. Both columns were therefore ordered to withdraw. For Beresford this meant the sad task of disabling the engines of the two remaining gunboats and, with the exception of the Gardners, throwing their armament and ammunition into the river. Buller was not the luckiest of commanders, but on this occasion he managed to disengage cleanly by night, leaving his campfires burning and buglers to sound routine calls until the Column's rearguard was well on its way into the Bayuda Desert.

Neither Queen Victoria nor the British public were inclined to forgive Gladstone. They were proud of the achievements of their soldiers and sailors who had failed in their impossible task by what seemed to be the narrowest of margins. The obvious inference was that if Wolseley's expedition had been despatched earlier, they would not have failed at all. Wolseley was made a viscount, promoted field marshal and became the British Army's Commander-in-Chief. As for the Mahdi, he survived Gordon by only five months, dying of smallpox. Under his successor, the Khalifa Abdullah, the Sudan would lapse into barbarism. Yet the story had some way to run and, in time, Abdullah was to see on the Nile more powerful and sophisticated gunboats than Charles Gordon could ever have dreamed of as he searched the northern horizon in vain for the relief column that never came.

7

REVENGE AT OMDURMAN
The Second Sudan War, 1896-8

Despite their tactical reverses, the dervishes followed up the British withdrawal from the Sudan. On the Nile sector their northwards advance was checked at Ginnis on 30 December 1885, the battle being otherwise remarkable in that it was the last occasion on which British infantry went into action in their traditional scarlet. Under British officers, the Egyptian Army was reformed, the men being given regular pay, decent conditions of service, the prospect of promotion and thorough training. Skirmishing continued along the frontier, escalating to a seven-hour pitched battle at Toski on 3 August 1889 in which the dervishes were decisively defeated with 1000 killed, a quarter of their strength, including one of their most notable commanders, the Emir Wad-el-Najumi.

In 1896 it was decided that the Sudan would be reconquered. This decision was not taken for the humanitarian cause of rescuing the Sudanese from the Khalifa's barbaric oppression, but for altogether more pragmatic reasons. The Italians, for example, had been seriously defeated by the Abyssinians at Adowa in 1892. The event damaged the prestige of all the colonial powers and there was a need to restore this. Even more pressing was the interest which other great powers, notably France, were showing in establishing control of the upper reaches of the Nile.

The Sirdar or Commander-in-Chief of the Egyptian Army was General Horatio Herbert Kitchener, who had been appointed to the post in 1892. He had performed intelligence duties during the Gordon Relief Expedition and considered the British withdrawal to have been a national disgrace. He had later commanded at Suakin. He was not a notable tactician but he was an expert in logistics, the very quality required for a campaign that would be conducted over such vast distances.

Egypt, goes the saying, is the gift of the Nile and so, largely, is the Sudan. The contribution made by Gordon's little gunboats during the

1884–5 war was such that Kitchener decided his own advance would have continuous gunboat support. When the new war started he had at his disposal four old stern-wheel gunboats, named after battles in the earlier war (*Tamai, El Teb, Abu Klea* and *Metemmeh*), all armed with one 12-pounder gun and two Maxim-Nordenfeldt machine guns. From 1896 onwards these were joined by three more stern-wheelers, *Fateh, Naser* and *Zafir*, armed with one quick-firing 12-pounder, two 6-pounders and four Maxim machine guns. In 1898 the flotilla was joined by three twin screw gunboats, *Sultan, Melik* and *Sheikh*, armed with one quick-firing 12-pounder, two Nordenfeldts, one howitzer and four Maxim machine guns. These last were built by Thornycroft and Company at Chiswick and shipped out to Egypt in sections. Some of the craft were fitted with powerful searchlights.

The gunboats' crews consisted of British, Egyptian and Sudanese service personnel and civilians. In command were junior officers drawn from the Royal Navy and the Royal Engineers most of whom would achieve distinction if they had not already done so. The flotilla commander, and also captain of the *Zafir*, was Commander Colin Keppel whom we have already met during the final stages of the Gordon Relief Expedition. Commanding the *Sultan* was Lieutenant Walter Cowan who, in 1895, had captured a rebel standard during a punitive expedition in East Africa; a born fighter, he will appear again in these pages and was still fighting in his seventies. Lieutenant David Beatty, commanding the *Fateh*, would command the battlecruiser fleet at the Battle of Jutland and go on to command the Grand Fleet itself. Lieutenant the Hon. Horace Hood, commander of the *Naser*, was to lose his life commanding the Third Battlecruiser Squadron at Jutland. Captain W. S. 'Monkey' Gordon, RE, was a nephew of General Charles Gordon and thus had a personal stake in the successful outcome of the campaign.

Curiously, when the Second Sudan War commenced, both Kitchener and the Khalifa had decided that the decisive battle would be fought near Omdurman, across the river from Khartoum, where the dervishes had made their capital. Both were aware that in desert warfare a victorious army becomes progressively weaker the further it advances from its sources of supply. The Khalifa's plan, therefore, was to offer only token resistance to the Anglo-Egyptian advance, drawing Kitchener further and further into the wilderness just as Hicks had been drawn to destruction in 1883. Kitchener, however, intended harnessing the most modern means of transport available, not only to keep his troops supplied but also to reinforce them with fresh British brigades at the critical moment so that when the battle was fought he would have *twice* the strength with which he had begun the campaign.

One by one the dervish outposts fell after varying degrees of fighting, these local successes doing much to raise the morale of the Egyptians. When Dongola was captured Kitchener took the decision which was to win him the campaign. This was nothing less than to build a railway through the 235 miles of arid and empty desert between Wadi Halfa and Abu Hamed, cutting across the northern arc of the Great Bend. Many doubts were expressed about the idea, for without water, steam locomotives were as helpless as men in the desert. Fortunately, Royal Engineer survey parties located suitable sources of water 77 and 126 miles out from Wadi Halfa. Construction commenced on 1 January 1897 and proceeded at an average rate of one mile per day. Simultaneously, Kitchener sent a diversionary force along the route taken by Stewart's Desert Column in 1885, hoping to convince the enemy that this was his chosen axis of advance.

During the early stages of the campaign the attack against the dervish positions at Hafir on 19 September 1896 received gunfire support from *Tamai, Abu Klea* and *Metemmeh*, which also sank an enemy steamer. During this action *Abu Klea* was extremely lucky in that a shell penetrated her magazine but failed to explode. On the 22nd the flotilla was joined by the *Zafir* and *El Teb*. The next day Dongola fell to a combined attack by the army and the gunboats.

The advance was renewed when the level of the Nile rose again the following year. On 5 August the flotilla commenced its ascent of the Fourth Cataract, led by *Tamai*. Some 300 local tribesmen had been recruited to assist by hauling on ropes from both banks and, with her stern-wheel thrashing at full power, the gunboat succeeded in climbing half the slope of water. The pull on the ropes, however, was uneven and her head began to pay off. The immense pressure of water would have capsized her had not the ropes been released in the nick of time. Bobbing like a cork, she was carried downstream.

Another 400 tribesmen were recruited and that afternoon *El Teb* tried the ascent. The same thing happened, but this time the gunboat capsized, flinging Lieutenant Beatty and his crew into the rushing water. All save three were picked up downstream by the *Tamai*. One man was known to have drowned but the fate of two more remained uncertain. Keel uppermost, *El Teb* floated down the river until she became trapped between two rocks. A party reached the wreck to see whether she could be salvaged and was about to leave when knocking was heard within the hull. Tools were brought and a plate removed from the keel. Somewhat battered by their ordeal and blinking, the two missing men, an engineer and a stoker, emerged from total darkness into brilliant sunlight. Raised and repaired over a period of months, *El Teb* was renamed *Hafir* to change her luck, and took part in the later stages of the campaign.

It was decided to try to ascend the cataract at another point, once the level of the river had risen a little more. The method of hauling was carefully revised and with yet more men on the ropes *Metemmeh* was successfully brought to the top on 13 August, followed by *Tamai* the following day, *Fateh, Naser* and *Zafir* on the 19th and 20th, and the unarmed steamer *Dal* on the 23rd. Abu Hamed had already been taken by the army and, to its surprise, Berber was occupied without the need for a fight. On 14 October the *Fateh, Naser* and *Zafir* steamed south and engaged the dervish fortifications at Shendi and Metemmeh. During the two-day operation 650 shells and several thousand rounds of Maxim ammunition were fired, inflicting about 500 casualties in return for one man killed and some minor damage.

The rounding of the Great Bend and the capture of Berber were of enormous strategic significance. Those dervish forces in the eastern Sudan found their position untenable and were forced to retire on Omdurman. This provided Kitchener with a second line of supply once the route from Suakin was re-opened. It also enabled completion of the Desert Railway. The line reached Abu Hamed on

31 October and was extended southwards. Along it came the three newest gunboats, the *Sheikh, Sultan* and *Melik.* These had been shipped in sections from England to Ismailia on the Suez Canal, then towed along the Sweet Water Canal and the Nile to Wadi Halfa. There, under Captain Gordon's supervision, the sections were loaded on to railway flats and transported to Abadiya. On arrival, they were launched and assembled by another Royal Engineer officer, Lieutenant George Gorringe, whom we shall encounter again in a later war, commanding a division in Mesopotamia. Lacking heavy lifting gear, Gorringe was forced to improvise, using railway sleepers, rails, ropes and muscle power. During the final fitting-out phase he was joined by Gordon.

On 1 November the *Zafir, Naser* and *Metemmeh* again bombarded Shendi and Metemmeh. Joined the next day by *Fateh,* they continued their raid as far south as Wad-Habeshi. During this foray three men were wounded when a shell struck the *Fateh.* By now the river had begun to fall and, rather than expose the gunboats to rapids which had appeared at Um Tiur, four miles below the point where it was joined by the Atbara river, a small fortified depot was established for them at Dakhila, just north of the confluence, becoming known as Fort Atbara.

With a growing sense of unease the Khalifa began to realise that he was engaged in a new type of war which he did not really understand. He had never seen a railway but its workings were explained to him and when his spies told him that each day a mountain of supplies reached Kitchener's army in this way he knew that the Desert Railway had to be destroyed. Although he still believed that the decisive battle would be fought at Omdurman, he despatched 16,000 men under one of his less popular followers, the Emir Mahmud, to execute this important mission. For his part, Mahmud, resenting the fact that the Khalifa seemed to regard him as expendable, declined to do much more than indulge in isolated skirmishes and dug himself trenches within a large zareba which had its back to the dry bed of the Atbara River. During their crossing of the Nile from Metemmeh to Shendi, his troops were badly shot up by the gunboats.

Meanwhile, Kitchener, seeing the critical final phase of the campaign approaching, had obtained two British brigades from the

War Office, the first of which joined his army in January 1898. Offensive operations began on 27 March when the *Zafir, Naser* and *Fateh*, with troops aboard or in towed boats, attacked and took Shendi. On 8 April Kitchener stormed Mahmud's zareba on the Atbara, killing 3000 dervishes and taking 2000 prisoners, the latter including Mahmud himself. The Anglo-Egyptian army's casualties amounted to less that 600. The gunboats were not directly involved in the battle but a landing party under Lieutenant Beatty used rockets to set fire to the zareba, opening the way for the troops' assault.

The road to Omdurman now lay open but Kitchener was not inclined to advance until the second British brigade had joined him and did not set his troops in motion again until August. On the 28th the flotilla sustained its most serious loss when, near Metemmeh, the *Zafir* suddenly sprang a serious leak and went down by the head in deep water before she could be run aground. Although no lives were lost, only the Maxim machine guns could be salvaged from the wreck. As no readily identifiable cause has been quoted, sabotage springs to mind as one possibility.

While the army kept pace, the rest of the flotilla passed through the Shabluka Gorge, a place of swirling water and precipitous cliffs covered by several now abandoned dervish forts. Well aware of the gunboats' potential, the Khalifa increased the number of batteries guarding the river approach to Omdurman and decided to mine the river itself by using two old boilers filled with explosive to be detonated by a pistol, the trigger of which would be pulled by cord from a safe distance. A former officer of the Egyptian Army, who had been a prisoner since the Mahdi's day, was put in charge of the project. As the first boiler was being lowered into the water the cord snagged, the pistol fired and the reluctant mine warfare expert and his team were blown apart. An emir was ordered to supervise the installation of the second mine. Being a canny man, he allowed water to leak into the explosive, rendering it useless, before sinking the device. The grateful Khalifa rewarded him with a number of presents.

On 1 September the gunboats landed their howitzers to supplement the army's artillery, then moved up-river to engage the river batteries at

Omdurman, Khartoum and on Tuti Island between. Lieutenant Cowan of the *Sultan* made the dome of the Mahdi's tomb his special target and punched several holes through it, causing dismay among the superstitious dervishes. Winston Churchill, then a junior officer attached to the 21st Lancers, had a grandstand view of the engagement, of which he has left us the following graphic account:

> At about eleven o'clock the gunboats had ascended the Nile, and now engaged the enemy's batteries on both banks. Throughout the day the loud reports of their guns could be heard, and, looking from our position on the ridge, we could see the white vessels steaming slowly forward against the current, under clouds of black smoke from their furnaces and amid other clouds of white smoke from their artillery. The forts, which mounted nearly fifty guns, replied vigorously; but the British aim was accurate and the fire crushing. The embrasures were smashed to bits and many of the dervish guns dismounted. The rifle trenches which flanked the forts were swept by the Maxim guns. The heavier projectiles, striking the mud walls of the works and houses, dashed red dust high in the air and scattered destruction around. Despite the tenacity and courage of the dervish gunners, they were driven from their defences and took refuge among the streets of the city. The great wall of Omdurman was breached in many places, and a large number of unfortunate non-combatants were killed and wounded.

Seven miles to the north, the army spent the night within a zareba centred on the village of El Egeiga, around which it curved in a half-moon with both flanks resting on the Nile. Outside the zareba lay a bare featureless plain which both sides recognised would be the morrow's battlefield. Throughout the hours of darkness the gunboats' searchlights probed the hinterland as a precaution against surprise attack. 'What is this strange thing?' asked the Khalifa, pointing to the distant, unblinking orbs. 'They are looking at us', he was told by those who understood.

At dawn the Khalifa led out his 60,000-strong army to launch an immediate attack on the zareba. The subsequent battle has sometimes been described as a triumph of firepower over fanatical courage, but that is simplistic. The dervishes had plenty of guns and their field artillery was actually on its way forward when the attack was launched. They also possessed machine guns, and although many of these were obsolete or damaged by rough handling, there were sufficient unscrupulous arms salesmen in the world to satisfy the Khalifa's needs had he chosen to contact them. The truth was that the dervishes regarded field artillery and machine guns simply as a preparation for the wild charge with sword and stabbing spear, borne forward on a wave of religious fervour.

At 06:25, with the enemy 2700 yards distant and closing rapidly, Kitchener's artillery opened fire. The gunboats joined in immediately, followed by the Maxim machine guns. At 06:35, with the range down to 2000 yards, volley firing commenced, and within ten minutes the whole of the Anglo-Egyptian line was ablaze. Disregarding their heavy casualties, the dervishes continued to press their attack, but few got closer than 800 yards on the British sector, or 400 yards opposite the slower-firing Egyptians. By 07:30, however, they had had enough and, in their usual way, turned about and walked off.

Elsewhere, matters had not gone according to plan. The Egyptian cavalry, accompanied by a horse artillery battery and the Camel Corps, had been operating outside the zareba and, while withdrawing over the Kerreri Hills, it succeeded in drawing off a large proportion of the dervish army. The slow-moving Camel Corps was soon in difficulty on the broken ground and began to suffer casualties from the enemy riflemen. Burdened with wounded, it was ordered to make for the northern flank of the zareba. With the dervishes in hot pursuit and on the verge of running their quarry to ground, it began to look as though a massacre would take place, but at that moment Captain Gordon's *Melik* took a hand. Churchill wrote:

The gunboat arrived on the scene and began suddenly to blaze and flame from Maxim guns, quick-firing guns and rifles. The range was short; the effect tremendous. The terrible machine, floating gracefully on the waters – a beautiful white devil – wreathed itself in smoke. The river slopes of the Kerreri Hills, crowded with the advancing thousands, sprang up into clouds of dust and splinters of rock. The charging dervishes sank down in tangled heaps. The masses in the rear paused, irresolute. It was too hot even for them. The approach of another gunboat completed their discomfiture. The Camel Corps, hurrying along the shore, slipped past the fatal point of interception, and saw safety and the zareba before them.

Somewhat prematurely, Kitchener ordered a general advance. As a result of this an Egyptian brigade came close to being overrun by a dervish counter-attack but was saved by the tactical skill of its commander. The 21st Lancers made their epic but pointless charge, during which Churchill shot his way through the enemy ranks with a privately purchased Mauser automatic pistol. By 11:30 the battle was over. The dervish loss amounted to 9700 killed and perhaps twice that number wounded. Anglo-Egyptian casualties were 48 killed and 428 wounded. Omdurman was occupied during the afternoon. On 4 September it was, fittingly, the *Melik* which ferried troops to Khartoum for a memorial service for General Gordon, held beside the ruins of the governor general's palace.

The Khalifa, his power broken, was now a fugitive who would have to be hunted down, but for the moment another matter claimed Kitchener's attention. On 7 September the *Tewfikieh* steamed into Omdurman from the south. Her dervish crew, promptly made captive, told a strange tale. The Khalifa had sent them up-river as part of a foraging expedition, but at Fashoda, 600 miles from Omdurman, they had been fired on by black troops commanded by white officers under a strange flag. Having sustained serious casualties, the foraging party had retired some way and sent the *Tewfikieh* back to Omdurman for further orders. Naturally, news of the presence of another European power on the Upper Nile was far from welcome. Having embarked two infantry battalions, two companies of Cameron Highlanders, an artillery battery and four Maxims aboard the steamer *Dal* and the gunboats *Fateh, Sultan, Naser* and *Abu Klea*, Kitchener set off in person to discover who these intruders might be. On 15 September the foragers' camp was reached. Rashly, the dervishes, 500 strong, opened fire on the gunboats and were quickly dispersed. Their remaining steamer, the *Safieh*, tried to escape but, for the second time in her history, a shell burst her boiler.

During the morning of 19 September the gunboats were met by a rowing boat containing a Senegalese sergeant and two men. They handed Kitchener a letter from their commander, a Major Marchand, which confirmed French occupation of the Sudan, offered congratulations to the Sirdar on his victory, and welcomed him to Fashoda in the name of France. Marchand's force, consisting of eight French officers and NCOs and 120 Senegalese soldiers, was found to be in occupation of the former government post. They had left the Atlantic coast two years earlier and had marched continuously across all manner of terrain before planting the tricolour at Fashoda. They were delighted by Kitchener's arrival as they had fired off most of their ammunition, had no transport and very little food, and were in touch with no one. Kitchener got on well with Marchand, congratulated him on his remarkable achievement and courteously suggested that settlement of the issues between them was best left to their respective politicians. Faced with so much firepower, Marchand could but agree. Kitchener established one Anglo-Egyptian garrison at Fashoda and two more 60 miles to the south, then, leaving the *Sultan* and the *Abu Klea* to support them, he returned to Khartoum. By December the diplomats had reached a conclusion that France had no interest in the area after all. Marchand and his men continued their journey by way of Abyssinia to the French territory of Djibouti, having marched right across Africa.

A period of pacification followed Kitchener's victory at Omdurman. There were pockets of resistance, notably east of the Blue Nile and in Kordofan province, whence the Khalifa had fled, but most Sudanese had had enough of dervish rule. Control of the major waterways by the gunboat flotilla, latterly commanded by Lieutenant Walter Cowan, was absolute. Often the mere appearance of a gunboat was enough not only to induce the surrender of the dervish garrison of a town, but guarantee a warm welcome from its inhabitants. By the end of the year the last dervish force in the eastern Sudan had been decisively defeated, leaving only the Khalifa and his most ardent followers at large. Finally, on 25 November 1899, he was cornered at Om Dubreikat and, together with his principal emirs, fought to the death.

Of the gunboats which served on the Nile during the period of the dervish wars, two survive. One, the *Bordein*, it will be recalled, saw much active service during the siege of Khartoum. The second is the *Melik*, which, after being decommissioned, served as the clubhouse of the Blue Nile Sailing Club until an exceptional flood left her stranded. The Sudan's Department of Archaeology and Museums is believed to be working on a repair and maintenance plan for both.

8

SPICER-SIMSON PULLS IT OFF

German East Africa, 1914–16

One of the Royal Navy's most important tasks on the outbreak of World War I was to clear the seas of German surface warships operating in widely separated areas of the world's oceans. Of these, one of the most elusive was the cruiser *Königsberg*, commanded by Captain A. D. Looff, based at Dar-es-Salaam in German East Africa, now known as Tanganyika. Looff took his ship to sea shortly before war was declared and on 6 August captured the 6600-ton merchant vessel *City of Winchester*. He kept his prize for a week, during which he helped himself to coal and other supplies before scuttling her. On 8 August, however, he lost contact with Dar-es-Salaam, where the radio transmitter had been destroyed by gunfire from the cruiser HMS *Astraea*. He therefore decided to establish a fresh base in the delta of the Rufiji River, the complex nature of which would also offer excellent concealment.

On 24 August the *Astraea* was sent off on convoy duties. This was most unfortunate as the only remaining British naval presence on the East African coast was the cruiser *Pegasus*, which had been in need of a major overhaul when the war began. By early September her condition was so bad that she was forced to make for Zanzibar, where all but one of her boilers were taken out of use for cleaning.

There were plenty of people in Zanzibar who were willing to make all this information available to Looff. At about 05:15 on 20 September the *Königsberg* appeared some four miles off the harbour entrance and opened fire on the completely immobile *Pegasus*. Even if the latter had had steam up, the contest would have been most unequal as not only was the range of her eight 4-inch guns a thousand yards less than those of the *Königsberg*'s ten 4.1-inch, her best speed of 20.5 knots left Looff with nearly four knots in hand, enabling him to maintain the distance between the two ships. This was what he chose to do now, for although the *Pegasus* hit back as best she could she was little better than a sitting duck. Salvos repeatedly crashed into her until she was reduced to a sinking condition. Reluctantly, the order was given to haul down her colours. Looff, having accomplished what he set out to do and not wishing to burden himself with prisoners, turned the *Königsberg* away and vanished below the horizon. Attempts to save the *Pegasus* by towing her to a sandbar were frustrated when she slid off and turned turtle in deep water.

The Admiralty, stung by this blow to British naval prestige and seriously alarmed that a powerful raider should apparently be loose to prey on the trade routes of the Indian Ocean, immediately diverted the cruisers *Chatham*, Captain S. R. Drury-Lowe, *Dartmouth* and *Weymouth* to the East African coast with the specific mission of seeking out and destroying the *Königsberg*. A report that she had returned to Dar-es-Salaam proved to be false, but interception of the German merchantman *Präsident*, sailing under dubious colours as a hospital ship, provided the first clue. When questioned, her crew admitted that she had recently delivered a full cargo to an unspecified location in the Rufiji River, and among her captain's papers was a modern chart of the river itself. A few days later a German reserve officer was captured by a landing party on Komo Island, off the Rufiji delta. The prisoner, who had been sent from Dar-es-Salaam to set up a signal station on the island, maintained a diary which contained reference to the *Königsberg* and an apparently encoded location. At the end of October another party, landing on the mainland, picked up a village headman and two of his men for whom rum proved to be a more potent incentive than threats. They divulged that the *Königsberg*, together with a supply ship and several smaller vessels, was concealed up a channel known as the Simba Uranga, the approaches to which were protected by artillery and machine gun posts.

By bringing the *Chatham* as close inshore as her draught would allow, Drury-Lowe could spot the German cruiser's distant masts across the dense mangrove swamps and jungle. Opening fire at extreme range, he was able to set the supply ship ablaze. The *Königsberg*, however, simply moved further upstream and camouflaged herself. Suggestions that she might be cut out were rejected on

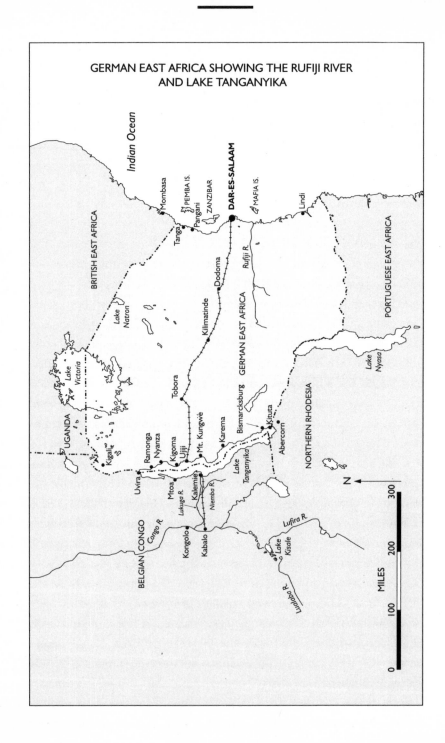

GERMAN EAST AFRICA SHOWING THE RUFIJI RIVER
AND LAKE TANGANYIKA

grounds of practicality, and the dismal failure of a landing intended to secure the German port of Tanga on 3 November ruled out any sort of joint land/sea operation against her. Nor could the British cruisers penetrate the river because of their draught and a sandbar which was passable only during the highest tides of the year. Drury-Lowe decided to close off the Simba Uranga channel, thus effectively imprisoning the *Königsberg*. On 10 November an old collier, the *Newbridge*, escorted by the armed tug *Duplex*, was towed into position under heavy fire from the shore and scuttled in mid-stream. The operation, however, was only a limited success, for during the highest tides the *Königsberg* could still slip past the obstruction. Drury-Lowe therefore requested the services of two river monitors which could penetrate the river and destroy the German ship with their gunfire.

The monitor, of course, was kin to the gunboat in that it drew little water and carried a powerful armament. During World War I this class of vessel provided naval gunfire support off the coast of Flanders, in the Dardanelles, the Eastern Mediterranean and the Adriatic. When war broke out, three light monitors being built in Britain for Brazil were taken into Royal Naval service. Two of them, the *Severn* and *Mersey*, each armed with two 6-inch guns, were despatched under tow from Malta to Mafia Island, off the Rufiji delta.

The stand-off continued well into 1915. Drury-Lowe and his successor, Rear Admiral Herbert King-Hall, tried attacking the *Königsberg* with aircraft of the Royal Naval Air Service, without result, although on 25 April an aerial photo was taken pinpointing the cruiser's exact position.

Meanwhile, early in the New Year, the German Admiralty decided that the *Königsberg* should run for home. A captured British freighter, the *Rubens*, was despatched from Germany with coal and munitions and given a neutral identity. She sailed from Hamburg on 19 February, successfully breaking through the British blockade of her home waters. By 9 April she was entering the Indian Ocean and at this point her commander, Lieutenant Christiansen, made his first mistake in trying to contact the *Königsberg* by radio using her AKO AKO AKO call-sign, which was known to the British. The transmission was intercepted and suggested that a blockade runner was in the vicinity. Two days later, it was repeated, the increased strength of the signal indicating that its source was now much closer.

King-Hall set off northwards in the *Hyacinth* and at dawn on 14 April spotted a strange vessel inshore, heading for Tanga, a few miles distant. It was the *Rubens*, and Christiansen, having given up hope of making a rendezvous at sea with the *Königsberg*, had decided that his priority must be to land his cargo as quickly as possible. Since she did not respond when challenged, *Hyacinth* gave chase and opened fire. At the critical moment, however, a piston rod in the cruiser's starboard engine snapped. Her speed fell away, enabling Christiansen to run his ship hard aground, light pre-set dummy fires on her decks, and escape with his crew in the boats. A boarding party from the *Hyacinth* correctly reported that the ship could not be refloated but, fired on from the shore, reached the hasty conclusion that the blaze was beyond control. After firing a few more rounds into the hulk, the *Hyacinth* repaired her engines and returned to her patrol off the Rufiji. Once she had gone, the Germans boarded the *Rubens* again and extinguished the fires. Subsequently their native labourers recovered not only her coal, but also 1800 rifles, four machine guns, 500,000 rounds of small arms ammunition, two 60mm guns, one thousand 4.1-inch shells, 6500 rounds of artillery ammunition, one ton of explosives, 200 tents and a quantity of communications equipment, all of which would be employed during the years to come.

The commander of the German forces in East Africa, Colonel Paul von Lettow-Vorbeck, offered Looff a train of porters to transport the *Rubens*'s coal to the *Königsberg*. 'It was,' he thought, 'a waste that the last of the German cruisers should allow herself to be immured in the jungle when she should be fighting for the Fatherland on the high seas.' Looff declined and was then required to land as many of his crew as possible to strengthen Lettow-Vorbeck's ground troops. He was left with just sufficient men to preserve his ship as a fighting entity, but not enough to take her to sea. On the other hand, he could claim with some justification that he was tying down British warships that could be found better employment elsewhere, whereas the alternative of breaking out carried with it little hope of reaching Germany and the strong possibility of a fight against odds ending in a needless German defeat.

Perhaps Loof might have thought differently had he known that the two monitors were even then making their sweltering passage under tow down the Red Sea, but by then the die was cast. On 5 July *Severn* and *Mersey*, under the overall command of Commander Eric Fullerton, entered the Rufiji just before dawn. Drawing only four feet nine inches of water, they experienced no difficulty negotiating the channel and, having been protected with additional plating and sandbags, they were able to ignore the fire directed at them from the banks. They dropped anchor at a point estimated to be 10,800 yards from the *Königsberg* and therefore beyond the range of the enemy's secondary armament. Their fire was to be corrected by a seaplane which would keep the German cruiser under observation. For his part, Looff had established forward observation posts in the trees and they enabled him to open fire first.

It was at once apparent that the Germans were firing broadsides. *Severn* was straddled, her decks plastered with river mud and a rain of dead fish. Fifteen minutes later the *Mersey* received a direct hit that knocked out her forward gun and caused casualties. Underwater explosions sprung the plating of both monitors so that they began to make water. The *Mersey* was forced to withdraw and make good her damage, the *Severn* following two hours later. Of the 635 shells they had fired, only one scored an important hit, knocking out one of the *Königsberg*'s forward guns. This was hardly impressive, but given that this was the first time aerial spotting had been used to correct gunfire directed against a warship, it is not surprising.

The engagement had, in fact, been Looff's swan song. The lessons were put to good use in sharpening up procedures so that when *Severn* and *Mersey* entered the Rufiji again on 11 July, their shooting, corrected by Lieutenant Cull in a spotter plane, was much better. *Königsberg* was hit repeatedly and even after Cull's aircraft was so damaged that it was forced to crash-land in the river, the German cruiser continued to receive brutal punishment. One after the other her guns fell silent. At 12:52 she was wracked by a terrific explosion that sent a pillar of dense smoke soaring above the trees; 50 minutes later she was further torn by a series of internal explosions, and within the next half-hour she became a blazing wreck. Satisfied that his elusive prey had finally been destroyed, King-Hall ordered the monitors to withdraw. With that it might be thought that the Royal Navy's part in the East African campaign had come to an end, save for guarding against the occasional blockade runner, but it was not.

Nor was it quite the end of the *Königsberg*'s story. Her crew volunteered to serve with Lettow-Vorbeck's troops and in due course salvaged all ten of her 4.1-inch and two 3.5-inch guns. Fitted to improvised field carriages, they provided the Germans with tremendous hitting power for many months to come. Lettow-Vorbeck was to conduct a brilliant guerrilla war in East Africa and was the last German commander to surrender in 1918. With never more than 3000 Germans and 12,000 native askaris, he tied down 160,000 British, Indian, South African, West Indian and East and West African troops together with large contingents of Belgians and Portuguese, becoming a national hero and earning the sincere admiration of his enemies, including that of his principal opponent, the future Field Marshal Jan Smuts.

It is sometimes forgotten that this strange war was fought out in a territory of vast distances. Some 400 miles to the west of the coast was Lake Tanganyika, 400 miles long and 47 miles wide at its narrowest, forming a natural boundary between German East Africa, the Belgian Congo (Zaire) and Rhodesia (Zimbabwe). Since 1914 the Germans had exercised total control of the lake because they possessed two armed steamers, plus a third fitting out, whereas the British and Belgians had none. Any operation against German East Africa from this direction was therefore hamstrung from the start by the fear that the enemy could easily prey on the Allied rear with amphibious operations anywhere on the lake.

This state of affairs might have continued indefinitely had not a big game hunter, Mr John Lee, called to see Admiral Sir Henry Jackson, the First Sea Lord, in April 1915. Lee was worried that Lettow-Vorbeck's raiding activities might produce tribal uprisings in the Congo and Rhodesia, but he was aware of the tactical problem facing Allied commanders, and he had a solution to offer, namely shipping out an armed motorboat which would sink the German warships. There was no direct rail link to the lake from Rhodesia, but in the Congo there was a line 175 miles long joining Kabalo with Lukuga on the western shore. Getting the motor boat to Kabalo would require a difficult overland journey involving traction engines and teams of oxen, but Lee had surveyed the route and believed that it was practicable.

Normally, the proposal might have been consigned to the Silly Ideas File, which already contained a suggestion that seagulls should be trained to perch on U-boat periscopes. This was, however, the best submission Jackson had received for solving the problem, and when the War and Colonial Offices confirmed Lee's assessment of the situation in Central Africa he decided to take immediate action. Two motorboats would be used rather than one and Lee, given the rank of lieutenant commander in the Royal Naval Volunteer Reserve, would accompany the expedition as its second-in-command.

Finding a suitable regular officer to command the operation was no easy matter as most of those approached had no wish to jeopardise their careers in a wild venture which seemed to have little chance of success. Nevertheless, having overheard one such refusal, Lieutenant Commander G. Spicer-Simson offered his services and was accepted.

Spicer-Simson was cursed with a difficult manner. He was autocratic, overbearing, unpredictable, eccentric, vain, unlucky and not terribly popular. After service in China gunboats he had received a series of dead-end appointments, including a survey of the Gambia River, which had led him to believe that he was being passed over for promotion, although he retained a belief that in the right circumstances he could distinguish himself. The war seemed to provide an answer to his problems. He was appointed Senior Naval Officer of the Downs Boarding Flotilla, consisting of two elderly torpedo gunboats, precursors of the modern destroyer, and six boarding tugs. Even then, misfortune seemed to dog him, for a fortnight after assuming command he ordered the gunboat *Niger* to anchor east of the Deal Bank buoy while he went ashore to entertain some ladies in an hotel. While he was thus engaged the *Niger* was torpedoed and sunk, the result being that he was posted to a desk in the Admiralty's Personnel Department. He may not, therefore, have been the wisest choice but he was an experienced officer and was at least sufficiently enthusiastic to have volunteered. Doubtless, few expected him to succeed and some may have harboured the unkind thought that it mattered little whether he returned or not.

Spicer-Simson nonetheless had the backing of the First Sea Lord and he set to with a will. Two 40-foot petrol-driven motorboats, capable of 15 knots, were acquired. Fitted with a 3-pounder gun forward and a Maxim machine gun aft, they became the smallest gunboats ever to see service and were named *Mimi* and *Toutou*. While they were fitting out and undergoing trials on the Thames, Lee was sent ahead to make the necessary arrangements for the difficult overland phase of the journey.

The expedition, consisting of four officers and 24 ratings, left Tilbury aboard the *Llanstephan Castle* on 11 June 1915, reaching Cape Town on 2 July. It then travelled 2700 miles by rail to Fungurume in the Congo, where it arrived on 4 August. The gunboats were transhipped to trailers constructed from the fore carriages of ox wagons. On 14 August two steam traction engines arrived and four days later the column began the most difficult phase of the entire journey, involving a 120-mile transit of bush and forest as well as crossing the Mitumba Mountains to reach the next railhead at Sankisia. By now, Lee, who had conceived the whole idea, had fallen victim to Spicer-Simson's unfortunate manner and been sent packing.

The party was plagued by intense heat, dust, insects and general shortage of water. This was needed not only for drinking but also for the traction engines' boilers. At times large numbers of native women were recruited to carry pots on their heads from the nearest water source, which might be as far as eight miles distant. The track, too, caused endless labour, being too narrow in some places, requiring reinforcement in others and frequent construction of bridges and culverts. Nevertheless, six weeks after leaving Fungurume, the expedition chugged slowly into Sankisia. The gunboats were transferred to the narrow gauge railway flats, a labour which must have seemed excessive after what had gone before, as the line to Bukama was only 15 miles long. The significance of Bukama, however, was that it lay on the Lualaba River, along which ran the next 200 miles of the route. There was barely enough water in the river to float the gunboats, let alone use their engines, but ingenuity being the keynote of the operation, this difficulty was resolved by lashing empty casks to their bilges to reduce their draught. Teams of native paddlers then took them downstream to Kabalo, which was reached on 21 October. Once again the gunboats were hoisted on to railway flats and a week later they reached Lukuga on the western shore of Lake Tanganyika. Since landing at Cape Town they had travelled a total of over 3200 miles by rail, river and overland.

As the lake was subject to sudden storms, Spicer-Simson asked the Belgians to construct a breakwater. This they did during the next six weeks by blasting rock from the cliffs, calling the newly formed harbour Kalemie. *Mimi* and *Toutou* were launched and on Christmas Eve completed trials to everyone's satisfaction. Spicer-Simson had meanwhile been briefed by the Belgians on the enemy's activities on the lake. The Germans now had three armed steamers, the largest being the *Graf von Götson*, which mounted two 4-inch guns plus two smaller guns salvaged from the wreck of the *Königsberg*, but was only capable of six knots. The *Hedwig von Wissmann* was much smaller, mounted two 6-pounder guns forward plus one 37mm Hotchkiss aft, and could reach ten knots. Smallest of the three was the *Kingani*, armed with one 37mm Hotchkiss forward, having a speed of seven knots. The Germans, based at Kigoma on the opposite shore of the lake to the north, therefore had much superior firepower but were at a serious disadvantage when it came to speed. It had to be assumed that they were aware of the British boats' presence as nothing remained a secret in Central Africa for very long. In fact, they had been informed of their approach but, well aware of the difficulties involved, they dismissed the idea as being preposterous.

On the morning of Boxing Day the Belgians reported that an enemy steamer was approaching from the north. It was the *Kingani*, engaged in a leisurely routine inspection of the Belgian fortifications at Lukuga. Spicer-Simson let her pass then took *Mimi* and *Toutou* out of Kalemie, followed by a British-manned Belgian motorboat with spare petrol aboard, intending to cut off the enemy ship from her base.

At first the *Kingani* paid them little attention. Then, as the range closed, their White Ensigns became apparent. Suddenly, her funnel began to belch smoke as she worked up to maximum speed, turning steadily to port in a vain attempt to escape. It was true that by swinging her head round she could bring her gun into action, but the tiny British gunboats were widely separated and she could only engage them one at a time. Once the range had closed to within 2000 yards, *Mimi* and *Toutou* opened fire. Trials had revealed that the 3-pounder's recoil could cause serious damage to the frail hull unless it was fired straight ahead. This, and choppy conditions, meant that at first the gunboats were firing only one round a minute. *Kingani* was engaging *Toutou* with her 37mm, causing her to zig-zag and open the range as shells fountained alongside, but was directing rifle fire at *Mimi*. This was a reversal of strict priorities, for it was *Mimi*, aboard which Spicer-Simson was standing behind the gun, eyes glued to his binoculars, that had begun to score hits. At length, with the range down to 1100 yards, one of her shells smashed through the enemy's gunshield, killing the German captain and two petty officers. When another hit killed the warrant officer who took over, some of the native crew began diving overboard and swimming for the shore. At this point the *Kingani*'s chief engineer emerged to haul down the German colours. *Toutou* came alongside to take possession of the prize, which was brought into Kalemie and beached in the nick of time as she was making water rapidly through a shellhole in her port bunker.

Spicer-Simson's men did not like him but for a brief moment after the engagement they were prepared to give him the benefit of the doubt. This he threw away by boasting about his own prowess as a gunnery expert, thereby denigrating the efforts of the two 3-pounder gun layers; in fact, the corrections he gave were delivered through teeth clenched around his cigarette holder and drowned by the roar of the engine. What finally cost him the men's respect was his taking a gold ring from the finger of the dead German captain and slipping it on his own. The Belgians, too, found him difficult to get on with. His manner apart, they did not expect a British naval officer to wear a native skirt with his shirtsleeve order, nor for him to sport tattooed snakes on his arms and thighs. Such manifestations, on the other hand, made him a figure of superstitious awe among the local Ba-holo-holo tribesmen to the extent that they erected an idol in his likeness, complete with snake markings, referring to him among themselves as The Lord in the Belly-cloth.

Patched up, the *Kingani* was refloated and given the new name of *Fifi*. A 12-pounder gun, supplied by the Belgians from one of their coast defence batteries, was mounted forward and a spare 3-pounder was fitted aft to cover her earlier blind spot. On 14 January 1916 a particularly violent storm swept down the lake. *Toutou* was driven against the stone breakwater and was so seriously damaged that she was out of commission for a while. *Fifi*, dragging her anchor, managed to get clear of the harbour and ride out the storm on a sea-anchor.

Early on 9 February lookouts reported that the *Hedwig von Wissmann* was approaching slowly from the north. *Toutou* was still out of commission but Spicer-Simson boarded the *Fifi* and immediately sailed to intercept her, accompanied by Lieutenant A. E. Wainwright, RNVR, commanding the *Mimi*.

The Germans still had no idea that a British flotilla was operating on the lake and attributed the sudden disappearance of the former *Kingani* to her destruction by Belgian coast defence batteries. In the growing heat, the thermals above the smooth water produced antipodal effects, depending on the viewpoint. Thus, to those ashore, mirage conditions made the British vessels appear much larger than they were, whereas the haze meant that they remained invisible to the *Hedwig von Wissmann's* captain, Lieutenant Odebrecht, until they were only four miles distant. He promptly put his helm over and headed for Kigoma.

Both steamers piled wood into their furnaces and soaked it with oil to raise pressure quickly. *Fifi* opened fire with her 12-pounder without apparent result save that the big gun's recoil all but brought the vessel to a standstill. As a result of this the *Hedwig von Wissmann* began to draw steadily away. Wainwright roared ahead in *Mimi*, opening fire on the German ship at a range of 3000 yards, beyond that at which the enemy's stern-mounted 37mm could reply. Some of *Mimi's* fire must have been effective, as the *Hedwig von Wissmann* began making a series of brief turns to port so that she could bring her forward 6-pounders into action. Whenever she did so, *Mimi* sheered away to starboard and the German shells fountained in empty space. The effect was to allow *Fifi* to catch up with the battle. Wainwright, who had been observing Spicer-Simson's shooting throughout, came alongside and informed him that his shells were falling ahead of the enemy. The necessary correction was made and the 12-pounder's next round struck home with dramatic effect, exploding in the *Hedwig von Wissmann's* engine room and blowing a hole in her side. Now ablaze, her steering gear wrecked and engines stopped, the German ship swung to starboard in a sinking condition. Fifteen minutes later she had gone to the bottom. Odebricht, eleven Germans and eight native crew were picked up.

Next day, when the *Graf von Götson* put in an appearance, no doubt existed in the minds of the jubilant British crews that they could deal with her, notwithstanding her much larger size. Inexplicably, Spicer-Simson declined to leave harbour and the German ship disappeared over the horizon. Sadly, this was not the last occasion on which his officers and men would feel ashamed of him.

In overall terms, however, the situation on the lake had improved sufficiently for the Allies to commence local land operations against German East Africa, the British from the north and south and the Belgians from the north-west. During April the flotilla was engaged in ferrying stores to Tongwe, some 20 miles north of Kalemie, where the Belgians were constructing a seaplane base. From this, air raids were mounted against the *Graf von Götson* at Kigoma. On 11 June they claimed to have hit her and when the German base was occupied the following month she was found to have been scuttled outside the harbour entrance.

Meanwhile, Spicer-Simson had been ordered to take his flotilla south to Kituta in Rhodesia and take part in operations intended to capture the German fortress of Bismarcksburg. His specific task was to watch the harbour entrance and ensure that the enemy garrison did not escape by sea. *Mimi*, *Toutou* and *Fifi* arrived off Bismarcksburg on 5 June but found no sign of the Rhodesian troops with whom they were to co-operate. Within the harbour were five dhows which the Germans regularly used to transport troops. Spicer-Simson declined to engage them, nor would he permit his officers to do so, on the grounds that this would bring their craft within range of the guns in the whitewashed fort on the hill overlooking the harbour. Instead, he withdrew to Kituta. On 9 June, believing that the Rhodesians would reach Bismarcksburg next day, he arrived off the enemy harbour again. To his horror, he found the dhows gone and the Union Flag flying above the fort. An army officer contemptuously asked why he had allowed the Germans to escape the previous night when the fort had been surrounded to landward, then told him to report to his commanding officer, a Colonel Murray. Unwisely, Spicer-Simson chose to wear his skirt, so that when he entered the fort's courtyard he was greeted with yells of derision from the Rhodesian riflemen sitting in the shade smoking their pipes. We do not know what passed between Murray and Spicer-Simson, but the latter emerged white, shaken and incoherent.

It was a sad end to a great adventure. Spicer-Simson's actions became ever more erratic until at length the flotilla's medical officer recommended that he should be sent home on the grounds of acute nervous debility. The recommendation probably saved him from serious trouble. His failure to act against the *Graf von Götson* and the dhows is difficult to understand, for he was certainly no coward. Possibly he believed that in capturing one enemy vessel and sinking another he had achieved the fame he sought, and that further risks were unjustified.

Whatever one's opinions about him, it could hardly be denied that he had overcome every obstacle in his path and, with two tiny gunboats and a handful of men, changed the face of the war in Central and East Africa without incurring a single casualty. He had already received promotion to commander and was further rewarded with the Distinguished Service Order, the Order of the Crown of Belgium and the Belgian Croix de Guerre with three palms. He applied to the Admiralty Court for prize money for the capture of the *Kingani* and several dhows, together with head money based on the enemy's casualties. The court found in his favour, taking as its precedent events on the Great Lakes of America during the War of 1812. His achievements were widely reported by the press in articles accompanied by drawings and photographs. He gave interviews and lectures during which his version of events was grossly at variance with what had taken place, particularly when it came to the *Graf von Götson* and Bismarcksburg episodes. There, a happy man at last, sitting at precisely the same desk he had occupied before leaving for Lake Tanganyika, we should allow him to slide into history, without forgetting the astonishing nature of his real achievements.

In a war involving so much mechanical slaughter, the human element almost seemed redundant. Such incidents as the destruction of the *Königsberg* and the story of what became known as Spicer-Simson's Phantom Flotilla therefore caught the imagination of the public and writers alike. Suitably adapted for fiction, the former inspired Wilbur Smith's novel *Shout at the Devil*, and the latter C. S. Forester's *The African Queen*, both of which were made into films under the same titles.

9

GENERAL TOWNSHEND HOLDS A REGATTA
The Mesopotamian Campaign, 1914–17

B y 1914 the German influence in the Ottoman Empire was para-
mount. As relations between Great Britain and Turkey deteriorated
steadily, the threat presented by the latter to the newly discovered Persian
oilfields, upon which the Royal Navy depended for fuel for its oil-driven
ships, was thrown into sharp focus. In particular, the oil terminal and
refinery situated on the island of Abadan on the Persian side of the Shatt
al Arab waterway was especially vulnerable.

The Shatt al Arab was the route followed by the combined waters of
the Rivers Tigris and Euphrates on the final phase of their journey to the
Persian Gulf. Upstream, both rivers flowed through the Turkish province
of Mesopotamia, known today as Iraq. There therefore existed a strong
potential for the Turks to inflict a severe blow to British interests as soon
as hostilities commenced. However, even before the United Kingdom
declared war on Turkey on 5 November 1914, an expeditionary force had
been assembled in India with the object of securing Abadan against attack.
Initially this consisted of one reinforced brigade of the 6th Indian Division
and supporting arms.

Two gunboats were, in fact, already on station at the head of the Gulf.
They were the *Odin* and the *Espiègle*, originally laid down between 1900
and 1903 as smallmasted cruisers, displacing 1070 tons. Too small for the
role, they were now classed as sloops, although they actually had more in
common with the Victorian gunboat. Taken together, their clipper bows,
cruiser sterns and three raked masts, albeit bereft of their yards, presented
a most elegant if somewhat dated appearance. Their armament consisted
of six 4-inch and four 3-pounder guns apiece and they were driven by
1400 hp triple expansion engines producing $13^1/_2$ knots. *Odin* and *Espiègle*
took it in turn to act as guardship off Abadan. On 6 November, with the
convoy carrying the expeditionary force approaching the mouth of the
Shatt, both went into action. *Espiègle*'s gunfire flattened some Turkish
entrenchments that had been built opposite Abadan. Downstream at Al

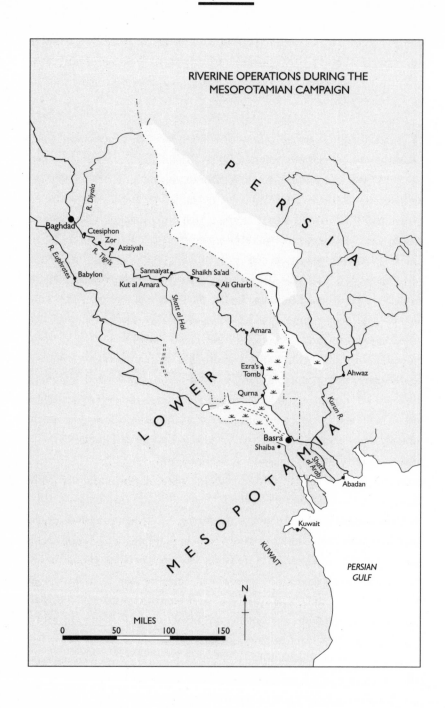

RIVERINE OPERATIONS DURING THE
MESOPOTAMIAN CAMPAIGN

P E R S I A

Baghdad
Ctesiphon
Zor
R. Diyala
R. Tigris
Aziziyah
R. Euphrates
Babylon
Sannaiyat
Kut al Amara
Shaikh Sa'ad
Ali Gharbi
Shatt al Hai
Amara
Ezra's
Tomb
Ahwaz
Qurna
Karun R.
L O W E R
Basra
Shaiba
Shatt al Arab
Abadan
M E S O P O T A M I A
Kuwait
KUWAIT
PERSIAN
GULF

N

MILES
0   50   100   150

Faw, where a spit of land marked the end of the Shatt, *Odin* silenced a four-gun field battery after a 40-minute duel during which she was hit only twice. When, on closing the shore, she came under fire from riflemen in trenches on the river bank, her gunners switched to shrapnel and chased the enemy off.

The expeditionary force entered the Shatt unhindered and on 8 November landed at Sanniya, two miles beyond Abadan. During the next few days a second infantry brigade, two squadrons of cavalry and three artillery batteries arrived. In command of the whole was Lieutenant-General Sir Arthur Barrett, who was set the new objective of Basra. On 15 November a reconnaissance in force made contact with the enemy and a full-scale battle developed, ending with the Turks being put to flight. *Odin* and *Espiègle* were sent up-river to verify a rumour that the enemy had abandoned Basra and, squeezing their way past sunken blockships, found it to be true. As the town was in the hands of its hooligan element, the crews had their hands full restoring order until Indian troops arrived by steamer the following day.

Whatever the original intention, ventures such as this have an unpleasant habit of escalating into full-scale campaigns. It was naïve to expect that the Turks would accept the status quo, or that they would tolerate a potential threat to Baghdad, one of the Holy Cities of Islam, towards which British thoughts were already turning. That being the case, yet more British effort would have to be directed into Mesopotamia.

Between 4 and 8 December, *Odin*, *Espiègle*, an armed paddle steamer, three armed launches and two river steamers mounting 18-pounder field guns, provided fire support for a turning operation which eliminated the Turkish garrison at Qurna, 46 miles north of Basra near the confluence of the Euphrates and the Tigris. Captain Hayes-Sadler, commanding *Espiègle*, received an enemy delegation as a result of which over 1000 Turks, including 42 officers, marched into captivity. British casualties amounted to 27 killed and 292 wounded, including two sailors killed and ten wounded. Little further occurred until April 1915 when, during a hard-fought soldiers' battle, the British ejected the Turks from an entrenched position at Shaiba, to the west of Basra.

Barrett had returned to India shortly before Shaiba. His successor, Lieutenant-General Sir John Nixon, was confronted by Turkish forces at An Nasiriyah on the Euphrates to the north-west, beyond Qurna to the north and, most dangerous of all, up the Kurun River at Ahvaz to the east where, though nominally on Persian territory, they could interfere with the oil pipeline supplying Abadan. Nixon now had two infantry divisions, the 6th Indian under Major-General Charles Townshend and the 12th Indian under Major-General George Gorringe, whom we last met commanding a gunboat at Omdurman, plus a cavalry brigade and supporting arms.

In May Gorringe was sent up the Kurun but the Turks declined to give battle and retired overland to Al Amarah on the Tigris. At the end of the month Nixon ordered Townshend to advance up the Tigris not just to Al Amarah, but to the town of Kut beyond. Townshend was a very capable soldier with a long and distinguished record. He had seen extensive service in the Sudan, having been present at the Battles of Abu Klea and Abu Kru and, later, at Omdurman. It was, however, his epic defence of the North-West Frontier fort of Chitral in 1895 that really brought his name before the public. He had become a major-general in 1911 but was driven by burning ambition and was constantly pestering his superiors about his personal advancement, to the point that he had received an official reprimand on the subject. At the moment, he was jealous of Gorringe and watched his every move carefully.

Nevertheless, he was a thorough, efficient commander. The Turkish position north of Qurna was located in swampland in which the only areas above water level were in enemy hands. What amounted to a series of amphibious operations would therefore be required to effect a breakthough, and in these the part of the Royal Navy would be crucial. *Odin* and *Espiègle* had now been joined by their sister *Clio;* there were also the armed tugs *Shaitan, Sumana, Miner* and *Lewis Pelly,* two naval horse-boats with 4.7-inch guns, two gun barges with 5-inch and 4-inch guns, and a variety of rafts and steamers carrying mountain artillery and machine guns. The assaulting infantry would follow behind in local canoes known as *bellums,* no less than 500 of which had been collected and, where possible, fitted with armoured shields.

The operation commenced at 05:00 on 31 May. Led by two of the tugs sweeping mines, *Clio*, *Espiègle* and the rest steamed slowly upstream, smothering every objective with gunfire. The sheer volume of it was more than the Turks could stand. Few were inclined to offer resistance, most preferring to wave white flags or paddle off into the reeds in their own boats.

So far, only the Turkish outposts had been captured. Their main line, two miles further on, was assailed next morning. There was no response and it was soon discovered that the Turks were retreating up the Tigris as fast as they could go. Townshend ordered an infantry brigade to embark in three paddle steamers and follow as quickly as possible while the gunboats set off in pursuit. Fortunately, the enemy officer responsible for mining the channel had been captured and, positioned in the bow of the leading tug, was extremely helpful. Two lighters had been sunk as blockships below Ruta but were just passable.

Townshend, his staff and a small escort had embarked on the *Espiègle* aboard which the general, keen to get on, had climbed the foremast to enter the lookout's position from which he keenly surveyed what lay ahead. In the far distance were two smudges of smoke, revealing the presence of the Turkish gunboat *Marmaris* and the steamer *Mosul*, both towing crowded barges, as well as numerous white sails indicating local *mahelas*, all heading for safety as fast as steam and wind could take them. There then followed what became known as Townshend's Regatta, one of the strangest episodes in military or naval history, in which, 150 miles from the sea and at the urging of a major-general in the crow's nest, the Royal Navy pursued the Turkish Army across mile after mile of desert.

By early evening the enemy were within range and the leading sloops opened fire. *Marmaris*, though armed with four 9-pounder guns, was more interested in escape than fighting and cast off her tow, as did *Mosul*. The blue dome of Ezra's Tomb, nestling among its palm trees, provided a welcome splash of colour in the drab, brown, featureless landscape and slowly slid astern. As the pursuit gained ground, the abandoned lighters and *mahelas* began making for the shore. *Odin*, bringing up the rear, was dropped off to round up the fugitives while the rest continued until darkness made navigation impossible.

Early next morning, 2 June, Townshend's flotilla got under way again. Six miles on, the battered *Marmaris* was sighted again, but now she was aground, burning and abandoned by her crew. A round from the *Clio* resulted in a white flag being run up by the distant *Mosul* and an armed tug went alongside to take possession.

Shortly after, the river became too shallow for the sloops to proceed further. Townshend and the senior naval officer, Captain Nunn, transferred to an armed tug, the *Comet*, which had caught them up the previous day. Al Amarah now lay less than 50 miles distant and, with *Shaitan*, *Sumana* and *Lewis Pelly* each towing a horse-boat mounting a 4.7-inch naval gun, the pursuit began again. White flags fluttered at every village passed until Qal'at Salih, half-way to Al Amarah, was reached during the afternoon. There, some cavalry and an infantry company were soon dispersed by shellfire and the village headmen quickly appeared to make their peace. A few miles beyond, the flotilla lay up for the night.

The next morning's progress along the tortuous river was very similar. It was by no means certain in what strength the Turks were holding Al Amarah, so at Abu Sidra, 12 miles short of the town, the *Shaitan* was sent to scout ahead while the rest followed. At about 14:00 *Shaitan* turned the last bend to find troops crossing a boat bridge to board a steamer with a lighter in tow. The bridge was opened to allow the steamer to escape, but a round from *Shaitan*'s 12-pounder promptly brought her to. The tug also passed through and found herself in the midst of the Turkish garrison. Infantry could be seen moving down the narrow streets towards the river, but made themselves scarce as soon as they saw the White Ensign. Seeing how matters stood, the captain of the *Shaitan*, with a mere 100 bluejackets and soldiers at his disposal, decided to embark on a colossal bluff. A corporal and 12 men landed by boat and cheerfully received the surrender of the entire garrison. This included a battalion of the Constantinople Fire Brigade which was not, as its name suggests, recruited from professional firefighters, but one of the most prestigious units in the Ottoman Empire. Most of the Turks were terrified of the local Arab population, whose hobby was slitting the throats of any stragglers, Turkish or British, who crossed their path. One officer is said to have despatched a reassuring telegram to his wife in Anatolia saying that he had been 'safely captured'! Nevertheless, even after the rest of the flotilla had arrived, the Turks began to suspect they had been sold a pup. The situation remained decidedly edgy until, on the morning of 4 June, infantrymen of the Royal Norfolk Regiment began landing from their paddle steamers. Townshend's Regatta was over. Apart from punching a hole deep into the enemy's hinterland, its results included the capture of 2000 prisoners and much booty, the destruction of a gunboat and the capture of two steamers and many smaller craft, all at trivial cost.

Once again, 'Chitral Charlie' Townshend was in the public eye and he revelled in it, not even caring that Gorringe had stabilised the Euphrates sector by capturing An Nasiriyah. After a short spell of sick leave in India he returned to find that Nixon had decided he should continue his advance to Kut el Amara, 120 miles upstream from Al Amarah. There were 6000 Turks with 30 guns holding entrenched positions at Kut, but on 27–28 September Townshend pitched them out of these in a brilliantly planned battle.

Beyond providing fire support from downstream, the flotilla played little part in the fighting, the reason being that the Turks were now well aware of the dangers of gunboats enfilading their trenches, let alone breaking away into their rear areas. They had, therefore, run barges aground on both banks, linking them by iron cables to a sunken *mahela* in mid-channel, covering the entire reach with artillery, machine gun and rifle fire. *Comet*, in the lead, had tried unsuccessfuly to ram her way through at full speed. With her guns silenced and most of the crew wounded, her captain, Lieutenant Commander Cookson, had leapt aboard the *mahela* with an axe but was shot dead at once. He received the posthumous award of the Victoria Cross.

Having taken Kut, a dirty, ramshackle little town lying on a peninsula, Townshend felt that the advance had gone far enough and that the gains made should be consolidated. Nixon, however, allowed wishful thinking to cloud his professional judgement. He saw Kut simply as a stepping stone on the road to Baghdad and obtained qualified permission to attempt the capture of the latter. Very properly, Townshend pointed out the difficulties, not least of which was the seasonal fall in water level which would affect his river transport, and also that if his small force received a check at the end of its long line of communications, the consequences would be very serious. Nixon remained obdurate, ignoring the probability that the Turks would make strenuous efforts to defend the ancient City of the Caliphs. Indeed, even as the 6th Indian Division and the cavalry brigade began marching north after five weeks' preparation for the advance at Aziziyeh, no less than 30,000 good quality troops under Khalil Pasha, one of the best generals in the Turkish service, were converging on Baghdad under the direction of the German Field Marshal von der Goltz, who had been appointed Commander-in-Chief of the Mesopotamian front. Nixon was aware of both developments but declined to recall Townshend.

On 19 November the naval flotilla received a welcome addition to its firepower with the arrival of HMS *Firefly*, the first of the Fly class gunboats which had been designed specifically for service in Mesopotamia and shipped in sections to Abadan for assembly. Displacing only 170 tons, they drew just 2 ft 6 in forward and 2 ft 10 in aft. Their original armament consisted of one 4-inch gun and four Maxim machine guns, but as the campaign progressed this was increased to one 4-inch, one 12-pounder, one 6-pounder, one anti-aircraft 3-pounder, one 2-pounder pom-pom and four machine guns. Their principal drawback was their 10 knot maximum speed, inadequate for the swifter-flowing reaches of the Tigris.

On 22–23 November Townshend mounted a determined attack on an entrenched Turkish position at Ctesiphon, 30 miles south of Baghdad. He succeeded in capturing the first line of trenches but not the second, and while he inflicted 6200 casualties on the Turks, his own losses amounted to 4600 of the 11,000 men engaged and his stock of ammunition had dwindled alarmingly. Once again, the gunboats were unable to intervene decisively, partly because they could not fire effectively over the high floodbanks, and partly because the Turks kept them at arm's length by covering the critical bend with impenetrable artillery fire. Indeed, they took *Firefly*'s mast as an aiming point, so that she had to change position constantly. When, on 25 November, air reconnaissance revealed that fresh Turkish formations were streaming out of Baghdad towards the front, Townshend had no choice but to withdraw.

It was now that the ramshackle nature of the Mesopotamian theatre's transport and medical services became apparent. After hours of jolting in unsprung carts, the seriously wounded were crammed aboard the steamer *Mejidieh* and two steel barges she was to tow. There was no room for them to move, nor protection against the sun and rain. Days later, she reached Basra beneath a cloud of flies, her deck and sides covered with excrement, while to the stench of human waste was added the sickly smell of gangrene from untreated wounds. The affair generated so great a scandal that a dramatic improvement in the medical service followed.

The retreating column reached Al Aziziyah on 26 November. During the day the falling water level had caused the armed tugs *Comet* and *Shaitan* to run aground. *Comet* was got off and struggled unsuccessfully to tow her companion free, as did *Firefly* and *Shushan*, harassed the while by local Arabs sniping from the banks. Only when the Turkish advance guard began to approach was the vessel abandoned.

The Turkish cavalry, joined by the Arabs, began looting the former British camp at Al Aziziyah. The Turkish infantry, however, marched on through the gathering darkness and, under the impression that their cavalry were still out in front, unwittingly camped in close proximity to the next British halting place at Umm al Tubul. Dawn on 1 December revealed their encampment less than a mile distant from Townshend's lines. It was promptly plastered with shellfire from the British artillery and gunboats. A counter-attack added to the Turks' confusion, but as soon as they showed signs of rallying, Townshend broke contact and resumed his retreat. Several hours elapsed before the Turks were able to sort themselves out and follow.

The affair at Umm al Tubul inflicted about 1500 casualties on the Turks, thrice that of the British, but the engagement cost the gunboats dear. Early in its course an enemy battery manhandled to the river bank managed to put a shell through the *Firefly*'s boiler, disabling her. *Comet* took her in tow but then both vessels went hard aground. With the Turks closing in fast, the *Sumana* went alongside and took off their crews, but both had to be abandoned. Very little now remained of the original flotilla.

Townshend reached Kut on 3 December and there took an evil deci-sion. His victories had apparently placed his star in the ascendant and if the last had been Pyrrhic and resulted in a necessary withdrawal, he now had the opportunity to repeat the feat of arms which had won him such fame on the North-West Frontier. Sending on the cavalry and the remnant of the flotilla, he announced, 'I mean to defend Kut as I did Chitral.' The flaw in his reasoning was that Nixon lacked the resources to mount an immediate attempt at relief. Inexorably, the Turks closed in around Kut and established strong defensive positions downstream to foil any effort to break the siege.

Much to the annoyance of the British government, Nixon and Townshend had succeeded in turning a sideshow into a major war front. Nixon was replaced by General Sir Percy Lake, but somehow Townshend had to be extracted from the mess he had got himself into and reinforcements were rushed to Mesopotamia.

The siege of Kut, and the vain attempts to relieve it, do not form part of our story. The Turks, rid of the burden of Gallipoli by the Allied evacuation, were able to devote plentiful resources to the operation. A brave attempt to supply the garrison by air came nowhere near meeting its needs. Throughout, Townshend continued to pursue the question of his personal advancement with authority, his reaction on learning of Gorringe's promotion being to burst into tears. By the fourth week of April 1916, 23,000 casualties had been incurred in abortive attempts to relieve a garrison numbering only 13,000 men and it would have been criminal madness to continue. On 24 April the supply ship *Julnur*, manned by a volunteer crew, made a last desperate attempt to break through but was driven aground. Townshend was authorised to seek terms, which were concluded on 29 April. He promised to share his men's hardships in captivity but spent the rest of the war in a luxurious villa on a pleasant island in the Sea of Marmara. Less than half the garrison survived years of malnutrition, disease and neglect. Neither those that did, nor the War Office, ever forgave him. Disgraced, he died in 1924 in the very obscurity he so dreaded.

In August 1916 Lieutenant-General Frederick Maude assumed command of the Mesopotamian Front and promptly set about restoring the bruised morale of his army. Like Kitchener, Maude believed that success depended upon a reliable logistic infrastructure. He rationalised road, rail and river transportation, the last of which was augmented by the arrival of a fleet of specially designed shallow-draught P class river steamers. Simultaneously, Captain Wilfred Nunn, responsible for naval operations in Mesopotamia, was steadily rebuilding the Tigris flotilla. Three more of the little Fly class were shipped to Abadan for assembly, to be joined by four of the more powerful Insect class, *Tarantula*, *Mantis*, *Moth* and *Gnat*.

The Insects, distinguished by twin funnels mounted in parallel, had originally, and somewhat optimistically, been designed for use against Austro-Hungarian monitors on the Danube but were now classed as China river gunboats. They displaced 625 tons, had a mean draught of four feet and were driven by 2000 hp triple expansion engines producing a maximum speed of 14 knots. Their armament consisted of two 6-inch guns on the main deck, two 12-pounder guns on a raised battery deck, and six machine guns. On arrival at Abadan, four of the machine guns were replaced by a 2-pounder pom-pom and a 3-pounder anti-aircraft gun. A kite balloon for artillery observation was also added and protection for the battery deck was provided first by sandbags and later by steel plating. Their first actions involved providing naval gunfire support for the abortive attempts to relieve Kut, during which they received their share of casualties and damage from the enemy's return fire.

After Townshend's surrender the front remained quiet for several months. As a result of Russian advances in Asia Minor and northern Persia, the Turks withdrew many of their troops from the Tigris in the belief that their lines below Kut were impregnable. By December, however, Maude possessed an army consisting of two corps and a cavalry division of two brigades, plus a strong naval flotilla. Aware that the Turks now had nothing in reserve, he decided to eliminate their less formidable defences on the right bank of the river one at a time, steadily working his way upstream past Kut, and then cross, the effect being to entrap his opponents unless they withdrew in good time.

The offensive began on 13 December with a feint attack on the left bank, in response to which the Turks concentrated their troops there. On the right bank steady, sustained progress was made until by the third week of February 1917 the advance had reached a point several miles north of Kut. On 23 February the demoralised defenders of the left bank, having endured weeks of shelling from across the river, were finally driven out of their trenches. Too late they decided to abandon Kut itself, for one of Maude's infantry divisions and the cavalry had already crossed at the Shumran Bend, behind them. Screened by strong flank and rear guards, they began a difficult retreat.

On the evening of 24 February the flotilla, consisting of the *Tarantula*, flying Captain Nunn's pendant, *Mantis* and *Moth*, plus two of the smaller Fly class, *Butterfly* and *Gadfly*, anchored off Kut. Nunn and a landing party took possession of the dismal, deserted ruins, hoisted the Union Flag on the tallest building and provided a garrison until relieved by the army.

Next day the gunboats moved slowly upstream, duelling constantly with the artillery of the enemy's rearguard. On the 26th Maude, having decided to reorganise the pursuit, asked Nunn to pound the Turks for all he was worth. Early that afternoon *Tarantula*, *Mantis*, *Moth*, *Butterfly* and *Gadfly* approached the little town of Bughaila to found it aflutter with white flags. *Gadfly* was detached to take possession, her commander personally capturing some 200 Turks and several trench mortars.

Pressing on, the flotilla reached the Nahr al Kalek Bend, where the river doubled back on itself in a complete hairpin. From three sides simultaneously the ships were assailed by heavy close-quarter fire from artillery, machine guns and rifles. They were hit repeatedly, sustaining casualties and damage, but there could be no turning back and, every gun blazing, they rounded each leg of the bend in turn. Aboard *Mantis* the native pilot and the quartermaster at the wheel were shot dead, only prompt action by the captain, Commander Bernard Buxton, preventing the ship from running aground under the very muzzles of the enemy guns. *Moth*, bringing up the rear, suffered most severely of all. She was struck by no fewer than five 5.9-inch howitzer shells – one through the port boiler, one through the port bunker and stokehold, one in the after storeroom and two glancing blows on the port side. Two of her ratings were killed and her captain, Lieutenant Commander Charles Cartwright, two of his three officers and eighteen ratings were wounded. Glancing anxiously astern, Nunn was relieved to see her rounding the final bend, wreathed in the smoke and flame of barking guns and bursting shells, her funnels and upperworks riddled by splinters and bullets, but with her Ensign streaming and gun crews hard at work. 'Commander Cartwright,' he wrote in his report, 'handled his ship magnificently.'

The flotilla had smashed its way through the Turkish rearguard and undoubtedly inflicted severe casualties in the process. The crews had been too preoccupied with the business in hand to observe the details but there had also been a distant impression of galloping horsemen and flashing swords emerging from a moving dust cloud as the British cavalry overran one of the enemy units. Several miles of quiet running followed, during which the damage control parties went about their work. Just below Sharqi, however, the river swung towards the road along which columns of Turkish troops and their transport could be seen marching. They were raked through and through with concentrated machine gun fire and dispersed with a rain of high explosive and shrapnel.

It might be thought that Nunn's flotilla had done enough for one day, but they were now thoroughly warmed to their task and luck was riding with them. Rounding the next bend, they sighted their opposite numbers, four Turkish gunboats steaming hurriedly north. While continuing to engage the enemy ashore with their automatic weapons, Nunn's vessels treated those ahead to some fast, accurate gunnery with their main armament. The rearmost enemy ship, mounting a 4.7-inch gun captured at Kut, was hit repeatedly and sank, fortunately without blocking the channel. The next ahead, the *Basra*, was also hit and ran herself ashore. Then it was the turn of the *Pioneer*, which was set ablaze and also run aground. The sole survivor was the *Firefly*, captured during the retreat from Ctesiphon. In no mood to share the fate of his colleagues, her captain ran her bows aground and escaped as soon as it was dusk, considerately leaving a full head of steam; by a strange coincidence, she re-entered British service under her original captain.

The pursuit ended at Al Aziziyah. Between 23 and 26 February over 4000 Turks were captured, together with guns, transport, ammunition and stores. The enemy army had been thoroughly routed, largely because of what Maude himself described as 'the daring pursuit of the naval flotilla' and its hard fight at the Nahr al Kalek Bend. Pausing only to allow his supply services to catch up, he continued his advance and on 11 March entered Baghdad, where the gunboats anchored under the walls of the former British Residency. Thereafter, apart from operations designed to keep the Turks at a respectable distance, the Mesopotamian Front remained relatively quiet for the rest of the war.

The reason for this was that a Turkish force assembled over a long period to recover Baghdad was diverted to Palestine because of the deteriorating situation there. During the first days of November 1917, General Sir Edmund Allenby broke the Turks' formidable Gaza–Beersheba line, which had held up the British advance for seven months. An important element in this success was an offshore bombardment force consisting of the cruiser *Grafton*, the old French coast defence ship *Requin*, armed with two 10.8-inch guns, the monitors *Raglan* (two 14-inch guns), *M.15* (one 9.2-inch gun), *M.29*, *M.31* and *M.32* (two 6-inch guns apiece), the Insect class gunboats *Aphis* and *Ladybird*, and seven British and French destroyers, spotting being carried out by seaplane and captive balloon. So efficient was the force that although ships returned to Port Said by rota to refuel and re-ammunition, there were never less than nine present in the bombardment line. As a result of this thorough preparation, tanks and infantry experienced no difficulty in breaking through the enemy lines on the coastal sector, and naval gunfire broke up such counter-attacks as the Turks were able to mount. Allenby continued to fight his way northward and on 9 December took Jerusalem.

Following as it did the loss of the other Holy Cities of Mecca and Baghdad, the fall of Jerusalem did the Turkish cause immense damage. Despite German support, Turkey was almost finished. She was, nevertheless, granted a prolonged reprieve, firstly because winter rains brought an end to the fighting in Palestine, and secondly because in the spring of 1918 Allenby was required to send troops to the Western Front because of the crises induced by Ludendorff's series of offensives. By September, however, he had recovered his strength and at Megiddo he shattered the Turks' Palestine Army Group in a matter of hours, carrying out a whirlwind advance that took him into northern Syria, where the enemy's rail link to the Mesopotamian Front was severed. On 31 October Turkey requested, and was granted, an armistice.

10

BOLOS, EMPERORS AND WARLORDS
Gunboat Operations Between
the World Wars, 1818–39

During World War I the Allies supplied many of Russia's needs through the northern ports of Murmansk and Archangel. When, in March 1917, revolution erupted among the war-weary population and the Tsar was forced to abdicate, it was hoped that the new Provisional Government would continue to prosecute the war against the Central Powers. Russia, however, was in no condition to continue fighting. When she mounted an offensive in July, it ended disastrously within days and was followed by the virtual disintegration of the Russian Army, much of which simply walked home. In October Lenin and his Bolshevik party seized power in St Petersburg and Moscow. This brought them into direct conflict with the more democratic elements of Russian society, known collectively as the Whites. Unfortunately, the Whites could not agree among themselves regarding war aims or anything else. The Bolsheviks, or Reds, on the other hand, enjoyed central control and were tightly disciplined. Utterly ruthless, they had few qualms about using terror to achieve their ends. For example, when their own ideologically inspired levies proved incapable of fighting a war, they did not hesitate to impress thousands of Tsarist officers, holding their families as hostages for their good behaviour.

The concern of the Allies was that if Russia collapsed completely, not only would German troops be transferred to the Western Front, the huge stockpiles of supplies in the northern ports, including 600,000 tons of munitions and 650,000 tons of coal at Archangel alone, would fall into enemy hands. In December 1917 the first of these fears became a reality when Lenin began negotiating an armistice with the Central Powers. The subsequent Treaty of Brest-Litovsk deprived Russia of huge areas but it left his hands free to deal with his internal enemies.

To safeguard the supply dumps as well as their own interests in Russia and provide assistance for their nationals fleeing from the civil war, the Allies decided to maintain their presence at Murmansk and Archangel. Relations with the Bolsheviks, or Bolos as they became known, deteriorated steadily when the latter announced their avowed intention of spreading revolution throughout the world. For Great Britain, the final straw came when Lenin's secret police, the Cheka, stormed the British Embassy on 31 August 1918. In the exchange of fire, Captain Francis Cromie, RN, a popular and successful submariner, killed two of the Chekists and wounded others but was shot dead in turn. The incident, breaching every accepted diplomatic protocol as it did, led to the Bolsheviks being regarded as barbarians with whom it was impossible to have civilised dealings. The international reaction, known as the Intervention, involved British, French, American, Canadian, Japanese, Greek and Italian troops placing Russia inside what amounted to a *cordon sanitaire* by maintaining an active military presence in such widely separated areas as North and South Russia, the Baltic, the Caucasus and Eastern Siberia, as well as supplying the White armies with war material and assistance.

In September 1918 the Insect class gunboats *Glowworm*, *Cicala*, *Cricket* and *Cockchafer* were warned for service in north Russia, their 12-pounders being replaced by 3-inch anti-aircraft guns and their Maxims supplemented by four Lewis light machine guns. They sailed for Archangel the following month and on arrival were laid up to await the coming of spring, when the melting of the ice would allow active operations on the Dvina River to commence. During the summer of 1919 the flotilla was joined by the *Mantis* and *Moth*, recently returned from Mesopotamia.

Although World War I had officially ended on 11 November the previous year, there was no respite for the Intervention forces. Bolshevik pressure on the Dvina Front was constant. The gunboats were in action daily and in one month fired over 1000 rounds of 6-inch ammunition apiece against targets as varied as enemy cavalry units, entrenched positions and gun barges. The Bolsheviks did not like them and made regular air attacks, without result. They also released mines into the river, hoping that they would strike the British ships as they were carried seaward by the current. This did produce a result, albeit by accident, for the *Cicala's* leadsman inadvertently struck one, the damage caused by the ensuing explosion requiring several weeks' repair work at Archangel. Enemy gunfire holed the *Cricket* in the bows below the waterline and the inrush of water caused her forward bulkhead to collapse. She ran heavily aground and remained fast for four weeks until she could be patched up and towed to Archangel. That she was allowed to survive so long says a great deal about the functioning of the Bolsheviks' command system. For their part, the Whites were no more efficient. On 24 August the *Glowworm* went to the assistance of a burning wooden barge moored against the river bank. The barge was not displaying any flags or warning signs to show that she was laden with explosives, but as the *Glowworm* came alongside, she blew up. The gunboat's captain, Commander Sebald Green, who also commanded the flotilla, was killed, as were seventeen of his officers and men, plus a further eighteen injured, and the ship was severely damaged.

As the summer wore on, it became apparent that the Allies were wasting their efforts in the area. The White troops became increasingly disheartened, disloyal and unreliable. British soldiers were offered commissions if they would serve with White units, but after several had been murdered there were few takers. It was decided to withdraw from North Russia altogether and under cover of a number of spoiling attacks mounted deep into enemy territory by the gunboats, the evacuation of Archangel and Murmansk was completed by the New Year.

On the Murmansk sector, progress had been better and much of the railway line between the port and St Petersburg was in Allied hands. On Lake Onega there were echoes of Spicer-Simson's adventures in Africa when a 70-foot motor launch, armed with 37mm guns and medium machine guns, was delivered by rail from Murmansk. Renamed *Jolly Roger*, she formed the nucleus of a miniature navy which included some motor boats and two steam launches abandoned by the retreating Reds. She was not a popular berth as her engines failed regularly and on 4 June they caught fire and exploded, killing several of her crew. That same day four armed Bolshevik steamers appeared to contest possession of the lake. Lieutenant Commander J. H. Mather gallantly took out four of his machine gun-armed motor boats to meet them, although the

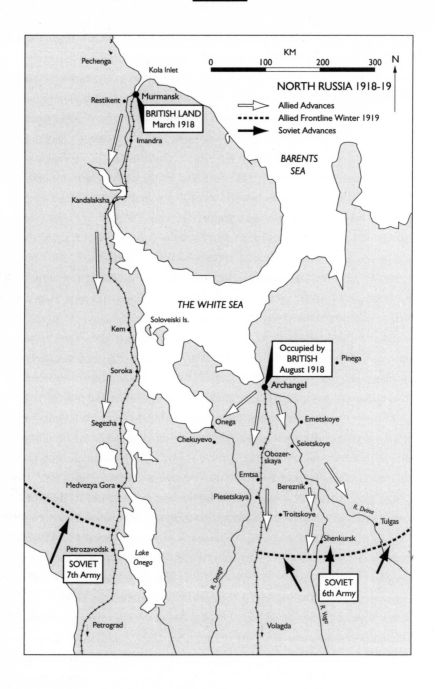

KM

0   100   200   300   N

NORTH RUSSIA 1918-19

⇨ Allied Advances
---- Allied Frontline Winter 1919
➡ Soviet Advances

Pechenga

Kola Inlet

BARENTS SEA

Restikent

Murmansk

BRITISH LAND
March 1918

Imandra

Kandalaksha

THE WHITE SEA

Kem

Soloveiski Is.

Occupied by
BRITISH
August 1918

Pinega

Soroka

Archangel

Segezha

Onega

Emetskoye

Chekuyevo

Seietskoye

Obozer-
skaya

Medvezya Gora

Emtsa

Bereznik

Piesetskaya

R. Dvina

Troitskoye

Tulgas

SOVIET
7th Army

Petrozavodsk

Lake
Onega

Shenkursk

SOVIET
6th Army

R. Onega

Petrograd

R. Vaga

Volagda

odds were very much in the enemy's favour. Fortunately, two flights of seaplanes intervened, bombing and strafing the Reds until they lost their nerve and turned for home with the motor boats in hot pursuit.

During the next few weeks, reinforcements arrived from England in the form of six 40-foot launches armed with 3-pounders and machine guns, and six 35-foot motor boats mounting machine guns. Under its new commander, Commander Curteis, RN, the little fleet now felt strong enough to tackle its opponents on their own ground and, with four seaplanes, set out for Petrozavodsk, the Reds' base on the western shore of the lake, on 3 August. When three of the Bolshevik gunboats appeared, the aircraft struck first, unsettling their crews once again. One of the enemy ships ran herself aground and was abandoned. The others, a 300-ton steamer and a gunboat armed with two 3-inch guns, suddenly found themselves surrounded by a swarm of snarling motor launches as they attempted to escape to the south. At length, their hulls riddled by 3-pounder fire, they surrendered. The northern half of the lake remained firmly in Allied hands until the general withdrawal from North Russia.

Although the operations of fast coastal craft armed with torpedoes are not strictly relevant to our story, it would be wrong not to mention them in the context of the Intervention, especially as they took place under the overall command of Rear Admiral Sir Walter Cowan, who as a lieutenant had captained the gunboat *Sultan* with such distinction at Omdurman. When Cowan assumed command of the Baltic Fleet in January 1919 he was already known as a strong-minded individualist with a passion for horses and field sport, clearly demonstrated by the riding boots with which he paced the quarterdeck and the hunting pink waistcoat worn under his uniform jacket.

Cowan had a most difficult task to perform in an area which was in turmoil. The newly created states of Finland, Estonia, Latvia, Lithuania and Poland all had their own interests to pursue, as did the Baltic German element of their population, in support of which substantial German forces remained active. His primary task, nevertheless, remained the support of the White armies and the containment of the Bolsheviks, and in this he was somewhat handicapped by having nothing heavier than a cruiser at his disposal, whereas the Bolsheviks possessed two battleships armed with 12-inch guns, the *Andrei Pervozvanny* and the *Petropavlovsk*, which would sometimes emerge from their heavily fortified base at Kronstadt to support their lighter units.

The approaches to Kronstadt, however, were familiar to a small number of young officers whose coastal motor boats were used to slip Allied agents in and out of St Petersburg. These craft were capable of over 40 knots and were armed with Lewis guns, depth charges and either one or two torpedoes. On the night of 17 June *CMB 4*, commanded by Lieutenant Augustus Agar and with Sub-Lieutenant John Hampsheir and Chief Motor Mechanic Hugh Beeley as crew, cheekily torpedoed and sank the Bolshevik cruiser *Oleg*. Agar was awarded the Victoria Cross, but as details of the action could not be published until long after the event it remained known as the 'Mystery VC'.

Naturally, Agar's exploit appealed to Cowan, who saw in it a way to destroy the enemy battleships. More CMBs arrived at Biörkö the base which had been established for them in Finland, and a raid on Kronstadt was planned jointly with the Royal Air Force. Ostensibly, the odds against it succeeding were high, for the Bolshevik base had the reputation of being the strongest naval fortress in the world, being defended by minefields, submerged breakwaters and twenty forts each armed with sixteen 11-inch, ten 9-inch and six 6-inch guns. Eight CMBs were detailed for the raid, which would be led by Commander C. C. Dobson, accompanied by Agar who would guide the craft through the chain of forts. In addition to its own three-man crew, each boat would have on board a Finnish smuggler familiar with Russian waters.

The raid went in during the early hours of 18 August, the sound of the CMBs' engines drowned by a diversionary air attack. Hydroplaning, the craft flashed over the minefields and submerged breakwaters to pass through the unsuspecting line of forts and penetrate the dockyard. There, the *Andrei Pervozvanny* and the *Petropavlovsk* were torpedoed and sent to the bottom, as was the submarine depot ship *Pamiat Azova*. The cost, mainly attributable to good shooting by the enemy guard destroyer *Gavriil* during the later phases of the attack, amounted to three CMBs lost, four officers and four ratings killed, and three officers and six ratings captured. It represented a high proportion of those involved, but at a stroke the raid eliminated the threat to Cowan's fleet and crippled Bolshevik naval power in the Baltic. Dobson received the Victoria Cross, and so did Sub-Lieutenant Gordon Steele, who took over after his commander, Lieutenant Dayrell-Reed, had been shot dead at the wheel, and completed the successful attack on the *Petropavlovsk*.

Unrest and violence were by no means confined to Russia. Across the whole of Eastern and Central Europe the old order had collapsed as emperors and kings lost their thrones. The peace-makers struggled to redraw the map along ethnic lines, dismembering the Austro-Hungarian Empire and founding the new states of Yugoslavia and Czechoslovakia. Naturally, they could not satisfy everyone and, inevitably, trouble flared whenever vested interests were damaged or political and economic aspirations remained unfulfilled. So it was that the Royal Navy despatched several Insect class gunboats, including the *Aphis*, *Ladybird* and the repaired *Glowworm*, to the Danube, for which waters they had originally been intended, to preserve order on the great international waterway.

There, in November 1921, *Glowworm* and *Ladybird* became involved in a remarkable series of events. The Austro-Hungarian Emperor Karl had abdicated in 1918 but after living in exile for a while he decided that he would like his empire back. On 22 October 1921, accompanied by a few followers, he crossed from Switzerland into Hungary, which was still nominally a kingdom and ruled by a regent, and set off for Budapest. There were plenty of people about who had no wish to see the Habsburg dynasty restored, notably the governments of Czechoslovakia, Romania and Yugoslavia, who threatened to invade Hungary if Karl ascended the throne. The Great Powers, anxious to preserve the peace they had so painstakingly created, insisted that the Hungarian government should formally dethrone Karl, who was now sitting in a train outside the capital, and banish him for life. The Hungarians complied and it was decided that the Emperor would begin his journey into permanent exile securely accommodated aboard a British gunboat, accompanied by the military representatives of Great Britain, France and Italy.

The *Glowworm*, commanded by Captain Arthur Snagge, Senior Naval Officer Danube, was then lying at Baja, a small port 90 miles downstream from Budapest, with *Ladybird* alongside. On a crisp November day a train drew into the adjacent station and the Emperor, accompanied by the Empress Zita and a small entourage, was escorted to the *Glowworm* through lines of soldiers by the three military representatives. After Snagge had signed for his distinguished prisoners, the imperial couple and the ladies were shown to the cramped cabin accommodation aboard the *Glowworm* while the rest of their party settled in on the *Ladybird*.

Dealing with the unexpected was part of gunboat life, but as the situation was difficult for everyone involved, Snagge suggested that if the Emperor would care to give his written parole this would dispense with the need for sentries. Karl did as he was asked, signing the document 'Emperor of Austria and King of Hungary'. Because of low water, the voyage only lasted as far as the Iron Gate on the Romanian frontier, after which bluejackets from the gunboats escorted the exiles across Romania in a convoy of cars. At Varna the imperial party boarded the cruiser *Cardiff* for transportation to the island of Madeira, where Karl died the following year.

Most gunboat activity between the world wars was still concentrated on the great rivers of China. Pirates were still a menace, but they had long since given up any idea of challenging professional navies on open water. Instead, they changed their tactics, mingling with the crowds of deck passengers who swarmed aboard the local steamers. In such circumstances it was almost impossible for a ship's crew to check for concealed weapons and, at a given signal, the pirates would storm the bridge and engine room. The pirates' numbers would be swelled by the crews of junks waiting conveniently in the offing and the steamer taken to one of their hideaways, where the cargo would be landed for sale and any passengers of note held for ransom. The steamer, stripped of anything of value, might then be allowed to proceed.

In reprisal for one such incident, in which the freighter *Kochow* was thoroughly looted on the West River, the gunboats *Cicala, Moth* and *Moorhen* flattened the known pirate villages of Taiphinghu and Shekki with the full approval of the provincial government, having given the inhabitants due notice to quit. In some circumstances shipowners were able to pay protection money as security against attack on certain sections of the river, but as a precaution the majority enclosed their bridges and engine rooms inside stout iron grilles, effectively turning the ship's central island into a fortress within which the officers had access to firearms if the need arose.

Unfortunately, pirates were not the only menace facing shipowners on China's rivers. In 1911 a revolution overthrew the Manchu dynasty and China became a republic. When the new President, Yuan Shih Kai, died four years later the country was left without a strong central authority. The result was that provincial governors and local warlords seized power for themselves, imposing whatever taxes and tolls they chose, the whole chaotic situation being overlaid by the conflicting political aspirations of north and south. More than ever, therefore, the situation in China resembled a giant jigsaw in which the pieces frequently changed position of their own accord, a state of affairs which was aggravated by the inevitable reduction in river patrols during World War I.

By the beginning of 1918 the British naval presence on the Yangtse had been reduced to the small and now elderly gunboats *Woodcock, Woodlark, Widgeon* and *Teal*, armed with two 6-pounder guns and manned by two officers and up to 30 ratings. It had already been decided, however, to strengthen the Yangtse and the smaller Si-Kiang Flotillas, and over the next two years all the Insects save *Aphis*, now laid up at Malta, and *Ladybird* and *Glowworm*, still patrolling the Danube, either made the passage under their own steam from the Middle East or under tow from home waters.

On reaching China the Insects' battery-deck 12-pounders were replaced by a 3-inch high-angle gun forward and a 2-pounder pom-pom aft, plus eight Lewis guns firing through slits in armour plating, and their two boats were supplemented by a motor sampan. The exception to this was the *Bee*, which became flagship of the Yangtse

Flotilla and had her armament reduced to one 3-inch high-angle gun and a pair of 3-pounders so that extra accommodation could be added for the admiral and his staff. The Insects also adopted the appropriate livery of white hulls with black boot-topping, white upperworks and buff funnels and masts.

It was appreciated that, interesting and popular though service in gunboats might be, health and morale could both be affected by over-long exposure to the cramped conditions of a small vessel in a hot, humid climate. Half the crews of the China gunboats were relieved annually, on the basis that they had completed a two and a half year commission by the time they reached England. Officers usually served for two years in what was considered to be a unique training ground. In accordance with long tradition, gunboat commanders were expected to act, using their own initiative, tact and common sense, rather than request instructions. For example, when warlords, bandits and pirates took to firing at merchant and naval vessels on both rivers, gunboat captains were authorised to reply immediately with their main arma-ment, and as a 6-inch shell trumps that from a field gun on most days of the week, the point was soon made. Face being so important a quality in the Orient, the rumour mongers who suggested the newly arrived Insects mounted wooden guns must have been stretched to provide a credible explanation!

Once patrolling the rivers had been re-established, it became possible to fit British merchantmen with radios, enabling them to report their progress to the nearest gunboat. Thus, the gunboats were often able to rescue merchant ships in difficulty, but all too often the radio operators on the latter were either corrupt or derelict in their duty and the pirates continued to make captures. Nor did it help when Chinese government gunboats such as the *Kong Ko*, whose task was to help preserve law and order, decided to go pirating on their own account. Those pirates who fell into British hands were given to the Chinese authorities to deal with, their usual fate being torture followed by decapitation.

In 1925, following the death of Sun Yat Sen, Chiang Kai-shek's southern Kuomintang Party emerged as the dominant force in Chinese politics. A year later, Chiang began a campaign to subdue the northern warlords, inadvertently provoking one of the most serious incidents in the entire history of the river patrols. The prosperous province of Szechuan, bestriding the upper reaches of the Yangtse some 1500 miles inland from Shanghai, was the domain of a warlord named Marshal Wu Pei Fu. On 27 August the China Navigation Company's steamer *Wanhsien*, flying the Red Ensign, anchored off the city of the same name, now known as Wangxian. Nearby was the gunboat *Cockchafer*, commanded by Lieutenant Commander Leon Acheson. During the evening shouts for help were heard coming from the *Wanhsien*, and Acheson set off in his motor sampan to investigate. On board the merchantman he found a Chinese divisional commander named Kuo Gu Tung and 100 armed soldiers. Kuo was a subordinate of Wu's local governor, General Yang Sen, and he was demanding transport for his troops. Told that he could not have it because that might be construed as British involvement in China's affairs, he had hysterics and told his men to level their rifles at the *Cockchafer*. Calmly, Acheson continued the discussion with Kuo's chief of staff, who seemed to be in a more reasonable frame of mind. The chief of staff informed Acheson that the general's troops had recently received transport aboard British merchantmen, to which the latter replied that the passage had been made at gunpoint before a gunboat could intervene. Unexpectedly, Kuo and his men left the *Wanhsien* without further comment. That, however, was only the beginning of the matter. Kuo, feeling that he had lost face, complained bitterly to Yang, who, egged on by a German trader, decided to assert his authority as governor.

On 29 August another of the China Navigation Company's steamers, the *Wanliu*, made a brief stop at Yunyang, 25 miles downstream from Wanhsien. While some of her passengers were disembarking, sixteen Chinese soldiers came aboard. Not liking this, nor the fact that several sampans full of troops were converging on his ship, the *Wanliu*'s skipper, Captain W. G. Lalor, rang down for full ahead. Everything then seemed to happen at once. One badly handled troop sampan collided with another in ths ship's wake and capsized, its occupants being drowned; rifle fire was directed at the

Wanliu from the shore; and those soldiers already aboard tried to storm the bridge, only to be beaten off by Lalor and his officers with their revolvers. So matters remained for the short passage to Wanhsien, where Lalor dropped anchor beside the *Cockchafer*. Acheson sent a boarding party over, disarmed the soldiers and sent them ashore in sampans. There they harangued a much larger group of soldiers who pointed their rifles at the *Wanliu*, only to scatter wildly when Acheson fired a burst from a Lewis gun into the water in front of them. Lalor then continued his voyage to Chunking (Chongqing), 300 miles up-river.

While Acheson was sorting out the *Wanliu*'s problems, Yang used the diversion to board the *Wanhsien* personally at the head of no less than 400 of his troops, telling her skipper, Captain Alexander Thomson, who had barricaded himself and his officers within the bridge structure, that until compensation was paid for the sampan allegedly sunk by the *Wanliu*, he would bring British river traffic to a standstill. Furthermore, he would have nothing more to do with Acheson and would negotiate only with the British consul in Chunking. During the evening his hand was reinforced when a third company steamer, the *Wantung* under Captain S. H. Bates, arrived at Wanhsien. Some 300 soldiers were immediately sent aboard and her British officers were imprisoned in the saloon. Simultaneously, an estimated 2000 troops and their artillery took up positions on both banks of the river and along the waterfront of Wanhsien itself, training their weapons on the *Cockchafer*. Acheson cleared for action but, knowing that the lives of the merchant marine officers would instantly be forfeit, was unable to do more.

Even by Yangtse standards, events were now apparently spiralling out of control. Fortunately, thanks to the gunboats' excellent radio net, steps were already being taken to support the beleaguered *Cockchafer*. Not only was Acheson's immediate superior, Commander Paul Berryman, aboard the elderly *Widgeon* at Chunking, aware of the situation, so too were the commander of the Yangtse Flotilla, the commander-in-chief, the Admiralty, the Foreign Office, the British Minister in Peking and the local consular service.

Whether Yang was alive to the uproar he was causing remains unclear. When three Chinese members of the *Cockchafer*'s crew went ashore on 31 August they were prevented from returning; worse still, the ship's sampan coolie was slashed to death.

The British consul at Chunking, a Mr Eastes, arrived by launch on 1 September. After conferring with Acheson, he visited Yang, who told him that the *Wanliu* had actually sunk two sampans, causing the deaths of 56 Chinese soldiers, and that by the unhappiest coincidence one of the stricken craft had been carrying $85,000 in collected taxes which it had been intended to place aboard the *Wanliu* under escort for safe transit. Working himself into a fury, Yang repeated that until reparation was made, the river would remain closed to British traffic. Eastes warned him that he was playing a dangerous game and that if any of the British ships were fired on, the *Cockchafer* would respond with her main armament.

Next day the gunboat's radio operator received a message from Marshal Wu ordering his unruly subordinate to release the British steamers. Eastes handed it to Yang who promptly tore it up, shouting that he was already in personal contact with the marshal. During the evening of 3 September Berryman arrived from Chunking in the *Widgeon*, relieving Acheson of some of the responsibility.

It had already been agreed by the commander-in-chief and the flotilla commander that, because of Yang's intransigent attitude, a cutting-out expedition would be required to free the trapped British merchantmen. The Jardine Matheson steamer *Kiawo* was chartered for the purpose, given extra protection in the form of steel plating and sandbags, and armed with a 2-pounder pom-pom, Maxim and Lewis guns. In command of the expedition was Commander Frederick Darley, whose boarders would consist of contingents from the cruiser *Despatch*, then at Hankow, and the gunboats *Mantis* and *Scarab*. Unfortunately, although strict security measures were enforced at Ichang (Yichang), where the expedition assembled, Yang's sympathisers were aware that something was afoot and kept the general informed.

At Wanhsien the war of nerves continued. On Sunday 5 September yet more troops boarded the captive steamers and the number of emplaced field guns rose to eleven. From the bridge of the *Wanhsien*

Captain Thomson semaphored that he had been physically threatened. Berryman hailed the senior Chinese officer aboard and warned him that the freighter would be blown out of the water if the British officers were harmed. To emphasise the point, both gunboats went to action stations and tension remained high throughout the afternoon.

At 18:15 that evening a column of funnel smoke signalled the arrival of the *Kiawo* from down-river. Despite her guise as a merchant vessel flying the Red Ensign she was clearly expected by the enemy, for as she rounded the final bend she attracted fire from the banks, even before the Red came down and the White went up. Passing the *Cockchafer*, she laid herself alongside the *Wanhsien*. The two vessels were grappled, the *Charge* was sounded, and the boarders, armed with rifles and truncheons, went over. Heavily outnumbered as they were, their task was no easy one, for the Chinese fought back with machine guns from behind sandbag barricades, while scores of riflemen opened fire from deckhouses, cabins, companionways, passages and the aft saloon. Although the vessel's British officers and five members of the crew were rescued from the bridge, fighting was bitter and casualties were heavy. When Darley was shot dead on the *Wanhsien*'s deck, his second-in-command, Lieutenant Oliver Fogg-Elliott, judged that the vessel was beyond recapture and, recalling his boarders, decided to attempt rescue of the *Wantung*'s officers.

Meanwhile, the engagement had become general. Heavy fire was directed at the *Cockchafer*, *Widgeon* and *Kiawo* from the shore. Acheson was wounded by a sniper but despite being in great pain, had himself propped up and continued to fight his ship. His 6-inch gun crews had long had Yang's headquarters in their sights and quickly reduced it to rubble; unfortunately, the general happened to be elsewhere. They then turned their attention to other targets in the city and along the waterfront so that fires soon began to rage. Simultaneously, the *Cockchafer*'s 3-inch guns, assisted by the *Widgeon*'s 6-pounders, began to blast the enemy's field guns. Throughout, shells continued to burst all round and rifle and machine gun fire rattled off the plating.

Elsewhere, Captain Bates, Chief Officer Paul and Chief Engineer Johnson had taken advantage of the confusion to break out of the

Wantung's saloon, clambering over the stern bulwarks to crouch on the rubbing strake. Paul and Johnson had then jumped into the river and struck out for a French gunboat, the *Doudart de Lagrée*, which was observing the battle passively from her anchorage across the river. Johnson was never seen again, but Paul was hauled from the water by the Frenchmen.

Having cast off from the *Wanhsien*, Fogg-Elliott now eased the *Kiawo* expertly towards the *Wantung*'s stern and, keeping the defenders' heads down with his automatic weapons, picked up Bates. In passing the *Widgeon*, he had attempted to inform Berryman that he was now in command, but his words were lost in the din. With the light failing, he recognised that nothing more could be achieved and set off down-river. Berryman evidently concurred, for he ordered *Widgeon* and *Cockchafer* to follow.

The three ships anchored for the night five miles below the burning city. The engagement had not been an unqualified success, for although most of the British merchant crews had been rescued, neither the *Wanhsien* nor the *Wantung* had been recaptured, while casualties amounted to three officers and four ratings killed, and two officers and thirteen ratings wounded. Chinese casualties remain unknown, although they were undoubtedly much heavier. As a result of subsequent high-level discussions, Yang returned the two merchantmen and, superficially at least, assumed a mellower outlook. In reality, he blamed Acheson for his troubles and put out a contract on his life; believing the risk to be real, the Admiralty posted the *Cockchafer*'s commander as far from China as possible. In the wider sphere, China lodged a formal complaint with the League of Nations and there was prolonged anti-foreign agitation across a wide area, involving riots, looting of western businesses and attacks on Europeans. The oddest thing about what became known as the Wanhsien Incident was that neither side had really believed that the other would dare to open fire first.

By 1927 Chiang seemed to be making some progress against the warlords. In the long term, despite his title of Generalissimo, he would never bring them completely under control and irreconcilable differences would arise between him and his communist allies, among whom Mao Tse-tung was to emerge as leader. For the moment, however, anti-foreign feeling in the newly 'liberated' areas reached such proportions that British troop reinforcements were rushed to Shanghai, the Royal Navy despatched an additional cruiser squadron from the Mediterranean to the Far East, and the *Aphis* and *Ladybird* sailed from Malta to supplement the river flotillas. The following year the new *Gannet, Peterel, Seamew* and *Tern* arrived to replace the old, pre-war British gunboats, being joined in 1931 by the *Falcon* and in 1934 by the *Robin* and the *Sandpiper*. The new arrivals, with 3-inch guns or 3.7-inch howitzers as their main armament, lacked the punch of the Insects but their accommodation was infinitely superior.

Despite Chiang's apparently firmer grip on the situation, life on the rivers continued much as before, although as the Thirties wore on, a new dimension was added by Japan's belligerent expansionism. By August 1937 periodic clashes between Chinese and Japanese troops had escalated into full-scale war. Whether it was by reason of arrogance or stupidity, or a combination of both, the better-equipped Japanese had no hesitation in opening fire on neutral ships, however clearly marked they might be.

Matters reached a critical level on 11 December. During the morning British ships near Nanking, including the *Wantung* with 600 passengers aboard, had first been shelled from the shore and then subjected to air attack. Also present were the *Scarab* (Lieutenant Commander C. B. Clitheroe) and the *Cricket* (Lieutenant Commander G. H. Ashby), which had hit back with their 3-inch and Lewis guns. The Japanese airmen, not having allowed for this in their calculations, swerved wildly away, dropping their bombs wide of the mark.

Early next morning, at Wuhu, some 50 miles up-river from Nanking, several Japanese field batteries and a number of machine guns opened fire directly on the *Ladybird* (Lieutenant Commander H. D. Barlow), which was clearly flying her White Ensigns. At point blank range six shells exploded aboard, killing a sick berth attendant, wounding Barlow, his officers and a rating, and causing considerable damage. As luck would have it, Barlow's passengers included Lieutenant-Colonel Lovat Fraser, the British military attaché, and the British consul at Nanking, who had made the journey to Wuhu with the object of preventing just this sort of incident. In fact, a boat was being lowered for the former when the Japanese opened fire. Disregarding the hail of shot, Fraser reached the shore and, incandescent with rage, stormed into the nearest battery. Grabbing the battery commander, he frog-marched him to the guns and forced him to cease firing.

Some 30 minutes later, Lovat was still engaged in his furious row with the battery commander when the *Bee* arrived; she was greeted by a single shell which fortunately went wide. Aboard her was Rear Admiral R. V. Holt, Senior Naval Officer Yangtse, on his way to meet his Japanese opposite number with a view to discussing measures that would ensure the safety of British shipping on the river.

Holt wiped the floor with the Japanese area commander, a Colonel Hashimoto, extracting an apology from him for the unprovoked attack and a promise to attend the dead seaman's funeral next day. This was honoured, due compliments being paid by two officers and a detachment of soldiers. Yet, even as Hashimoto was apologising to Holt, his aircraft were committing an even greater atrocity.

Halfway between Nanking and Wuhu the gunboat USS *Panay*, commanded by Lieutenant Commander James Hughes, USN, was escorting a convoy of American merchantmen. Hughes had informed the Japanese of the movement, and also that the convoy would anchor at a point 28 miles upstream from Nanking, which it did at 11:00. There could be no possible doubt as to the gunboat's nationality as, in addition to her ensign, two large Stars and Stripes flags were laid across her awnings. Nevertheless, at 13:00 the entire convoy came under heavy and sustained air attack. The *Panay* was hit repeatedly by bombs and began to settle. Hughes, seriously wounded, gave orders for the wounded to be taken off, only to see their boat deliberately machine gunned by two aircraft. The sinking gunboat was then abandoned. If any doubt still existed as to Japanese intentions it was dispelled when one of their landing craft appeared, opening fire on two chief petty officers who had returned to the ship to collect medical supplies. Once the *Panay* had been disposed of, the Japanese airmen concentrated their attacks on the American merchant vessels, sinking two and driving a third aground.

So sudden had been the attack that the *Panay* had been unable to use her radio. At Shanghai, Admiral Yarnell, Commander-in-Chief of the US Asiatic Fleet, therefore remained in ignorance of her fate. Growing anxious at her continued lack of communication, he asked his British counterpart to enquire whether there had been any sightings. Holt at first did not believe anything was seriously amiss, but after the funeral on the 13th he was informed of the air attack. He promptly hurried to the scene with *Bee* and *Ladybird*, but all that remained were two burning oil company lighters, an abandoned, gutted freighter, and the *Panay*'s bullet-riddled motor sampan. In response to blasts on the *Bee*'s siren, several figures appeared on the bank. Some belonged to the gunboat's crew, others to the merchantmen. Shortly after, Chinese militiamen told Holt that the rest of the survivors had been taken to an inland village for their own safety. They were brought back and accommodated on the *Bee* and the *Ladybird*. It all but beggars belief that while their rescue was in progress two Japanese gunboats arrived from Shanghai 'to render assistance'. This may have been their mission, or it may not, for the uncharitable thought arises that elimination of the witnesses would have suited the Japanese very well. Whatever the truth, not one American would set foot on a Japanese deck and it was aboard the British vessels that the survivors were returned to their own people. Once again, far from home, blood had proved thicker than water, and for this Admiral Yarnell was duly grateful.

The incident cost the lives of two American ratings, the master of one the merchantmen and an Italian journalist; five American officers, 35 ratings and several civilians were wounded. The Japanese government had little alternative but to bow to the storm of international protest generated by the attack, acceding to Washington's demand that Hashimoto be dismissed and paying an indemnity of two million dollars. Hashimoto was a particularly strident member of his army's fervently nationalistic war party which, unfortunately, had become a dominant force in Japan's political life.

In fact, the Sino-Japanese War had already ensured that the days of the Western gunboat flotillas were numbered. Once Japan had secured control of China's coastline and the lower reaches of the great rivers, the conduct of normal commercial activity became virtually impossible. The need for gunboat operations therefore declined and some of the older vessels were sold for scrap. When war broke out between the United Kingdom and Hitler's Germany in 1939, a number of British gunboats sailed west. Japan promptly requested the withdrawal of the remainder on the grounds that their presence in 'her' neutral waters was not acceptable, a specious submission that nevertheless led to a further reduction of strength on the Yangtse. In the immediate aftermath of Pearl Harbor, two gunboats, *Peterel* at Shanghai and *Cicala* at Hong Kong, went down fighting against impossible odds, while *Tern* was scuttled to prevent her capture. *Moth*, salvaged from the graving dock at Hong Kong, was taken into Japanese service as the *Suma* but struck an American mine near Nanking and went to the bottom. The *Sandpiper*, *Gannet* and *Falcon*, still on the upper reaches of the Yangtse, were presented to Chiang's Nationalist government in 1942.

11
INSHORE SQUADRON
The Mediterranean, 1940–4

The rapid victory won by Germany over Poland in 1939, followed by her stunning conquest of all Western Europe save the United Kingdom the following year, had left Benito Mussolini, the Italian dictator, feeling somewhat up-staged. On 10 June 1940, with the French Army already beaten to its knees and the British Expeditionary Force driven from the continental mainland, he declared war on France and Great Britain, commenting to his army chief of staff, Marshal Pietro Badoglio, that he 'needed a few thousand dead so that he could sit at the conference table as a man who has fought', and therefore share in the spoils. He did so against the advice of his service chiefs who warned him that in their present condition the Italian armed forces were only capable of fighting a short war, and that it would be 1942 at the earliest before they could be equipped on a scale suitable for a modern European conflict.

This did not trouble him unduly as he did not believe that Great Britain could possibly resist the might of Hitler's Wehrmacht beyond September. Furthermore, within the Mediterranean and the Middle East, which was his own particular sphere of interest, the British were stretched so thinly that, on the basis of simple mathematics alone, an Italian victory seemed assured.

It was true that in the Middle East General Sir Archibald Wavell commanded some 50,000 British and Imperial troops, but these were deployed across a vast area stretching from the Syrian border to Somaliland. In Egypt itself, the very pivot of British power in the region, there were only 36,000 men, short of supporting armour and artillery, and it was difficult to see how this small force could possibly resist the 250,000-strong Italian Army in Libya. In Italian East Africa there were a further 200,000 men, poised to strike into the Sudan, Kenya and British Somaliland, the largest of whose garrisons numbered only 9,000.

At sea the revitalised Royal Italian Navy not only enjoyed a wealth of bases in the central Mediterranean, but also outnumbered Admiral Sir Andrew Cunningham's Mediterranean Fleet, although in capital ships the Royal Navy had a slight advantage, opposing six Italian battleships with seven of its own. In other classes of warship the Italian strength was as disproportionately overwhelming as it seemed on land, 21 cruisers being deployed against eight, 50 destroyers against 37, and 100 submarines against eight. It hardly seemed to matter that the Royal Navy had two aircraft carriers in the area, for it had been planned, a little optimistically, that the Italian fleet would receive massive support from the land-based Regia Aeronautica, which could put up about 2000 aircraft against the RAF and Fleet Air Arm's handful of more or less obsolete types. Thus, when Mussolini spoke of the Mediterranean as *Mare Nostrum*, it seemed far from being an idle boast.

Unfortunately, the Royal Italian Navy, while containing some outstandingly courageous officers and men, did not relish the task it had been set. Psychologically, it was in awe of the Royal Navy and was further handicapped by limited fuel supplies; it also had to take into account British striking forces operating from the heavily fortified island of Malta, just 60 miles south of Sicily, which was to remain a permanent and very painful thorn in its side. When the two battlefleets clashed briefly on 9 July the Italians sustained some damage and retired. Although Mussolini claimed a victory, presumably because he still had a powerful fleet in being, his admirals thereafter remained shy of fighting a general engagement. On the night of 11/12 November Swordfish torpedo bombers, flying from the carrier *Illustrious*, crippled the Italian battlefleet in Taranto harbour.

We are, however, getting a little ahead of ourselves, for events on land had been almost as dramatic. Italy had obtained possession of Libya following her war with the Ottoman Empire in 1912. The establishment of a North African colony proved to be a difficult undertaking, largely because the Libyans themselves remained bitterly opposed to the idea. In Tripolitania, the western province, a degree of settlement had taken place, although it did not extend far inland. In Cyrenaica, the eastern province, a barren hinterland and

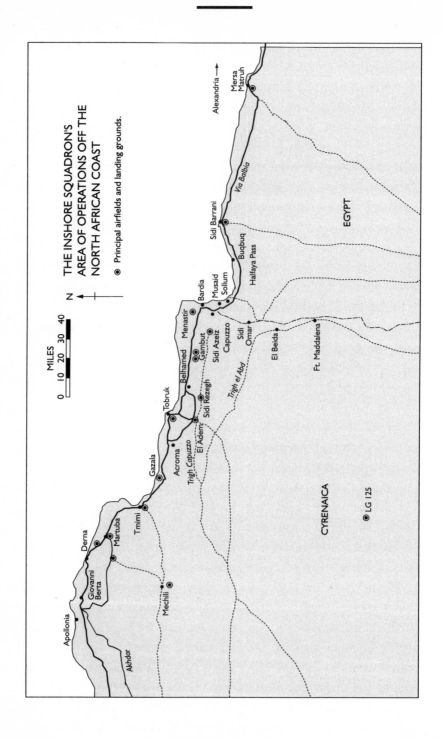

THE INSHORE SQUADRON'S
AREA OF OPERATIONS OFF THE
NORTH AFRICAN COAST

⊚ Principal airfields and landing grounds.

Libyan intransigence meant that the Italians were even more confined to a coastal strip, where they had constructed elaborate defences around the ports of Bardia and Tobruk. It might, perhaps, be thought that in June 1940 the huge Italian army in Cyrenaica was brimming with self-confidence and looking forward to an easy victory. Such a mood, if it ever existed, was quickly dispelled when Wavell despatched his mechanised elements across the Egyptian frontier. During the next three months they beat up isolated garrisons, snapped up convoys, captured generals and made life very unpleasant for the Italians, inflicting some 3000 casualties in exchange for only 150 of their own. A visiting German officer was startled to be told that the Italian 'will to resist' remained unshaken and reported that 'everyone seems scared stiff of the British'.

Despite his immense responsibilities, Admiral Cunningham was anxious to provide Wavell's tiny army with as much gunfire support as possible. For the moment, all he could offer were three now elderly Insect class gunboats, of which he commented in his memoirs:

> I had gladly accepted the offer of these little ships for service in the Mediterranean, as their small size and shallow draught made them difficult targets for bombs or torpedoes, while their two 6-inch guns, though old, were useful weapons. Of these the *Ladybird*, *Aphis* and *Gnat*, later joined by the monitor *Terror* with her pair of 15-inch guns, all gave grand service off the Libyan coast in 1940–41 on the sea flank of the army. Over long periods they bombarded every night, paying particular attention to Bardia and Tobruk as the battle on shore surged to and fro.

First into action was *Ladybird*, which, under Lieutenant Commander J. F. Blackburn, was ordered to proceed west from Mersa Matruh and, disguised as far as possible as a merchant vessel, penetrate Bardia harbour and destroy any shipping there. After dusk on 23 August the enemy's coast defence gunners spotted her approaching and opened a heavy but inaccurate fire to which *Ladybird* replied with her 6- and 3-inch armament. She then slid into the harbour, a narrow inlet surrounded by cliffs, but found it deserted. For the next 25 minutes Blackburn pounded installations and buildings ashore, quickly destroying a solitary field gun which opened fire in return. Emerging into open water again, *Ladybird* once more became the target of the coastal artillery, the aim of which had improved considerably. As heavy shells threw up fountains of water all round her, the gunboat replied with her heavy weapons and pom-poms. Blackburn took sharp evasive action and laid smoke, making good his escape, covered by the Australian destroyer *Waterhen*. As Bardia was one of the most heavily fortified ports in North Africa, this astonishing piece of cheek could have done nothing for the morale of its Italian garrison.

Meanwhile, Mussolini had been nagging his commander-in-chief in North Africa, Marshal Rodolfo Graziani, to invade Egypt or face the sack. To his credit, Graziani recognised that while he had by far the bigger army, it was insufficiently mechanised to fight a successful desert war. Nevertheless, on 13 September he began a ponderous advance which, four days later, brought him to Sidi Barrani, just 60 miles into Egyptian territory. There, having established an advance post at Maktila, he began digging himself in with a chain of fortified camps stretching south-west into the desert, refusing to budge further.

Near the Egyptian–Libyan frontier the escarpment between the desert plateau and the coastal plain can be crossed by two routes, one at Sollum and the other at nearby Halfaya Pass. The Italian army had perforce to advance through these. On 14 September the *Ladybird* appeared off Sollum, battering the enemy's transport and artillery at the very point where it was unable to escape off the road. Satisfied that he had caused damage, casualties, confusion and panic, Blackburn withdrew before any coherent response could be organised. On her return to Mersa Matruh, *Ladybird* was joined by *Aphis* under Lieutenant Commander J. O. Campbell. During the next few weeks the two Insects, now known collectively as Force W, carried out many similar harassing missions.

Wavell's devastating counter-offensive, codenamed Operation Compass, began during the night of 8/9 December. Spearheaded by a regiment of Matilda II tanks, which at that stage were invulnerable to any gun the Italians possessed, the counter-attack force passed through a gap in the chain of fortified camps, isolated Sidi Barrani from the west, and proceeded to storm each camp in turn. On 10 December Sidi Barrani itself was taken and the routed Italian army was streaming back towards the frontier, leaving 38,000 of its men to be taken prisoner.

Force W had now been joined by the monitor *Terror*. During Operation Compass the enemy's advance post at Maktila had been pounded by *Terror*, standing well offshore, and by *Aphis*, which closed in to a point-blank 3000 yards; badly shaken, the Italians tried to escape westwards to Sidi Barrani, which had been simultaneously bombarded by *Ladybird*, only to find that it was already in British hands. For the next few days the two Insects harried the retreating army without mercy while *Terror* pounded targets within the Bardia perimeter with her 15-inch guns. Sometimes the enemy responded with an air attack on the ships and sometimes with MAS (motor torpedo) boats, all attacks being beaten off without casualties or damage.

On the night of 16/17 December the *Aphis* crept stealthily along the coast towards Bardia. By 06:30 she had reached the harbour entrance undetected and glided inside. Within, she found three supply ships at anchor, using just six rounds of 6-inch to reduce them to blazing wrecks. During the next hour Campbell's main armament fired a further 100 rounds, turning a fuel depot into an enormous fireball and engaging every likely target within sight. Each time the guns fired, the cliffs sent back a quadruple echo, so that the cumulative noise level was deafening. Out at sea, those aboard the watching *Terror* could also see dense black smoke clouds boiling up out of the enclosed harbour.

'Seems to be having a good time!' mused Commander Hayes, her captain.

At length, with his gun crews exhausted and the *Aphis* coming under increasingly heavy machine gun and mortar fire, Campbell decided to head for open water. This was the moment that the outraged coast defence artillerymen had been waiting for. For ten miles they pursued the little gunboat with their heavy shells, but her sudden twists and turns left them baffled and the covering fire provided by the *Terror*'s 15-inch guns cannot have helped. There can be little doubt that the battery commanders received a furious tongue lashing from the fortress commander, General Bergonzoli, better remembered by his nickname of 'Electric Whiskers', for when *Aphis* reappeared off the port the following day they were much quicker off the mark and Campbell wisely decided not to press his advantage. Both he and Blackburn were awarded the DSO for their forays into Bardia.

By the New Year Wavell's troops, under the operational command of Lieutenant-General Richard O'Connor, had caught up with the fleeing Italians and were ready to mount an assault on Bardia. The devastating preliminary bombardment was delivered not just by O'Connor's artillery, but also by the battleships *Barham*, *Valiant* and *Warspite* and their escorting warships, supplemented inshore by Force W, which had been joined by a third Insect, the *Gnat*.

It was enough to stretch the resolve of even good troops to breaking point, and that of the Italians was already shaky. When the assault went in on 3 January, the combination of Matildas and aggressive Australian infantry proved unstoppable. By the evening of 5 January all of Bardia was in British hands. Immense quantities of equipment were captured and another 38,000 men began their weary trudge into the prisoner of war cages. 'Electric Whiskers' Bergonzoli was not among them, having successfully evaded capture and made his way to Tobruk. British casualties amounted to 500, of whom only 150 were killed.

As Force W had retired from the bombardment phase it had come under air attack. Aboard *Aphis* several men were killed or wounded when the gunboat was strafed. With two of his loaders dead and another man wounded, Petty Officer Leslie Poore served B gun alone until he was joined by a stoker and a cook. Simultaneously, Able Seaman Bennett Chapman, though seriously wounded, continued to man the 2-pounder pom-pom until he collapsed. Both were awarded the Conspicuous Gallantry Medal.

Immediately after the fall of Bardia, Force W became the Inshore Squadron under the command of Captain H. Hickling and was joined by three minesweepers, four anti-submarine trawlers and a variety of smaller vessels including schooners, lighters and store ships. On land the advance continued and Tobruk was invested. Once again *Terror*, *Ladybird* and *Gnat* took part in a preliminary bombardment against selected target areas within the defences. The same careful preparation went into the assault on Tobruk as had gone into that on Bardia. At 06:30 on 21 January the Matildas and Australians broke into the perimeter and by the afternoon of the following day all resistance had ended. Yet more guns, tanks and supplies were captured and another 25,000 prisoners were taken.

Following the Sidi Barrani débâcle, Marshal Graziani had complained bitterly that he was being compelled to wage 'the war of the flea against the elephant', recommending that the army should be withdrawn as far west as Tripoli. Since this meant abandoning the entire province of Cyrenaica, Mussolini thought that he had lost his mind. However, the loss in succession of Bardia and Tobruk placed a different complexion on the matter. After making a brief stand along the line of the Wadi Derna, the Italians did decide to retire into Tripolitania, using the coastal route through Benghazi. Alerted as to what was happening, O'Connor despatched the 7th Armoured Division across the base of the Benghazi Bulge while the 6th Australian Division pursued the retreating enemy along the coast. On 5 February the Italian Tenth Army suddenly found itself trapped between the two at Beda Fomm. During repeated attempts to break through, its commander, General Tellera, was mortally wounded. Following the failure of his last attack on the morning of 7 February his successor, General Bergonzoli, surrendered. Over 25,000 prisoners were taken, as well as over 100 tanks, 216 guns and 1500 wheeled vehicles.

In addition to their bombardment duties, the Insects had been kept extremely busy throughout the campaign. Their shallow draught enabled them to act as supply carriers, and at one time they were delivering 100 tons of urgently needed drinking water daily to the army. They also brought reinforcements forward and ferried hundreds of tractable prisoners back to Mersa Matruh on their decks.

Only a single Italian division and fugitives from vanished formations lay between O'Connor and Tripoli. The probability is that if the advance had continued Tripoli would have been taken and the Desert

War would have ended there and then. That, however, is hindsight. At the time, Churchill decided that once the threat to Egypt had been decisively dealt with, Wavell should send troops to Greece to assist in the defence of that country, leaving a screening force in Cyrenaica to guard against an Italian revival. Unfortunately, the campaign in Greece ended in defeat, as did the subsequent defence of Crete, and the Royal Navy was required to pay a high price in lost or damaged ships during the subsequent evacuations.

The second consequence of the British victory in Africa was that Hitler was forced to provide support for his tottering Italian ally, who from that point became the junior partner in the Axis alliance and something of a liability. While Italian reinforcements and German armoured units were hastily shipped into Tripoli, the Luftwaffe quickly made its presence felt. In command of the German element of the new Axis army in Libya was the then Lieutenant General Erwin Rommel. It quickly became apparent that while he was nominally subordinate to the Italians, in practice it would be he who made the going. On 31 March he opened his first offensive, cutting across the base of the Benghazi Bulge and provoking a hasty British withdrawal. He failed to capture Tobruk but entered Bardia unopposed and secured the Halfaya Pass and Sollum escarpment crossings on the Egyptian frontier.

Having been assured by Cunningham that Tobruk could be supplied by sea, Wavell decided that it would be held, thereby depriving Rommel of the deep-water port he needed to ease the strain on his long supply line. Initially the garrison would consist of Major-General Leslie Morshead's 9th Australian Division, supported by British artillery and armour. Unable to make any impression on the defences, Rommel was forced to spend the rest of the year maintaining a regular siege, simultaneously fending off British attempts to relieve the fortress. Two such attempts, the first in May and the second in June, resulted in failure and Wavell being replaced by General Sir Claude Auchinleck as Commander-in-Chief Middle East.

The Inshore Squadron had not escaped unscathed during these events. The Luftwaffe's Ju 87 dive bombers, the legendary Stukas,

were especially troublesome. Whereas the Italians had preferred to
area bomb from high altitude, the Stukas bored straight down on their
targets like black-crossed pterodactyls, sirens howling and bombs
screaming. To anyone beneath a Ju 87's attack-dive it seemed as
though he had become the pilot's personal target and until one got
used to it the experience was very frightening. The Stukas were, of
course, very vulnerable to fighter attack, but for the moment the
British had few fighters to deploy and their only worry was the
volume of anti-aircraft fire that could be directed at them. As the principal target of the German dive bomber squadrons during this period,
the Royal Navy quickly developed a grudging respect for their profes-
sionalism and courage. At Benghazi *Terror* was narrowly missed by a
bomb on 22 February, the damage being such that several of her
compartments were flooded. This was compounded when, on her way
back to Tobruk, she struck two mines. She was then subjected to
further air attacks, the combined effect of which was to break her
back. On 25 February her captain took the decision to abandon her
and two hours later she rolled over and sank.

Naturally, the dive bombers were drawn to the increased maritime
activity centred on Tobruk, which Rommel mistakenly believed was
an evacuation rather than a reinforcement of the garrison. On 10
April *Ladybird* slid into the harbour, having taken part in an abortive
attempt to secure the island of Castelorizo, off the Turkish coast, as
a motor torpedo boat base. Castelorizo, it should be mentioned, was
part of the Dodecanese group, which Italy had also won from the
Ottoman Empire in 1912, and lay within comfortable striking
distance of Rhodes, the principal island in the group. The operation
was badly planned, although *Ladybird* had nothing with which to
reproach herself. After the initial landings, the Italian defenders had
retired to a fort on a hill above the town. This Blackburn turned into
a ruin with a dozen well-placed 6-inch shells, so that when the
landing force closed in, the defenders streamed out with their hands
raised. Now short of fuel, the gunboat set off for Cyprus and at this
point the enemy on Rhodes began to react. *Ladybird* was subjected to
a series of air attacks, and although her triple rudders gave her the

ability to twist and turn unpredictably, she was hit by a small bomb which wounded all the forward 3-inch gun crew. Drawing as little water as she did, she began to roll wildly as bombs churned up the sea all round her. Evidently satisfied, the airmen departed; to his surprise, Blackburn learned later that the Italian radio had reported his ship as being sunk. Meanwhile, the enemy had further reacted by landing fresh troops of his own on Castelorizo, and as the British landing force lacked heavy weapons it was agreed that it should be taken off. Disappointing as the Castelorizo operation was, several valuable lessons were learned, among which was that the poor performance of the Italians in North Africa could not be taken for granted everywhere.

On her return to Alexandria, *Ladybird*, accompanied by *Gnat*, was sent through the Suez Canal into the Red Sea, where an Italian destroyer flotilla based at Massawa was thought to be on the point of interdicting the route between Suez and Aden. In the event, the threat did not materialise and, after undergoing a brief refit at Port Said, *Ladybird* sailed west to Tobruk.

While the Luftwaffe's intervention had originally been made from bases in Sicily, Rommel had recovered so much territory that it was now operating from airfields in Cyrenaica. The Stuka squadrons menacing Tobruk harbour were based at Tmimi, supported by more bombers and fighter escorts at Gazala and Derna, all a comparatively few minutes' flying time to the west. The harbour was also within range of the German heavy artillery, so for her own protection *Ladybird* took up her berth in the lee of the sunken freighter *Serenitas*. On the night of 14/15 April the purpose of her presence became apparent. Blackburn took her out into the darkness and sailed west until she reached a position off Gazala. She proceeded to pound the airfields savagely, her shells exploding among parked aircraft, bomb dumps, barracks and a tank leaguer in which several vehicles were set ablaze. Satisfied with the night's work, Blackburn withdrew into his lair. Every few nights *Ladybird* repeated the treatment, her attack on 28 April being particularly successful in that a large concentration of enemy transport vehicles, the very lifeblood of desert warfare, was left wrecked and burning. Elsewhere, she used her guns in support of sorties made by Morshead's belligerent Australian garrison.

Naturally, the Luftwaffe did not take kindly to all this. It was fairly obvious that the source of their troubles lay somewhere in Tobruk harbour, against which they mounted a heavy raid during the afternoon of 7 May. Mistakenly, the Stukas took the fleet minesweeper *Stoke* as their target. She sank after being hit repeatedly, her survivors being rescued by the *Ladybird*'s crew. *Stoke*'s captain has left a vivid account of the attack:

> All knew that under existing conditions in the harbour and with no fighter protection and the enemy aircraft doing as they liked it was only a matter of time before a ship was hit, but there were no complaints. Guns' crews stuck to their weapons until either they were blown away or there were no aircraft left to shoot at.

If the German airmen thought they had solved their problem they were mistaken, for on the night of 11/12 May *Ladybird* was back battering their airstrips. It was, therefore, in a vengeful spirit that a total of 47 Ju 87s and Ju 88s returned to the attack at about 15:15 the following afternoon. With a quiet efficiency born of familiarity the *Ladybird*'s crew went to action stations, manning her anti-aircraft armament. This included the 3-inch guns, the 2-pounder pom-pom, and Lewis light machine guns, supplemented by captured Italian weapons including a 20mm Breda cannon and two 8mm Fiat machine guns.

Three Stukas led the attack on the gunboat, howling down through the tracer that snaked up to meet them. One bomb from the first plane burst on the pom-pom mounting, destroying the weapon and killing its crew. Shards of flying metal cut down the two Fiat gunners. Almost simultaneously a second bomb penetrated the boiler room and exploded within, blowing out the sides of the hull. *Ladybird*, mortally hurt and afire aft, began to settle by the stern with a list to starboard.

The second explosion had flung the Breda crew off their feet. Led by CPO Albert Thornton-Allen, who had already been awarded the

Distinguished Service Medal for the probable destruction of two Italian aircraft during the Castelorizo affair, the semi-stunned men quickly got their weapon back into action. All round them every one of the ship's remaining anti-aircraft weapons was hammering away at the attackers. One of the Stukas, its pilot shot dead at his controls, failed to pull out of its dive and plunged into the harbour; another, trailing smoke and flames, disappeared behind the town to explode in a fireball in the desert beyond.

Lieutenant Diack, the ship's first lieutenant, gave Blackburn his damage control report. The fire was approaching the after magazine, which could not be flooded because the valves could no longer be reached; it was impossible to raise steam; the ship's back was all but broken and she was continuing to settle. Blackburn gave orders that the wounded should be taken off in the motor sampan and waited with the rest of his crew for the boats which were already approaching the stricken vessel.

The fire spread throughout the ship, sending up a dense cloud of black smoke until she settled into the mud on an even keel in just ten feet of water. The White Ensign continued to fly from her broken fore-mast for the remainder of the siege as though the fighting *Ladybird* refused to die. Nor did she. Her 3-inch gun remained above water and, having been returned to working order by the Royal Artillery, was manned by them during subsequent air raids.

The *Ladybird* had been a ship with her own personality and a strong *esprit de corps* among her crew. As she was well known to the Mediterranean Fleet and the army, her loss was a matter of great sadness. General Morshead, by no means the most sentimental of men, sent Blackburn a sympathetic note. Admiral Cunningham received the following message from the commanding officer of the South Staffordshire Regiment:

All ranks of South Staffords having had opportunity of getting to know officers and crew of HMS *Ladybird* and seeing so much of their co-operation in the Western Desert, wish to express their sympathy at the loss of this gallant little ship.

Cunningham himself had something of a soft spot for *Ladybird*.

> The *Ladybird's* sailors were intensely proud of their ship and her record. I visited some of her wounded in hospital and was greatly struck by their cheerfulness. Two young men in adjacent beds with only one leg between them made a very deep impression on me. They took their disability in such a fine spirit.

Aphis and *Gnat* had meanwhile been active in the Gulf of Sollum. On 12 April, as Rommel's advance units began consolidating their positions on the Egyptian frontier, Campbell received orders to investigate how matters lay in Bardia. Once more the *Aphis* penetrated the harbour in darkness and Campbell had himself rowed to the wooden jetty on its north shore. He had barely set foot upon it when he heard voices nearby, talking in German. The port was clearly in enemy hands and he quietly retraced his steps to the boat. So absorbed were the sentries in their conversation that neither its departure, nor that of the *Aphis* herself, attracted their interest.

Both gunboats duelled regularly with enemy artillery in the Sollum/Halfaya Pass area. On one occasion *Gnat* sustained minor damage but wiped out the offending battery in return. Having completed repairs, she replaced *Ladybird* at Tobruk and on the night of 14 May eliminated a heavy battery that had been bombarding the port area. Captain Poland, now commanding the Inshore Squadron, suggested that Davenport should strike his topmast to make her less conspicuous, and this was done. He also directed the gunboat to berth in a small creek which was eventually named *Gnat's* Cove. There, during the day, she sweated out the North African summer beneath camouflage nets, emerging at night to make the enemy's life as much a misery as had *Ladybird*. By now, *Cricket*, commanded by Lieutenant Commander Edwin Carnduff, had also reached Port Said from the Far East. After a long and difficult passage she required a refit but had to wait her turn while the dockyard dealt with larger warships damaged during the fighting off Greece and Crete. At length the work was completed and in June 1941 she received her first assignment, which was to join the sloop *Flamingo* and the whaler *Southern Isle* in escorting a small convoy bound for Tobruk.

At this stage almost anything that could float was being used to supply the embattled fortress. The convoy consisted of two small and very elderly Greek coasters, one of which was 50 years old and could only slop along at $4^1/2$ knots, thereby reducing the speed of the rest to a snail's pace. Air cover was provided by British and South African fighters but as the ships approached Tobruk during the afternoon of 30 June, these became involved in dogfights with enemy fighters escorting waves of dive bombers.

Carnduff successfully avoided damage during the first three attacks by waiting until he saw the bombs leave the aircraft and then jamming his triple rudders hard over, leaving the bombs to explode in the spot where she would have been. When the fourth German attack came in, however, the enemy had clearly decided to limit his options. While a Stuka approached from abeam, a Ju 88 came in from ahead. Carnduff delayed his helm order until the last possible minute, causing the Stuka to miss, but the Ju 88's 1000-pound bomb fell close alongside. The gunboat staggered under the impact of the explosion. Her decks were swamped with cascading water which flooded the engine and boiler rooms, wrecking the dynamo. Several men sustained leg and ankle injuries from the transmitted shockwave. Worst of all, the ship's frame was buckled, her bottom plating was distorted into metallic ripples, her machinery was damaged, she was making water and was down by the stern. While *Flamingo* escorted the convoy into Tobruk, *Southern Isle* stood by the crippled *Cricket* until nightfall and then towed her back to Mersa Matruh. The gunboat had fought her last fight.

Aphis relieved *Gnat* at Tobruk, continuing the work of battering the enemy's airfields and heavy artillery. The months of August, September and October were taken up with the relief by sea of the 9th Australian Division with the British 70th Division. During the early hours of 21 October, *Gnat*, having rejoined the fray after a rest period, was escorting several 'A' lighters – motorised landing barges – on their return journey from Tobruk, when she was torpedoed by *U.79*. The explosion blew off her bows, threw up such a column of water that she was all but swamped and flung on to her beam ends, and started fires. Slowly she righted herself but remained with a list to starboard and down by the head. While the crew were tackling fires and shoring up bulkheads, two more torpedoes were fired. One missed. The other, though running true, simply grazed its way under the gunboat's after part without exploding; imagining that he was dealing with a conventional warship, the U-boat captain had failed to allow for the fact that the gunboat's stern was drawing even less water than before.

The immediate danger past, Davenport was able to go slow ahead for a while in the hope that the shored bulkhead would hold. Gradually, however, with her deck awash, settling slowly by the head and steerage way lost, he was compelled to shut down the boilers. Help arrived in response to his report of the incident and the gunboat was taken in tow stern-first by the destroyer *Griffin*. Even so, as the sea rose during the night, it was considered unlikely she would survive. The crew were taken off but at dawn *Gnat* was still afloat, albeit with her rudders now clear of the water. The tow continued at four knots through a moderating sea until, west of Mersa Matruh, the naval tug *St Monance* appeared. Davenport and eleven of his men returned to the ship to transfer the tow from the *Griffin*. At 13:00 on 22 October, over 30 hours after the torpedo had struck, *Gnat* entered Alexandria to receive Admiral Cunningham's congratulations on a fine piece of seamanship. Some consideration was given to welding the undamaged bow of the *Cricket* to the *Gnat*'s still serviceable afterpart; that, after all, had happened in World War I to the similarly damaged destroyers *Zulu* and *Nubian*, thereby creating a new destroyer, the *Zubian*. Unfortunately, such were the difficulties involved and the pressures on the dockyard that the idea did not proceed. Though decommissioned, *Gnat* ended her days, still fighting, as an anti-aircraft gun platform at Fanana.

On 18 November Auchinleck's troops in North Africa, now designated the Eighth Army, commenced Operation Crusader, designed not only to relieve Tobruk but also to smash the Axis forces in Cyrenaica. During its advance, the Eighth Army, commanded in the early stages of the operation by Lieutenant-General Sir Alan Cunningham, the admiral's younger brother, and later by Major-General Neil Ritchie, bypassed the fortified frontier zone of Sollum–Halfaya Pass–Bardia, and advanced on Tobruk along two separate axes; simultaneously, the Tobruk garrison commenced a break-out operation intended to effect a junction with the relief force. The battle proved to be a far tougher and more protracted struggle than anyone had imagined, so that it was not until 7 December that Rommel took the decision to abandon Cyrenaica in order to save the remnant of his army. His isolated frontier garrisons, beyond hope of relief, were then methodically crushed. Overall, Axis casualties amounted to 38,000 killed, wounded and missing as against 18,000 British and Commonwealth; some 300 German and Italian tanks were destroyed compared to 278 British, although a high proportion of the latter could be recovered and repaired.

During the battle, *Aphis*, now commanded by Lieutenant John Cox, shelled the Gazala airfields on the night of 24/25 November, evidently to such good effect that over the next two days Tobruk harbour was subjected to a vindictive bombardment. Secure beneath their camouflage nets in *Gnat* Cove, *Aphis*'s crew watched the shells burst among the wrecks littering the water. On the night of 1/2 December, *Aphis* sallied forth again, but this time set her course eastwards to Gambut, around which elements of the 15th and 21st Panzer Divisions were leaguered. During an hour-long shoot, eighty-four 6-inch shells slammed into these already mauled formations. The treatment was repeated on 4 December, and again three days later. *Aphis* supported the Eighth Army's advance as far as Derna, ferrying stores and personnel as well as escorting smaller vessels. While so engaged, she contemptuously evaded a torpedo dropped by a Heinkel He 111, turning so quickly on to a parallel course that the pilot was mortified to see his fish miss by a good 50 yards.

By now the ship's 6-inch guns were completely worn out. They were replaced by *Cricket*'s, which retained their accuracy but were so slow to run out from full recoil that they required manual assistance. On 31 December, while the 2nd South African Division was fighting its way into Bardia, *Aphis*, *Southern Maid* and the cruiser *Ajax* of River Plate fame provided gunfire support. As the enemy's return fire was falling uncomfortably close, Cox led the two smaller ships out to extreme range, dropping a smoke float which effectively distracted the enemy's gunners. The 8000-strong garrison surrendered at dawn on 2 January. The South Africans also took Sollum, although Halfaya Pass held out until 17 January, by which time many of its garrison were close to dying of thirst.

With the relief of Tobruk, the most important function of the Inshore Squadron came to an end. Three of the four gunboats to serve with the squadron had been lost and, for the moment, *Aphis* alone remained, her contribution eclipsed by great events on land and the epic siege of Malta.

Just as, a year earlier, Wavell had been forced to send troops to Greece, so now Auchinleck was required by Japan's entry into the war to despatch reinforcements to the Far East, thereby weakening the Eighth Army. In the third week of January 1942, Rommel, having himself been reinforced, returned to the offensive. He did not achieve quite the same runaway success as he had the previous year, but he did recover the Benghazi Bulge. The line was stabilised at Gazala and a new front established, running south to Bir Hacheim. Both sides prepared for the next round but it was Rommel who struck first, on 26 May. During the ensuing Battle of Gazala/Knightsbridge the Eighth Army sustained the worst defeat in its history. It was during this that one of the Royal Navy's most famous gunboat captains, Admiral Sir Walter Cowan, whom we have already met bombarding the Mahdi's tomb and in the Baltic, went into captivity. Although long retired and in his seventies, the outbreak of World War II provided him with a chance for yet more fighting. He was absolutely adamant that he was not going to be left out and in due course he was found the task of naval liaison officer to an Indian brigade with the honorary rank of commander. His duties cannot have been exacting, for during the Gazala battle the brigade was operating 40 miles from the sea. When it was overrun, Cowan climbed stiffly from his slit trench and emptied his revolver point blank at a German tank.

Gentlemanly instincts still existed on the battlefield, for the crew did not return fire and led him away with the respect due to his age and rank. The following year he was exchanged for an Italian officer of equivalent standing. On his return he swore to Admiral Cunningham that if he had been properly supported, and possessed a few more rounds of ammunition, he would have captured the tank!

In the immediate aftermath of his victory Rommel stormed Tobruk, an event which won him his field marshal's baton. He then decided to use the huge quantities of captured fuel and stores to pursue the badly rattled British into Egypt. As his advance rolled eastwards beyond the frontier, it captured Mersa Matruh, the former base of the Inshore Squadron. Auchinleck assumed personal command of the Eighth Army and in the month-long, bitterly contested First Battle of Alamein fought the Axis army to a standstill. Despite this, Churchill felt that a change at the top was needed. General Sir Harold Alexander took over as Commander-in-Chief Middle East while Lieutenant-General Bernard Montgomery arrived from England to command the Eighth Army.

Across the lines, Rommel was beginning to regret his opportunism. He now lay at the end of a long and very difficult supply line, had burned most of the fuel captured at Tobruk. and was receiving barely sufficient to meet his daily requirements. At Alam Halfa on 31 August, he made one last attempt to regain the initiative but was thwarted by a rock-solid defence.

Montgomery continued to restore his own army's morale, building up its strength until he was confident of victory. The Second Battle of Alamein, commencing on 23 October, reduced Rommel's German divisions to skeletons and destroyed most of the Italian divisions where they stood. Rallying such survivors as he could, Rommel began his long retreat, knowing that this time there could be no halting on the Egyptian frontier or on the border of Tripolitania, for on 8 November the Anglo-American First Army had landed in French North Africa. In such circumstances the best he could hope for was to reach Tunisia, which Hitler and Mussolini had decided would become a Fascist redoubt.

During the final stages of the North African campaign, *Aphis*, commanded by Lieutenant Commander Frank Bethel, was based first at Tripoli and then at Sousse. On 21 March 1943, as part of a feint to distract the enemy's attention while Montgomery outflanked the prepared defences of the Mareth Line, she carried out a bombardment of Gabes, flattening the railway station and reducing a staff officers' accommodation block to rubble. More importantly, wild rumours circulated that the entire Mediterranean Fleet was firing the preparatory bombardment for a landing resulted in troops being withdrawn from the Mareth Line, as intended.

Following the Axis surrender in North Africa, plans were immediately made for the invasion of Sicily. Before they could be activated, however, the heavily fortified Italian island of Pantellaria, lying between Sicily and Tunisia, would have to be neutralised. On 11 June *Aphis* formed part of the bombardment force which softened up the defences, firing accurately at targets in the harbour area. Hardly had the assault wave gone in than the island's commander, Admiral Pavesi, indicated that he wished to surrender because of a water shortage. This was simply an excuse, for his men were already giving up in droves, providing a clear indication that the average Italian was no longer interested in fighting for Hitler and Mussolini.

It was now apparent that impending naval operations in the Mediterranean theatre of war would again involve a considerable amount of inshore activity. Because of this two more Insect class gunboats, the *Cockchafer* under Lieutenant Arthur Dow, RNVR, and the *Scarab* under Lieutenant E. Cameron, RNZVR, were detached from their station at Basra in April 1943 and sent under tow to join the Mediterranean Fleet. They joined *Aphis* at Malta, where final preparations for the invasion of Sicily were under way. As a result of experience, the Insects' light automatic anti-aircraft weapons had been augmented, most being mounted forward. In addition to her heavier weapons, *Aphis* now possessed an Oerlikon and two 20mm Bredas, while *Cockchafer* and *Scarab*, having disposed of their pom-poms, mounted seven Oerlikons each.

Thereafter, the Insects took part in the preliminary bombardment for the landings in Sicily, where *Cockchafer*'s gunners shot down an enemy aircraft off Catania, and in the toe of Italy, being joined sometimes by the monitor *Erebus*, sister ship to the *Terror*. By now, however, the elderly gunboats were beginning to show their many years of hard usage, *Cockchafer*'s engines·in particular giving much cause for anxiety. In normal circumstances the Insects would have been scrapped long since, but the fact was they were doing a useful job and, since they could not be replaced, they were sent to Egypt for overhaul. As part of this they were each rearmed with a later and more powerful mark of 6-inch gun.

During the autumn of 1943 the French had gained control of Corsica. The following spring it was decided that this would serve as a base from which the island of Elba, lying off the west coast of Italy and dominating the coastal shipping routes between with its coastal batteries, could be captured. Elba, once the pocket kingdom of Napoleon Bonaparte's first exile, is eighteen miles long, nine miles across at its widest point, and mountainous. Its garrison was said to consist of some 800 Poles and Czechs who had been conscripted into the German Army and whose morale was low. The truth was that there were 2600 good-quality German troops manning well-prepared defences throughout the island.

Nevertheless, nothing was left to chance. The assault force, consisting of French Commandos and the French 9th Colonial Division, would receive gunfire support from *Aphis*, *Cockchafer* and *Scarab*, the last now commanded by Lieutenant E. A. Hawksworth, RNVR. Having completed their refit, the gunboats sailed via Malta to Porto Vecchio in Corsica where the invasion fleet was assembling. It consisted of the headquarters ship *Royal Scotsman*, flying the flag of Rear Admiral Thomas Troubridge, 124 landing craft of various types and a flotilla of minesweepers, escorted by 28 British and American torpedo boats.

The invasion force sailed on 16 June, approaching Elba during the early hours of the following day. The gunboats commenced their bombardment and the commandos slid ashore in their assault boats to neutralise the coast defence batteries. Then, as in any military operation, unforeseen events induced a radical change of circumstances. At Marina di Campo, the principal landing area, a British naval beach commando unit stormed into the harbour to capture an armed lighter and cut the wires of the enemy's demolition charges on the mole. Unfortunately, enemy artillery fire detonated the charges. The immediate result of the explosion was that 35 of the beach commando were killed and 18 wounded; furthermore, as the light strengthened, yet more enemy guns began concentrating on the area and the landing craft standing off the beaches. At this point the Insects, which had been engaging their designated targets, joined in the fray, systematically eliminating the enemy's field batteries one after another under the direction of their Royal Artillery Forward Observation Officers, enabling the landing to continue. Elsewhere, although a commando attack on a coast defence battery at Cape Enfola destroyed four of its 6-inch guns, a similar battery at Cape Ripalti beat off its attackers and was only neutralised when the gunboats intervened. Throughout the day, while the French consolidated their gains ashore, the Insects continued to engage numerous targets, earning the highest praise from the FOOs for the accuracy of their shooting. By evening they had expended a total of some 500 rounds of 6-inch ammunition. *Scarab*, her magazine empty, returned to base to replenish, followed the next day by *Aphis* and the day after by *Cockchafer*, which at one stage had become the target of heavy coast defence guns firing from Piombino on the Italian mainland. On the morning of 19 June the remnant of the garrison surrendered, having sustained the loss of over 500 killed. French casualties amounted to 400 killed and 600 wounded, while those of the Royal Navy were 65 killed and 58 wounded. The operation had succeeded, but at such a price that it was later described as 'a bloody little sideshow'.

In the wider sphere the Allies were now firmly ashore in Normandy, though facing a fanatical defence. The Supreme Command decided that the moment had come to activate Operation Dragoon, a landing on the French Riviera by the French First and US Seventh Armies which would effectively turn the flank of the German army groups in northern France. As *Cockchafer*'s engines were again giving trouble, *Aphis* and *Scarab* alone were detailed to work under American naval command as part of a group known as Task Force 80.4, the function of which was to jam the enemy's radar and, using reflector balloons, create false radar targets with the object of confusing the Germans as to precisely where the landings would take place; once this phase had been completed, the two Insects were to close the range and bombard targets between Antibes and the River Var for an hour. Operation Dragoon took place on 15 August and was a complete success. According to German radio broadcasts seeking excuses for the invaders' success, Antibes and Nice had been shelled by four or five battleships, a claim which gave the gunboat crews much satisfaction.

On the misty, drizzling morning of 17 August, Task Force 80.4 was approaching the main assault area when one of the American torpedo boats picked up strange contacts on her radar. When challenged, the strangers opened fire. The PT boat turned away, signalling a warning of the hostile presence to those astern.

The enemy ships were the former Italian corvette *Capriola*, armed with two 3.9-inch and eight 37mm guns, and an armed yacht, the *Kemid Allah*, both now flying the German naval ensign. Hoping to make a killing among the smaller craft, they pursued the retreating PT boat. Simultaneously, *Aphis* and *Scarab* broke out their battle ensigns, working their speed up to a rivet-rattling 15 knots for which they had not been designed. Some 20 minutes after the initial contact report they had the enemy in sight and opened fire at a range of 12,000 yards.

During the ensuing battle most of the technical advantages lay with the enemy, for although the British ships threw the heavier weight of metal, the Germans had the better fire control system and were much faster. Soon the gunboats' decks were being lashed with spray and shell splinters. It was known that the American destroyer *Endicott*, with Lieutenant Commander John D. Bulkeley, Task Force 80.4's commander, aboard, was coming up fast, and that she would soon be in a position to cut off the enemy's retreat. To conceal the fact, the Insects made smoke. From time to time they would emerge from the screen to loose off a salvo or two, then retire into concealment. An hour after the engagement had begun, one of their shells penetrated the *Capriola*'s hull amidships. The corvette blew up in a tremendous eruption of flame and smoke.

Simultaneously, another 6-inch shell burst on the foredeck of the *Kemid Allah*. The auxiliary made off to the west as fast as she could go but she was already too late. With her ensign streaming and a bone in her teeth, the *Endicott* was already closing in at 36 knots. Three of her four 5-inch guns were overheated after bombarding coastal batteries at La Ciotat and the fourth could only be operated with difficulty, firing one round a minute, so Bulkeley also engaged with his 40mm anti-aircraft armament. Within an hour the gunboats and the destroyer had reduced the German ship to a burning wreck. Over 200 survivors were picked up, the older hands pleased that their war was over, the younger still sufficiently self-confident to give the Nazi salute as the *Kemid Allah* rolled over on her way to the bottom. It was a reaction that the gunboatmen found difficult to understand, given that the days of Adolf Hitler and his evil regime were now so obviously nearing their end. During the battle the only casualties sustained by the Allies were three of *Endicott*'s men wounded by shell splinters. In passing it should be mentioned that Bulkeley was a distinguished PT boat commander who, two years earlier, had rescued General Douglas MacArthur from the besieged fortress of Corregidor in Manila Bay, for which feat he was awarded the Medal of Honor; also that one of the PT boats forming part of Task Force 80.4 was commanded by Lieutenant Commander Douglas Fairbanks, Jr, the film star.

Aphis and *Scarab* were rewarded with permission to splice the mainbrace, followed by a rest period in Naples. Shortly after, they moved to a new base at Ancona on the Adriatic coast of Italy. During the autumn of 1944 they provided gunfire support for the Eighth Army as it fought its way through the formidable defences of the Gothic Line. There we shall leave them to fade away, as old warriors do, for early in 1945 they were, like *Cockchafer*, reduced to care and maintenance status.

The Insect class, hard working and hard hitting, had served their country well throughout two world wars and the years between. *Scarab* was the last of them to go, being sold for scrap at Singapore in 1948.

12
IMPERIAL ECHO
The Detention and Escape of HMS *Amethyst,* 1949

Although Japan had been decisively defeated in 1945, her earlier victories over the colonial powers, and in particular the capture of Singapore, marked an historical turning point in the relationship between East and West. Never again would the peoples of the Far East regard their former masters in quite the same light as of yore, for their fallibility had been ruthlessly exposed by an Oriental power.

China, as always, had special problems of her own. From 1927 onwards, a state of civil war had existed between General Chiang Kai-shek's Nationalist Party and the country's communist element, led by Chou En-lai and Mao Tse-tung. An uneasy truce existed between them for much of China's struggle against Japan, but the war was resumed with renewed vigour once the Japanese had been defeated. The fighting was centred on the northern industrial areas of Manchuria. Chiang, the recipient of American aid, retained the upper hand until 1947. The following year, however, the situation began to change dramatically when the Russians handed over the tanks and artillery they had taken from the Japanese when they overran Manchuria during the last weeks of World War II. With both sides now equipped with comparatively modern weapons, the contest was between Nationalist corruption, incompetence and poor leadership on the one hand, and communist discipline and determination on the other. In November 1948 the Nationalist stronghold of Mukden fell. Quickly redeploying, the communists trapped four Nationalist armies in the area of Huai Hai. Following one of the greatest and most decisive battles of the century, the Nationalists surrendered on 10 January 1949. As Chiang had no more armies to field, the communists were able to overrun central and southern China at their leisure. By October 1949 their hold on the mainland was complete, Chiang and his followers having withdrawn to Taiwan and a few offshore islands under American protection.

For commercial organisations trying to re-establish their trading links in China the situation was fraught with difficulties and potential violence. Anyone who wanted could obtain access to arms. There were weapons a-plenty left behind by the defeated Japanese, American-supplied weapons for sale by corrupt Nationalists, and British weapons captured by the Japanese in Hong Kong, Malaya and Burma. It was, therefore, hardly surprising that the ancient trade of piracy should enjoy a resurgence, nor that the Royal Navy should react by sending warships to police those trade routes that had been reopened.

Sometimes, both sides received an unpleasant shock. It was bad enough that the pirates should be able to lay their hands on automatic weapons of various calibres with which to arm their motorised junks, but the mounting of modern field guns was a stage worse. Against this, the Royal Navy's use of submarines and aircraft in coastal waters would have been viewed by the pirates as being distinctly unfair. During one such encounter a submarine surfaced near a suspect junk to find the enemy baring his teeth in the form of a former British 25-pounder gun-howitzer. The pirates got off the first shot but, as they did not under-stand the characteristics of the howitzer, their shell more or less fell out of the muzzle to land between the two vessels. Under no such handicap, the submarine's 4-inch gun crew quickly finished the matter.

Useful though submarines might be in coastal waters, the task of safeguarding British interests on the great rivers could only be performed by small surface warships. One such was the frigate *Amethyst* of the Modified *Black Swan* class. Displacing 1350 tons, *Amethyst* was driven by two-shaft geared turbines producing 4300 shp, giving her a maximum theoretical speed of 20 knots. Her arma-ment consisted of six 4-inch guns, plus two 40mm Bofors anti-aircraft guns and two 20mm Oerlikon cannon. Launched on the Clyde in 1943, she claimed a share in the destruction of *U.482* off the Scottish coast in January 1945 and the following month sank *U.1208* in the Western Approaches. She had then moved to the Far East and was present at the surrender of the Japanese forces in New Guinea. More recently, she had been patrolling the Malayan coast during operations to counter communist terrorism.

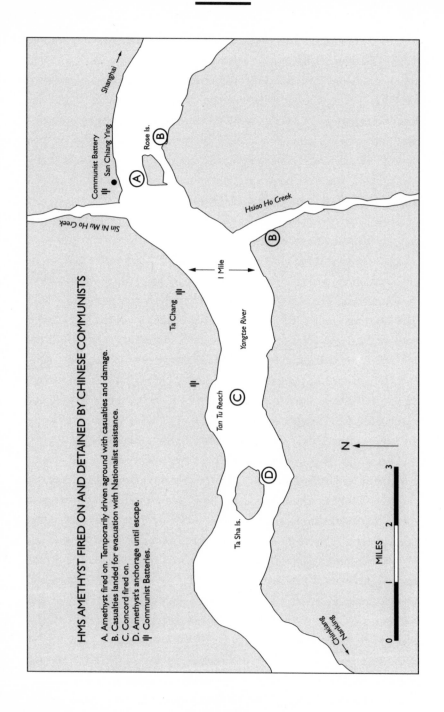

HMS AMETHYST FIRED ON AND DETAINED BY CHINESE COMMUNISTS

A. Amethyst fired on. Temporarily driven aground with casualties and damage.
B. Casualties landed for evacuation with Nationalist assistance.
C. Concord fired on.
D. Amethyst's anchorage until escape.
⫿ Communist Batteries.

On 20 April 1949, under the command of Lieutenant Commander
B. M. Skinner, *Amethyst* was proceeding up the Yangtse with the
intention of relieving the destroyer *Consort* as guardship at Nanking.
Her crew numbered in all 160 officers, ratings and Chinese, the last
being employed in their usual tasks as cooks, stewards, laundrymen
and tailors. The Nationalist forces on the south bank of the river had
been forewarned of her movement but, perhaps unwisely, the communist Chinese People's Liberation Army, already preparing to mount a
crossing from the north bank, had not, although she was flying the
White Ensign and had large canvas Union Jacks ready to unfurl along
her sides, clearly demonstrating her neutrality. Aware of the potential
dangers, Skinner kept his crew at first-degree readiness.

At about 08:30, opposite Low Island, small arms fire was directed at
the ship from the north bank, supplemented by ineffective artillery fire.
Skinner broke out his battle ensigns, ordered the Union Jacks to be
unfurled along the sides, and instructed the gunnery officer to open fire
as soon as a target could be identified. The mist prevented this and, after
firing a dozen or so rounds, the communist battery lapsed into silence.
Having made no reply, *Amethyst* continued on her way, expecting to
reach Nanking that afternoon.

Forty minutes later she was running parallel with Rose Island, flat
and marshy, to port. To starboard was a small village named San Chiang
Ying at the junction of Sin Ni Mu Ho Creek with the Yangtse. Moored
in the creek were a number of craft the communists intended using in
their planned assault crossing. At 09:20 a battery near the village
opened fire on the frigate. Skinner ordered his engines to full ahead and
turned *Amethyst*'s bows towards the friendly Nationalist bank in the
hope of opening the range. Almost immediately, enemy shells burst in
the wheelhouse, killing or wounding most of those within. The ship
continued to turn to port. Her first lieutenant, Geoffrey Weston, had
run for the bridge as soon as the battery opened fire. As he arrived,
Skinner ordered him to open fire in return. Hardly had he passed the
authorisation to the director tower than two shells exploded on the
bridge, killing or wounding everyone present. Skinner was mortally
wounded and semi-conscious. A shell splinter penetrated Weston's

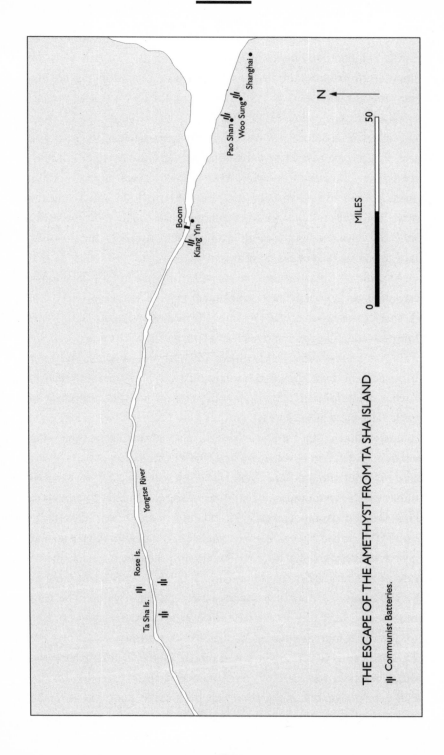

THE ESCAPE OF THE AMETHYST FROM TA SHA ISLAND

╫ Communist Batteries.

chest, damaging his lower lungs before lodging itself in his liver. Coughing blood and in intense pain, he assumed command, ordering the wheel to be put hard a-starboard and the engines full astern. It was too late. Very gently, *Amethyst* slid on to a mudbank beside Rose Island, leaving her stern exposed to the enemy.

Weston despatched a 'flash' radio signal to the effect that the ship was under heavy fire, aground and had already sustained a large number of casualties. Wondering why the guns were not replying to the enemy, he discovered that the low-power room, which generated much of the ship's electricity, had been damaged by another hit. As a result of this, the vital gun-control circuits between the director tower and the gun positions had been severed. Weston therefore authorised X gun, located aft and the only mounting that would bear on the target, to engage under local control. It continued to bang steadily away until a direct hit killed most of the crew. The communists continued to hammer the ship, punching a waterline hole into the tiller flat and inflicting further damage. The deck was now covered with dead and dying men. When a shell wrecked the sick bay, Surgeon-Lieutenant Alderton and Sick Berth Attendant Baker attended to their patients on deck; both were killed by the same bursting shell.

From time to time Weston collapsed or passed out. He decided upon a partial evacuation of the vessel until nightfall, using the only remaining boat to ferry the wounded to Rose Island, 150 yards distant. This seemed to enrage the communists, who opened fire with machine guns, indiscriminately shooting at swimmers and the wounded in the boat. After some 60 men had been put ashore, the evacuation was stopped. As if by tacit agreement, the shelling also stopped, although the enemy continued to play his machine guns along the ship's upperworks. Below, repair parties began the work of restoring the electricity supply, plugging the hole in the tiller flat and carrying out other essential repairs.

Heat and humidity rose as morning turned to afternoon. At about 14:30 the lookout left in the comparative security of B gun reported that a warship was approaching from the direction of Nanking. She was *Consort*, under Commander I. G. Roberston, responding to *Amethyst*'s 'flash' message, and she was doing so in some style.

Although she was flying no less than seven White Ensigns and three Union Jacks, she had come under fire herself as she entered the Tan Tu Reach, downstream of Chinkiang. Now, with her 4.5-inch guns blazing to port, she was coming on at 29 knots, a speed never seen before on the Yangtse, creating a huge bone in her teeth. At least three field guns were blown apart and the enemy was obviously sustaining casualties. As she drew level with *Amethyst* she enquired by signal lamp whether it would be possible to tow the stricken ship off the mudbank. Weston replied that it would not until the communist guns had been silenced, but was confident that she could get off under her own steam that night. *Consort* reversed course below Rose Island, turning to make another pass at the enemy. By now, however, the communists were frantically hauling anti-tank guns from their landing craft. At a range of only 400 yards these began pumping high-velocity solid shot into the destroyer. The bridge and wheelhouse were hit and both forward gun turrets were put out of action. Having completed her second pass, *Consort* had no alternative but to retire down-river. She had sustained no less than 56 hits, eight of her crew were dead and 30 were wounded.

Once more, *Amethyst* was alone. At 16:00 Weston was hailed by his men ashore on Rose Island. They had, it seemed, made contact with Nationalist troops who were arranging for their evacuation. Weston therefore decided to land the remainder of his wounded at the more suit-able location of Hsiao Ho Creek, some four miles upstream. During the evening the engines were started and, after a quarter of an hour's pulling, *Amethyst* was refloated at 00:15 on 21 April. Proceeding stealthily up-river, she anchored off the mouth of the creek. During the next evening the wounded were taken ashore and, as at Rose Island, the Nationalists did everything they could to care for them and speed their evacuation.

By now, news of the outrage had spread around the world, causing uproar in diplomatic circles. On the morning of 21 April the cruiser *London* and the *Black Swan* tried to fight their way up to *Amethyst* from the river mouth but were forced to retire with casualties and damage. Inevitably, the unwelcome question arose as to how many lives and ships could be risked in further attempts to rescue the trapped frigate. It was decided to discontinue direct action but later in the day a Sunderland flying boat put down beside the ship. Coming under shellfire at once, the aircraft was forced to take off immediately, but not before an RAF doctor, Flight Lieutenant M. E. Fearnley, had jumped aboard a Nationalist sampan to be ferried to the *Amethyst*. His first decision was that Weston should be evacuated with the rest of the wounded, but the latter refused.

In fact, after receiving a dose of benzedrine to keep himself awake, Weston returned to the bridge to comply with an order he had received to take the ship about ten miles upstream, where the anchor was dropped off the eastern end of Ta Sha Island. Once more the *Amethyst* came under fire, forcing him to move two miles upstream. During the afternoon of the 22nd Lieutenant Commander J. S. Kerans came aboard from a Nationalist craft and assumed command. Kerans, attached to the embassy in Nanking, had been ordered to board *Amethyst* two days earlier and although he had just missed the frigate as she left Hsiao Ho Creek, he had been able to arrange transport for the wounded in very difficult circumstances. Weston, whose physical condition had begun to deteriorate, was ordered ashore for medical treatment and evacuation. After this Kerans conducted a funeral service for the dead, 17 in number, committing their bodies to the river. There was, at this time, no predicting how the communists would behave. Sometimes they fired at *Amethyst* only when she was moving, and sometimes only when she dropped anchor. The following day, therefore, Kerans moved the ship a mile or so downstream to a point where there was no cover for the enemy's artillery and snipers on the shore of Ta Sha Island. There she would remain during the most protracted phase of her ordeal. Instructions to scuttle her were modified to include the possibility of escape or proceeding down-river under a safe conduct, the terms of which were apparently being negotiated.

By the following morning the Nationalists had vanished from the south bank of the mile-wide river and that afternoon the communists began ferrying their own troops across in hundreds of junks, sampans and small motorised craft. The majority soon disappeared in pursuit of their retreating enemy. The only opposition came from nine Nationalist warships coming down-river from Nanking after dark, but after an hour-long engagement they continued on their way to the sea. Kerans toyed with the idea of slipping out under their cover but rejected it because of possible accusations of collusion with the Nationalists at a time of great political sensitivity.

On 26 April the communists requested a meeting ashore. Kerans was unwilling to risk losing one of his few officers but Petty Officer W. H. Freeman volunteered for the task. To give him 'face' he was dressed in an officer's uniform. In a dirty farmhouse Freeman met a 'Major Kung' who said he commanded the battery at San Chiang Lin. He accused the *Amethyst* of opening fire first, which Freeman hotly denied, and remarked that the fire of the two British warships had caused 252 casualties and much damage. He then said he was unable to issue a safe conduct, which was a matter for higher authority in Nanking, but that if the ship remained where she was and gave no trouble, she would not be molested. Continuing in English, he commented that the British and Chinese had always been friends and, in view of the damage to *Amethyst*'s boats, placed a sampan at her disposal.

Freeman's report of the interview enabled Kerans to interpret the situation correctly. The communists had made a serious error of judgement, but as they never admitted to such things, the question of 'face' was involved, particularly in view of the hostile international reaction to the outrage. This became clearer when Kerans personally attended a meeting with the communist area commander, General Yuan Chung-hsien, who was accompanied by a Colonel Kang Mao-chao, political commissar of the 3rd Artillery Regiment, who bore a startling resemblance to 'Major Kung' and who, like the alleged battery commander, could speak English when the mood took him. As the weeks passed, further meetings were held. General Yuan rarely attended but, reading between the lines, it became obvious that he expected Kang to sort out his own mess. Kang tried bullying and intimidation, demanding an admission of guilt and the promise of compensation, without result. Then he tried the communist tactic of appearing to soften his demands at the end of one meeting, only to begin the next with even harsher requirements. Kerans quickly saw that he was desperate for an acceptable form of words and took advice via the radio from the diplomatic service. This allowed him to use the words 'indiscreet intrusion', but they did not go far enough for the commissar, who preferred to talk in terms of 'brutal acts'.

In fact, while *Amethyst* might remain a virtual prisoner, Kang was skating on very thin ice whenever Kerans took the offensive. Two wounded seamen, too ill to be moved from hospital, had been detained in Chinkiang when the communists overran the town. Kerans, pointing out that their continued detention would damage not only Sino-British friendship but also the international reputation of the CPLA, demanded their return at once. Kang complied. When Kerans complained that even the Japanese treated their prisoners better that the CPLA was treating the crew of the *Amethyst*, Kang immediately arranged for a contractor's boat to visit the ship and sanctioned the barter of supplies for fresh vegetables, albeit at an extortionate rate. Worried by his diminishing supply of fuel oil, Kerans asked for more. Kang said there was none. Kerans pointed out that there was a British dump at Nanking, bought and paid for by the Admiralty. Kang was forced to give way, but charged £500 for its delivery.

And so it went on, with the frustrated Kang becoming ever more belligerent as he failed to get what he wanted. The possibility also had to be borne in mind that the commissar was capable of provoking an 'incident' involving loss of life that would prove he had been right all along. By the fourth week of July the prospect of a safe conduct seemed as far away as ever and the fuel supply was beginning to run low again. The morale of the crew, now only some 70 strong, remained good despite 100 days of heat, humidity, confinement and boredom. The overall situation had changed, too. It was true that there were batteries covering *Amethyst*'s position, and more batteries down-river, but the war had moved away to the south and the passage, while hazardous, would not present the dangers it had in April. Taking all these factors into account, Kerans discussed the possibility of a break-out with his superiors, who promised to respect his judgement. He decided to break out on the night of 30 July, when the new moon would set at 23:00, but kept his thoughts to himself until the last possible minute. At 17:00 he despatched a 'flash' message to the commander-in-chief and *Concord*, now lying off the mouth of the river.

Top Secret C-in-C, repeat Concord, *from Kerans. I am going to try and break out at 10 p.m. tonight 30 July.* Concord *set watch 8290 kilocycles.*

He briefed his officers in turn during the afternoon, then summoned the chief and petty officers and key ratings to his cabin at 19:45. The anchor would be slipped, its passage through the hawsehole muffled with heavy grease and bedding. A canvas screen was to be erected from A gun to the bow, giving the ship a passing resemblance to a Chinese landing craft. Green-over-red yard-arm lights, as carried by civilian river traffic, were to be prepared. As the ship was now short-handed, only B gun and one of the Oerlikons would be manned. After dark, noise and movement on the upper deck were to be kept to an absolute minimum. A special watch was to be kept on the Chinese crewmen, just in case some of them had changed their allegiance since coming within the sphere of communist influence.

As 22:00 approached, all was ready. There was a sense of keen anticipation throughout the ship. In the engine room machinery hummed quietly, awaiting the demands that would be made upon it. High above, the young moon had begun its descent, but Kerans decided to wait a few moments longer until it was obscured by an approaching cloud. Suddenly, a fully lit merchant vessel, the *Kiang Ling Liberation*, rounded the bend of Ta Sha Island, travelling down-stream. At last *Amethyst* had been granted a slice of luck, for here was an unwitting pilot who would lead her down-river past Rose Island, the one stretch for which Kerans lacked a chart. He gave the order for Slow Ahead. Gently, *Amethyst* closed up to her anchor cable.

'Slip!'

The pin was knocked out and the cable slid noiselessly into the water below.

'Wheel hard a-starboard. Half astern starboard, half ahead port.'

Slowly, the frigate turned until she was in midstream, her bows pointing towards freedom.

'Stop starboard. Half ahead both. Midships.'

Now, unknown to those aboard the freighter, *Amethyst* was dogging the footsteps of the *Kiang Ling Liberation*. The mood of exhilaration grew as the gentle breeze created by the ship's passage freshened the air. Half an hour passed without incident until they were opposite Ta Chang, the known location of an enemy battery. A flare soared into the air from the shore. The *Kiang Ling Liberation* responded with a coded siren signal. At this point Kerans observed the lights of an armed landing craft off his port bow. A second flare soared skywards, illuminating the *Amethyst*.

All hell broke loose. The landing craft fired a machine gun across the frigate's bows. It entered the battery position opposite. The next minute guns on both banks opened a wild fire and tracer criss-crossed the river.

Amethyst shuddered as a shell exploded close to her starboard water-line. The ship's Brens and the Oerlikon replied, joined by a single round from B gun.

'Full ahead both engines – make smoke! Make to C-in-C: *I am under heavy fire and have been hit!*'

The *Kiang Ling Liberation* had hastily turned off her lights and was swinging to port. *Amethyst*, her oily smoke screen smothering the scene as she worked up to her maximum speed, raced past, avoiding collision by a mere 18 inches. The worst of the danger was now past. With grim satisfaction, those on deck watched the comrades fighting their increasingly furious battle astern. The *Kiang Ling Liberation* had already been smashed into a blazing wreck and the landing craft was in serious trouble, too.

Making 22 knots, *Amethyst* passed Rose Island at 22:50. The temperature in the engine room rose to 120 degrees, that in the boiler room to 170 degrees. Shortly before 01:00 the frigate was approaching Kiang Yin, a former Nationalist naval base. Here she was again challenged and for about 15 minutes came under inaccurate fire from the shore and a ship. At Kiang Yin itself there was known to be a boom across the river. A channel through the boom was normally marked by two lit buoys, but only one was visible. Kerans decided to shave it as close to starboard as possible. Belching smoke from her funnel, *Amethyst* charged past the hazard, all but running down a small boom defence vessel in the process.

At 02:45 Kerans sent a brief signal to Admiral Sir Patrick Brind, the Commander-in-Chief, informing him that *Amethyst* had covered 100 miles. *A magnificent century*, Brind replied. Shortly after, to Kerans's regret, *Amethyst* ran down an unlit junk which simply disintegrated under her bows. By now, those in the engine and boiler rooms were beginning to suffer from heatstroke. Fearnley, the RAF doctor, had them placed under fans and revived them with salt and water. All insisted on returning to duty. Most drank a gallon of tea during the night.

There remained only one serious obstacle – the coast defence batteries at Pao Shan and Woo Sung, which were armed with 6-inch guns capable of crippling the frigate with a single direct hit. *Consort* was known to be standing off the river mouth and Kerans made arrangements for her to support him if the need arose, estimating his time of arrival as being 05:30. By 05:00 the cold white beams of the forts' searchlights could be seen probing the waters of the estuary. Kerans ordered the engine room to give him everything it had got, even if it involved damage to the engines themselves. Trailing smoke, *Amethyst* entered the danger area. The tense silence aboard was broken by a collective intake of breath as the ship was briefly caught in peripheral light, but there was no response from the enemy and not one of their beams touched her directly. After what seemed very long minutes the frigate left the illuminated area astern and again tasted the salt water of the open sea.

'We're out, lads! We're out!' were the jubilant shouts from all quarters as the word was passed. The time was 05:29. Ahead was the hazy outline of a warship which soon solidified into *Concord.* Her signal lamp began to blink.

Fancy meeting you again!

The depth of Kerans's relief can be judged by his reply:

Never, repeat never, has a ship been more welcome.

He then signalled Admiral Brind: *Have rejoined the Fleet south of Woo Sung. No damage or casualties. God save the King.*

Brind replied promptly: *Welcome back to the Fleet. We are all extremely proud of your most gallant and skilful escape and that endurance and fortitude displayed by everyone has been rewarded with such success. Your bearing in adversity and your daring passage tonight will be an epic in the history of the Navy.*

After *Concord* had replenished *Amethyst's* all but empty fuel tanks the frigate proceeded to Hong Kong, where she was cheered into harbour and received a tumultuous welcome. Among those waiting to greet her were the Governor, the Commander-in-Chief, the General Officer Commanding, the Air Officer Commanding and all the colony's dignitaries. Then the telegrams and messages of congratulation began to arrive by the sack-load, including a personal signal from King George VI himself:

> *Please convey to the commanding officer and ship's company of HMS* Amethyst *my hearty congratulations on their daring exploit to rejoin the Fleet. The courage, skill and determination shown by all on board have my highest commendation. Splice the mainbrace.*
>
> George R.

There were similar messages from all over the world, from the sister services, from the United States Navy, from cities, towns, commercial organisations, schools, scout groups, clubs of all sorts and from numberless private individuals in many countries. Simon and Peggy, respectively the ship's cat and dog, also received vast quantities of fan mail.

At the end of September, repaired and spruced up, *Amethyst* began the long voyage home, being fêted at whatever port she called. When she docked at Devonport on 1 November, there were, among those waiting on the quay, those who had been evacuated after the action at Rose Island, some still showing signs of their wounds. The ship's company then marched through the streets of the town to a civic luncheon. Later, they joined the ships' companies of *London, Consort* and *Black Swan* and the crew of the Sunderland flying boat for a march through the beflagged, crowded streets of London for a reception at the Guildhall, followed by a march to Buckingham Palace for a special investiture. Among those who were honoured, Kerans received the Distinguished Service Order and Weston a Bar to his Distinguished Service Cross.

Naturally, the Chinese communists were incoherent with fury. What had happened went far beyond loss of 'face', for one little ship had exposed them to the whole world as a set of bungling, incompetent fools. In a wild and rather pointless reaction the Yangtse was closed to traffic for two days. For a while foreign residents, especially Westerners, went in real fear for their lives. No doubt the party carried out its own inquest into the disaster, and the party was seldom inclined to show mercy to those who failed it.

It was not until 3 August that the *New China News Agency* found its voice. It described the *Amethyst*'s escape as 'infamous', harked back to the events of 20 April, then accused the frigate of every possible atrocity relating to the loss of the *Kiang Ling Liberation*. What seemed to rankle most deeply, however, was the sheer ingratitude displayed by those aboard the *Amethyst* to their captors. They had been allowed mail, supplied with oil and permitted to purchase fresh fruit and vegetables, yet their response to all this kindness had been to escape! This, commented General Yuan Chung-hsien sagely, was how imperialists repaid good with evil! On balance a dignified silence might have been more appropriate, or even a suggestion that *Amethyst* had been released, but subtlety never was a communist forte.

The communists have never explained why they opened fire on *Amethyst* on 20 April, nor will they. One explanation, put forward by C. E. Lucas Phillips in his book *Escape of the Amethyst*, seems probable. The CPLA had apparently bribed the captain of a Nationalist warship to stand aside during their crossing of the Yangtse and join them afterwards. When *Amethyst* appeared, Colonel Kang, whose knowledge of naval matters did not extend to the White Ensign, thought that the Nationalist captain was escaping with the ship and the money, and he ordered his gunners to open fire. Once the mistake had been discovered, it became Kang's responsibility on behalf of the CPLA to save 'face' by obtaining some confession of British guilt, however long it took.

As for *Amethyst* herself, in 1951 she returned to fight her old enemies during the Korean War. In 1954 she was placed on Reserve but two years later she came out of retirement to make a film of her own exploits entitled *Yangtse Incident,* with Kerans acting as technical adviser and ship's captain. That task completed, she went to a Plymouth breaker's yard in 1957. She served in a world of opposed ideologies, surrogate conflicts and nuclear threat in which gunboats had no place, yet her action provided a magnificent postscript to their story. Kerans was cast in the same mould as Sherard Osborn and Lambton Loraine, and in comparative terms his ship was no more powerful than theirs had been. The difference was that he had exposed a brutal system to the one thing it feared and against which it had no defence, namely international ridicule.

13

EPILOGUE: RETURN TO BROWN WATER
Riverine Operations in Vietnam

The gunboat, in various forms, returned to active service during the long Vietnam War. In the south-eastern corner of South Vietnam lay the Mekong Delta, a maze of rice paddies and swamps subdivided by river channels of various widths, streams and canals. In most places it was impassable for vehicles. Wet paddies, booby-trapped ditches and steep-sided dikes, intense heat and high humidity all combined to make movement difficult even for the infantryman. To the communist Viet Cong the delta was not only a refuge but also an area through which arms and supplies could be smuggled by means of junks from North Vietnam and Cambodia. It was, therefore, of critical importance to both sides.

The French and the South Vietnamese both conducted riverine operations in the delta, but these reached their climax during the period of American involvement. The Americans established Mobile Riverine Bases at various points on the delta. These consisted of anchored barrack and supply ships protected by monitors and armed patrol boats, plus troops and artillery on the banks. From such bases it was possible to conduct operations against objectives up to 30 miles distant, the object being to eliminate elusive bands of Viet Cong guerrillas wherever they might be found.

Once the enemy was known to be present in a specific area, the assault force would approach, covered by fire support bases, which might consist of field artillery firing from barges, air attack and, where possible, naval gunfire. Supported by direct gunfire from monitors and assault support patrol boats, the infantry would disembark into the suspect area. Simultaneously, more patrol boats would move up adjacent channels to cut off the enemy's line of retreat while helicopters landed a blocking force in his rear. The assault infantry would then methodically drive the enemy forward against the blocking force, in the manner of beaters driving game on to a line of guns.

These tactics caused the Viet Cong serious losses. Even when they retired into swamplands unsuited to assault landings and helicopter insertions they were likely to be assailed by air cushion craft gliding effortlessly over the soft terrain. Attempts to ambush Mobile Riverine Force convoys from the banks did inflict casualties on the Americans, but the sheer volume of return fire made such forays unprofitable. Since the delta was a major rice growing area, the measure of American success was the quantity of the crop reaching Saigon, which continued to rise as more and more areas were returned to government control.

If Henry Walke and the others who had fought their way down the Mississippi a century earlier had been present, they would not have felt unduly out of place. True, the vessels of the Mobile Riverine Force possessed neither tall belching smokestacks nor protected paddle wheels, but the lines and purpose of the monitors and armoured troop carriers were recognisable and unmistakable. The return of the gunboat to brown water warfare, if temporary, was a curious case of history repeating itself in a slightly different form; and, human nature being what it is, it is likely to do so again.

BIBLIOGRAPHY

Archibald, E. H. H., *The Fighting Ship in the Royal Navy 897–1984,* Blandford, 1984

Barker, A. J., *Townshend of Kut,* Cassell, 1967

Braddon, Russell, *The Siege – The Kut Disaster,* Jonathan Cape, 1969

Churchill, Winston S., *The River War,* Four Square, 1960

Clowes, William Laird, *The Royal Navy – A History from the Earliest Times to 1900,* Vols 5, 6 and 7, Chatham, 1997

Croizat, Lt Colonel Victor, *Vietnam Riverine Warfare 1945–1975,* Blandford, 1986

Duncan, John and Walton, John, *Heroes for Victoria,* Spellmount, 1991

Earl, Lawrence, *Yangtse Incident – The Story of HMS* Amethyst *April 20–July 31 1949,* Harrap, 1950

Featherstone, Donald, *Victorian Colonial Warfare – Africa,* Cassell, 1992

Fleming, H. L. Le, *Warships of World War I,* Ian Allan, 1967

Fox, Grace, *British Admirals and Chinese Pirates,* London, 1940

Goldsmith-Carter, George, *Sailing Ships and Sailing Craft,* Hamlyn, 1969

Gosnell, H. Allen, *Guns on the Western Waters – The Story of River Gunboats in the Civil War,* Louisiana State University Press, Baton Rouge, 1993

Greene, Jack and Massignani, Alessandro, *The Naval War in the Mediterranean 1940–1943,* Chatham, 1998

Hampshire, A. Cecil, *Armed With Stings – The Insect Class Gunboats,* William Kimber, 1958

Haythornthwaite, Philip J., *The Colonial Wars Source Book,* Arms & Armour Press, 1995

Katcher, Philip, *The American Civil War Source Book,* Arms & Armour Press, 1992

— *Great Gambles of the Civil War,* Arms & Armour Press, 1996

Kemp, Paul J., *Gunboats of the Royal Navy,* ISO Publications, London, 1997

Lenton, H. T., *Warships from 1860 to the Present Day,* Hamlyn, 1970

Lenton H. T. and J. J. Colledge, *Warships of World War II,* Ian Allan, 1980

Macintyre, Donald, *The Battle for the Mediterranean,* Batsford, 1964

Marley, David F., *Pirates – Adventures on the High Seas,* Arms & Armour Press, 1997

New York Times, The, various dates between 14 April and 8 May 1874 relating to the visit of Commander Sir Lambton Loraine, RN

Perrett, Bryan, *Desert Warfare from its Roman Origins to the Gulf Conflict,* Patrick Stephens, 1988

— *At All Costs – Stories of Impossible Victories,* Arms & Armour Press, 1993

— *Impossible Victories – Ten Unlikely Battlefield Successes,* Arms & Armour Press, 1996

Phillips, C. E. Lucas, *The Escape of the Amethyst,* Heinemann, 1957

Preston, Antony and Major, John, *Send a Gunboat – A Study of the Gunboat and its Role in British Policy 1859–1904,* London, 1967

Shankland, Peter, *The Phantom Flotilla,* Collins, 1968

Ziegler, Philip, *Omdurman,* Collins, 1973

INDEX